The Making of Prussia

The Work of Johann August Sack

and Baron Karl von Stein

In Remembrance of
Dr. Johann August Sack,
who died 100 years ago on June 25, 1831 in Stettin,
since 1816 Crown President of the Province of Pomerania
and the most faithful student and friend of
Baron Karl von Stein
Dedicated to the Privy Councillor Simon Heinrich Sack
Family Foundation
From the Book by Gertha von Dieckmann in German 1931
© 2020 Translated by Stephen A. Engelking

*"Just as the greatest gospel was a biography, so the life story of
every good man is still an unquestionable gospel, preaching to
the eye and heart, indeed to the whole man, its most joyful
proclamation: Man is born in heaven. Not a slave to circumstances and necessity, but the victorious conqueror of the same"*
Schopenhauer.

The Making of Prussia
The Work of Johann August Sack and Baron Karl von Stein

In Remembrance of
Dr. Johann August Sack,
who died 100 years ago on June 25, 1831 in Stettin,
since 1816 Crown President of the Province of Pomerania
and the most faithful student and friend of
Baron Karl von Stein
Dedicated to the Privy Councillor Simon Heinrich Sack
Family Foundation

From the Book by Gertha von Dieckmann in German 1931
with additional notes and illustrations.

© 2020 Translated by Stephen A. Engelking
Texianer Verlag
www.texianer.com
ISBN: 978-1-64921-805-6

Cover illustration: Entry of Napoleon I into Berlin, 27th October 1806 by Charles Meynier. (Public Domain PD-Art)

Foreword to this Edition

This monumental work by Gertha von Dieckmann found its fundament in her love and dedication for the cause of the *Privy Councillor Simon Heinrich Sack Family Foundation* — a cause to which she dedicated her life.

She was also a very proficient writer and researcher of Prussian history and, whilst this book was primarily targeted at the audience to be found amongst the family members, it contains valuable insights into the Prussia of the early 19th century and details of the operation of the Prussian bureaucracy both under the time of the conquest of Napoleon and the efforts at rebuilding the structures of Prussia after his defeat. Much of the effort was carried out by the visionary leadership of the two characters which are portrayed in this book.

It paved the way for the modern society in Germany and was to influence the rest of Europe in the future — no less because of the considerable connections between these characters and England, Austria, Russia and France.

The original edition was set in old German Fraktur and in a large format. Initially I transcribed and edited the book completely into latin script to make it easier to commence the formidable task of translating into English. Some of the translation is particularly difficult because the documents go back into the eighteenth century and the meaning of many terms have been lost or forgotten. I would request the reader for forgiveness should the desire to lean in the favor of readability have introduced any oversights. For scientific research I would point the student to the original German text that has also been published by this house.

I have provided considerable additional notes to those provided in the original (marked with *) to assist the reader of English who may not be familiar with the Prussian customs and terms of the time. These have either been extracted from wikipedia.org or translated by me from wikipedia.de, unless otherwise stated. They are thus in the public domain and I would suggest that the interested reader might wish to search those sources for further information which would go beyond the scope of this book.

In addition to the illustrations provided in Gertha von Dieckmann's book, I have also added a number of illustrations which are in the public domain (PD-US) also sourced as above.

I have tried to retain the style of the original German whilst hopefully making this accessible to the modern English reader. I hope you will enjoy reading this piece of valuable historical literature.

Stephen A. Engelking

Zum Gedächtnis

des vor 100 Jahren am 28. Juni 1831 zu Stettin verstorbenen

Dr. Joh. August Sack

seit 1816 Oberpräsident der Provinz Pommern,

des Freiherrn Karl vom Stein treuester Schüler und Freund

Der Hofrat Simon Heinrich Sack'schen Stiftungsfamilie
gewidmet

„So wie das höchste Evangelium eine Biographie
„war, so ist auch die Lebensgeschichte eines jeden
„guten Menschen noch ein unzweifelhaftes Evangelium
„und predigt dem Auge und Herzen, ja dem ganzen
„Menschen seine freudenreichste Verkündigung; Der
„Mensch ist himmlisch geboren. Nicht Sklave der Um=
„stände und Notwendigkeit, sondern der siegreiche
„Bezwinger derselben"   Schopenhauer.

Original Frontispiece

Contents

First Section

Foreword by the Author

Having set myself the task of collecting everything that was available about him from within the circles of the Sack Family Foundation and from the life stories of the contemporaries of this immortalized man that were known to me, in order to commemorate the centenary of the death of this most important citizen. Because he has been given to the German fatherland by our Sack family in the 500 years of its proven ancestral line, I decided to lay a wreath of remembrance at his place of rest on June 28, 1931. I am well aware that my contribution can offer only a modest and very inadequate summary of the outstanding importance of that ardent admirer of the Fatherland and loyal official of his King, that fighter and servant for his German people and devoted friend of the fiery spirit Stein, with whom he worked tirelessly for 28 years in the closest possible cooperation for the preservation, promotion and liberation of Prussia from the yoke of French bondage. This latter accomplishment is expressed mainly in the first half of my compilation and at the same time, in order to be grateful to his former mentor, Baron Karl von Stein, who followed into eternity on the day after Joh. August Sack, June 1831, I conclude the first section with Stein's official departure from the Prussian civil service. The second half of this commemorative volume, which will show Sack's independent leadership in the realization of the beneficial Stein transformations in the administration of the liberated fatherland, is to follow on his birthday on October 7 in this year or writing [now included with this edition]. This contains his work as Governor General and Crown President[1]

---

1 "Crown President" ist the translation chosen in this book for the German "Oberpräsident". The chief president of a Prussian prov-

of the Rhine Province, as well as his 15 years of activity in the reorganization of the Province of Pomerania, as whose Crown President he dedicated his life.

In the first half of the historical events, I have taken into account the presentation of P. H. Pertz in his "Steins Leben"[2] and the memoirs of Heinrich and Amalie von Beguelin (No. 3880 [36/144]), edited by Adolf Ernst[3] (mar. no. 3880 [36/144!]), until the hitherto unknown publication from the state archives of Herman Granier[4] revealed to me the strangely heavy burden that Sack carried on his shoulders alone during his years as civil governor of

---

ince was the highest representative of the Prussian crown in the province. As early as in the 17th and 18th century he was appointed by the elector or king and was responsible only to him.

From 1808 and 1815 respectively, the Crown President exercised the right of inspection – the supreme supervision of the administration in his province – on behalf of the king. However, he was not a superior of the regional presidents, who were directly subordinate to the Prussian Ministry of the Interior in Berlin. The Crown President had the right to be informed by the District Presidents about all matters of the province, he could inspect all administrative procedures and was also allowed to intervene himself in case of imminent danger. He exercised important constitutional control over the district presidents and the administration. He had the right of "Immediate Action" and was only subordinate to the Prussian Prime Minister. For the fulfilment of his task he had only a small staff of employees at his disposal and was the civil counterpart of a Prussian general inspector in terms of task and authority.

In addition to senior and government presidents, the highest officials of the provincial association were the provincial governors, who exercised the self-administration powers of the provinces and were elected by the provincial assemblies.

2   Verlag von Georg Reimer, Berlin 1856.*
3   Verlag von Julius Springer, Berlin 1892.*
4   Verlag von F. Hirzel, Leipzig 1913.*

Berlin and governor of the Kurmark, Neumark and Pomerania. As editor of the family magazine *Die Taube*, the treasure of letters from Dr. Joh. August Sack's estate, had once been given to me for publication, so I mostly used the articles which had already been published in *Die Taube* many years ago as family chronicles.

The second half is based on Neigebaur's[5] account of the provisional administrations on the Rhine[6] The significance of the Pomeranian region can be found in the Pomeranian Provincial Gazette founded by Sack himself, the two-volume biography[7] of Friedrich von Motz[8] written by Hermann von Petersdorf and various letters and Pomeranian local newspapers I received from the family. For all the kind assistance, especially for the photographs of the portrait of his wife, the house of his birth and the grave, I hereby express my most sincere thanks.

Should my small compilation happen to inspire a historian to write the detailed life story of Dr. Joh. August Sack, which has long been awaited in literary collections, it would be a particular success. My hope today is that it will create within the family of the foundation a double meaning. It's dove coat of arms was found in the letter seals of the Crown President in the form as reproduced from the ti-

---

5   Johann Daniel Ferdinand Neigebaur (1783-1866) was a German writer and lawyer. He wrote numerous books, especially on regional studies, travel descriptions and current affairs.

6   Verlag von Johann Veter Bachem, Köln 1821.*

7   Verlag von Reimar Hobbing in Berlin 1913.*

8   Friedrich Christian Adolf Motz, since 1780 von Motz (1775-1830) was a Prussian statesman, Prussian Minister of Finance, Crown President of the Province of Saxony and District President of Erfurt and Magdeburg.

tle page. The coat of arms of cousin Captain Lieutenant Werner Reger, Kiel (No. 303 [1/4354]), is tastefully grouped around it as a wreath of remembrance, the upper one in youth, the lower one in later manhood, guiding this great citizen through life to strengthen and edify himself in the memory of this exemplary ancestor. This was at a time of a new threatening domination and enslavement and exorbitant taxation on the part of the French neighbor.

Note: The numbers behind names in brackets are those under which the members of the Privy Councillor Sack Family Foundation are listed in the family tree lists of 1926, in the second volume of the "Silver Book of the Sack Family". [The translator of this edition has also added the new numbering system employed in recent editions of the "Silver Book" enclosed in square brackets].

Arolsen, June 1931.

Johann August Sack's Homeland, Childhood and Youth.

On October 7, 1764, a fourth son was born to the Judicial Councillor Karl August Sack and his wife Marie Gertrud, née Nottemann[9] of Cleve on the Lower Rhine. He was named Johann August in the holy baptism on October 10, receiving the first name Johann August and was always known by the latter of the two.

Both the marriage certificate of his parents and the baptismal registrations of his brothers and sisters are still kept in the files of the Reformed Church in Cleve and are listed in the appendix to this document among the family documents.

The city of Cleve, situated at the gateway to the Kingdom of Prussia on the Rhine, endowed with special natural beauty almost grander than the gateway to Westphalia (Porta Westfalica) on the Weser, had been the capital of the former duchy of Cleve, which, as one of the oldest hereditary lands of the House of Prussia-Brandenburg acquired by marriage, only finally came into the possession of Prussia after the fates of the Thirty Years' War, in the Peace of Westphalia, through a settlement with the contender to the inheritance rights, the Duke of Palatinate-Neuburg.[10]

---

9   Margarete Gertrude Sack (née Nottemann) was born in 1736, to Gerhardt Notteman and Charlotta Sophia Notteman (née Hermesen). Margarete married Carl August Sack in 1757, at the age of 20.
10 Wolfgang Wilhelm von Palatinate-Neuburg (1578-1653 was a German imperial prince from the House of Wittelsbach.

The Soldier King Frederick Wilhelm the Second[11], in order to select the old Cleve officials, whose names are still in evidence there today, had already decided to transplant a number of State officials to Cleve, his son Frederick the Great[12] having later followed his father's example. Thus, in 1748, the State Magistrate Karl August Sack, who was also a legal adviser, was appointed to the Justice Commission at the Cleve War and Domain Chamber.

Because of Cleve's exposed border location in the far west of the Prussian kingdom, its supreme government had been granted a particularly privileged position and the ex-

---

11   Frederick Wilhelm II (1744-1797) was King of Prussia from 1786 until his death. He was in personal union the Prince-elector of Brandenburg and (via the Orange-Nassau inheritance of his grandfather) sovereign prince of the Canton of Neuchâtel. Pleasure-loving and indolent, he is seen as the antithesis to his predecessor, Frederick II. Under his reign, Prussia was weakened internally and externally, and he failed to deal adequately with the challenges to the existing order posed by the French Revolution. His religious policies were directed against the Enlightenment and aimed at restoring a traditional Protestantism. However, he was a patron of the arts and responsible for the construction of some notable buildings, among them the Brandenburg Gate in Berlin.

12   Frederick II (1712-1786) ruled the Kingdom of Prussia from 1740 until 1786, the longest reign of any Hohenzollern king, at 46 years. His most significant accomplishments during his reign included his military victories, his reorganization of Prussian armies, his patronage of the arts and the Enlightenment and his final success against great odds in the Seven Years' War. Frederick was the last Hohenzollern monarch titled King in Prussia and declared himself King of Prussia after achieving sovereignty over most historically Prussian lands in 1772. Prussia had greatly increased its territories and became a leading military power in Europe under his rule. He became known as Frederick the Great (Friedrich der Grosse) and was nicknamed Der Alte Fritz ("The Old Fritz") by the Prussian people and eventually the rest of Germany.

ercise of many sovereign rights. For in the second half of
the 18th century it was still the capital of two large parts of
the country, the county of Cleve and Mark with 48 towns,
and thus united in its government a very important administrative apparatus of state justice, guardianship, council for criminal matters, provincial fiscal authority, council
of the commissions of justice and the supreme court of justice with its judges and notaries. Also attached to this government was the very respectable Council of Cameral,
called the War and Domain Chamber, which also had to
serve the smaller neighboring areas of Geldern and Mörs
and to which the provincial government with the state war
treasury, as well as the entire medical, forestry, mining and
metallurgy, construction, shipping and bridge administration with its financial departments, the tax and excise system were subordinated.

At that time, the judicial business of our present courts of
justice (district and local courts), the administrative business of our present government and the cash transactions
of the present tax offices were united in the government of
the state domain. Well over one thousand legal transactions were heard each year before the councils of justice
there.

It is obvious that it took not only the best and most reliable
officials, but also the brightest and most educated minds
to support and represent the main government of Berlin.
Apart from its official and functionally patriotic importance, Cleve, with its mercantile border traffic at the entrance to Holland, was of great importance for trade,
which was also subjected to official supervision.

Finally, in the 1740's, Cleve had acquired the special charm of a spa and bathing resort through the private deep drilling by one of its most important physicians, the Medical Councillor Schütte. It had a strong ferric acid spring for curative purposes. Especially because of its mountainous forest area with wonderfully wide views from the Dutch plains and the flat lowlands of the Lower Rhine, Cleve enjoyed a welcome influx of foreigners, particularly in summer. As a result, spa and bathing facilities, bathing hotels, well-maintained bridleways, driveways and promenades were created for the spa guests who wished to be looked after and cared for.

In this city of Cleve our Johann August Sack grew up among his rich siblings, three older and two younger brothers, as well as three sisters and a fourth one who had died early. He was a strong, bright and kind boy, a popular fellow student and playfellow, as well as a particularly gifted and diligent pupil.

Together his parents owned major property holdings in Cleve city and the surrounding countryside. His parents' house alone was a two-storey long house having a later baroque façade with a nine window front, an adjoining house and a large garden. In older times it must have been a house belonging to a knight or minister, who was related to the nearby "Schwanenburg", the castle of Cleve[13]. The

---

13   To which the Lohengrin saga is linked.* Lohengrin is a character in
      German Arthurian literature. The son of Parzival (Percival), he is a
      knight of the Holy Grail sent in a boat pulled by swans to rescue a
      maiden who can never ask his identity. His story, which first ap-
      pears in Wolfram von Eschenbach's Parzival, is a version of the
      Knight of the Swan legend known from a variety of medieval

overgrown hill of trees behind it stretched up to the castle and the name of the street on which the large stately residential building of Sacks was situated – the Stechbahn – a name which has been preserved even today for the narrow side street of the main road leading to the castle, indicating that in the Middle Ages the tournament grounds of the knighthood had been established there.

On February 22, 1754, three years before his marriage, the Judicial Councillor Karl A. Sack had acquired the house and ancillary building, together with a narrow courtyard behind it and a higher-lying strip of trees, which was parcelled out from the slope as was the garden belonging to it, for the price of 1,611 Reichstaler at a public auction of the municipal authorities. At that time it bore the house numbers 303 and 304, because it had three entrances: a front gate, a main front door and a side entrance which led from the street through the house directly into the courtyard. Today [as the author writes] the house is still standing, only the middle part bears number 34, because the whole is divided into three small houses and serves shopkeepers downstairs as shops and upstairs as living quarters, which were gradually built by adding walls in the 19th century.

In Sack's time, the stately building had retained much of its character as a former exclusive residence. Even in 1906, the main entrance hall is said to have had a beautiful open fireplace and even in 1931, faint remnants of murals here and there were still visible in the main room, which was

---

sources. Wolfram's story was expanded in two later romances. Richard Wagner's opera Lohengrin of 1848 is based upon the legend.

Joh. August Sacks Birth House in Cleve a.
Rh., Stechbahn Nr. 303/4

fragmented by additions. 180 years ago, these certainly
served their original decorative purpose, as the murals described below were still clearly visible in 1906.

The largest one represented four noblewomen, two
knights and a squire. The latter receives the knighthood
from one of the two knights, clothed in armor and kneel-
ing with his hands up. The knight holds a sword in his
right hand and a book in his left. One of the noblewomen
is handing the knight a sword, another holds a bowl in her
hands, and the third is sitting at a table with a wooden
bucket on top. In the background one sees a landscape
with a mountain (perhaps the Eltenberg opposite Cleve,
which is the only single elevation in the vicinity).

In another painting you can see noblewomen and knights preparing for a hunt.

Another hunting painting depicted a knight and two noblewomen on horseback.

One of the noblewomen is carrying a falcon on her right hand whilst the other carries a quiver with arrows on her back.

The fourth largest hunting painting depicted the hunt itself. A boar had to be shot. One knight is going at the game with drawn sword, supported by other knights armed with spears, while hounds are angrily attacking the boar. Several noblewomen are seen emerging swiftly from the thicket of the forest, the first of whom hurries towards the boar with a javelin but is being held back by a knight. Other participants are fleeing to a nearby tree. Nearby, a spring is gushing forth from which a horse is quenching its thirst.

In addition to these larger murals, there were also several smaller ones (lunettes[14] and overdoors[15]) — at least in pre-

---

14   In architecture, a lunette (French lunette, "little moon") is a half-moon shaped space, either filled with recessed masonry or void. A lunette is formed when a horizontal cornice transects a round-headed arch at the level of the imposts, where the arch springs. If a door is set within a round-headed arch, the space within the arch above the door, masonry or glass, is a lunette. If the door is a major access, and the lunette above is massive and deeply set, it may be called a tympanum.

15   An "overdoor" (or "Supraporte" as in German, or "sopraporte" as in Italian) is a painting, bas-relief or decorative panel, generally in a horizontal format, that is set, typically within ornamental mold-

historic times the room had been the banqueting hall of the aristocracy. The Reichswald[16], which is still adjacent today, had been a popular hunting ground for some time.

In this venerable and historic house, well-to-do parents raised their eleven children in the simple piety of the Reformed faith. The cheerfulness brought by the Dutch-born mother was joined by the serious outlook on life which the father had acquired for his career as a civil servant from his parental, princely and Anhalt parish in Hecklingen. In addition to the happy tone in his parents' home, our Joh. August Sack also owed the vivacity of the senses, the versatility of opinion, the amiable temperament and his fiery restless activity to his Lower Rhine home, which characterizes and distinguishes the Rhinelander but which also often presents them in a false light, as opposed to the more reserved tribes of other parts of the country, through their open innocuousness. Later in life our Sack strongly felt the kinship of fine character with that of his compatriots and was deeply rooted in his homeland. His highest wish in life was always to be allowed to work among them but this was only to be granted to him during short periods of his eventful career.

---

ings, over a door, or was originally intended for this purpose.

16 The Kleve Reichswald is an Imperial forest in North Rhine-Westphalia (Germany) between the Rivers Rhine and Meuse at the German Dutch border. The forest is located in the municipal territory of Kleve, Goch, Kranenburg and Bedburg-Hau. It is the largest coherent wooded area of the lower Rhine and the largest coherent public state forest of North Rhine-Westphalia with an area of 51^2 km (5100 ha).

The Stechbahn street, with its hilly trees behind it, gradually becoming gardens of the row of houses, which, having smaller courtyards, were built with the front facing the main street, i.e. Schlosstrasse, forming the southern boundary for the civil servants' quarter, which stood out from the lower-lying bathing and spa quarter, in Sack's time, when the Prussian administrative government and its subsidiary departments were housed in the palace itself.

Anyone who had business at the castle lived in the immediate vicinity of it at that time, so that one can imagine the tree hill behind the Sack's house divided into neighboring gardens, just like today, where the children of the families Jacobi, Sethe, Rappard, Focke, von Harthausen, Bernuth, Reimann, etc. romped about. As the Silver Book of the Sack family records, even some bridal and married couples sprang up out of the neighboring gardens. However, as yet our J. August Sack was still a diligent student who, like his older brothers before him, attended the lower classes of the Cleve High School. On August 8, 1780, Joh. August had lost his promising eldest brother Friedrich Gerhard Sack, who had just been employed as a 22-year-old trainee teacher by the Glogau State Government, to a severe fever within a few days. The next oldest brother, Karl Heinrich Theodor, had hurried from Cleve to visit the sick man but only arrived in time to see the young life be placed in a coffin and to bury the dear brother in the ground on August 10th at the Reformed cemetery in Glogau. He himself, working as a trainee teacher in Cleve, then had to return home to comfort his grieving parents and siblings. This was the first serious loss in Joh. August's parental home, when he himself, just like his older brothers, then from 1780-82 completed the higher classes under

t SLOT te CLEEFF langs het Rieviertje Kermisdal te zien.

Schwanenburg Castle seen from the south, 1758

the outstanding teacher Engel and the highly important school reformer Meierotto[17] from Stargard in the famous

---

17 Johann Heinrich Ludwig Meierotto (1742-1800) was a German geographer and pedagogue. He was a son of the rector of the Stargard Reformed School. From 1760 to 1762 he was a pupil at the Joachimsthal High School in Berlin, where his grandfather Heinrich Meierotto (1671-1717) had already worked. He then studied philology and theology at the University of Frankfurt (Oder). Afterwards he was a private teacher from 1765 to 1771 on behalf of the banker David Schickler. From 1771 Meierotto worked again at the Joachimsthal High School, this time as professor of rhetoric, Latin and classical literature. From 1775 he was headmaster of the school.

He advocated reforms in the school system. Thus his commitment led to the introduction of the school-leaving examination in Prussia, with the support of the Minister of Culture Karl Abraham von Zedlitz.

From 1786 he took up the post of church and secondary school councilor for the school system in Pomerania and Prussia. In the

Joachimthal Gymnasium[18] (High School) in Berlin. Here he enjoyed the paternal guidance of the State Court Preacher Sack (3388 [33]) and his brother Christian Cornelius (No. 1106 [9]), who was a cathedral candidate there. Not yet 18 years old, in 1782, the knowledge-thirsty student went to the University of Halle, which appointed him forty years later as honorary doctor. Two years later, in 1784, he moved to Göttingen, the main seat of lawyers and chamberlains. There he heard the famous scholar and publicist A. L. Schlözer (1735-1809)[19], with whom he also lived, certainly an advantage during his intellectual development years. He loved to be a hiking companion of his roommates, the later Professor Lüder and the later historian

---

same year he became a member of the Academy of Sciences and Mechanical Arts.

18 The Joachimsthalsches Gymnasium (also: Joachimsthaler Gymnasium) was a secondary school (Fürstenschule: princely school) for gifted boys, founded in 1607 in Joachimsthal, Brandenburg, which was located in Berlin from 1636 and from 1912 in Templin.

19 August Ludwig von Schlözer (1735-1809) was a German historian who laid foundations for the critical study of Russian history. He was a member of the Göttingen School of History.
Since Schlözer opposed a strictly European perspective, the scope was the entire mankind. Moreover, he included all classes of society and social and cultural developments. The development of glass by the Phoenicians and the introduction of potatoes in Europe were more important than the names of the Chinese or German emperors.

Gatterer[20], and to increase his knowledge practically in forests and mines.

Sack later spoke of his teachers with great love and esteem and showed his gratitude by taking special care of the teaching profession and raising the standard of education. The spirit of humanism and classicism had always remained alive in him, which is evident not only in his tendency to weave Latin quotations into his letters but above all in his whole way of looking at things, in his high respect for science and for an ideally directed intellectual culture.

In 1785 Sack joined the War and Domain Chamber of Cleve as an auscultator (trainee), soon passed the assessor examination with flying colors and attracted the attention of his superiors with his knowledge and skill in practical

---

20 Johann Christoph Gatterer (1727-1799) was a German historian who was a native of Lichtenau. He was the father of cameralist Christoph Wilhelm Jacob Gatterer (1759–1838) and poet Magdalena Philippine Engelhard (1756–1831). He was a member of the Göttingen School of History.
From 1747 he studied theology at Altdorf, where his interest later changed to history. In 1752 he became a school teacher of history and geography in Nuremberg, and in 1756 gained his professorship in natural history. In 1759 he was appointed professor of history at the University of Göttingen, where he remained for the next forty years. Gatterer was a pioneer of "universal history", and with fellow Göttingen historian August Ludwig von Schlözer (1735–1809), he was instrumental in developing a modern, hermeneutical approach to history. He believed that historical events needed to be systematically arranged by describing their causal relationships, rather than simply providing a chronology of events. Gatterer used the phrase *nexus rerum universalis* to represent "a universal connection of things in the world".

Johann Heinrich Ludwig Meierotto

service, so that his highest superior, Minister v. Heinitz[21], chose him in 1788 to be a mining judge and mining councilor in Wetter a.d. Ruhr.

21 Friedrich Anton von Heynitz, also Heinitz (1725-1802) was one of the founders of the Freiberg Mining Academy and the most important Prussian state economists of the 18th century. He is regarded as the reformer of the Braunschweig mining industry. His main achievement was the reorganization of mining and metallurgy in Prussia.

First Meeting and Collaboration of Sack with the Imperial Baron Karl von und zum Stein

How could the young, albeit exceptionally well-informed and intelligent mining councillor have guessed that the next four years at Wetter a. d. Ruhr would be a particularly gracious coincidence of the heavens, which would be of decisive importance for his whole later life.

However, for his immediate superior there, the State Mining Councillor Frhr. v. Stein, too, this short time turned out to be a significant experience in another sense. When this statesmanlike genius, in his later position as a European celebrity, saviour of the fatherland and first advisor to the Emperor and King, was once asked by Bishop Eylert where in the world he had enjoyed himself most, Stein's answer was without hesitation: "At Wetter on the Ruhr, for there I was touched by the greatest purity in humanity and in nature".

I believe that we can indisputably attribute this highest praise to the man who Stein chose there as his most intimate friend and his most zealous disciple, for in Wetter the rare friendship was established which bound Stein and Sack together in the closest possible bond until the end of their lives.

But we are only at the beginning of both careers and, in order to be able to pursue them properly, we must first go back to a time several years before they met.

But we are only at the beginning of both careers and, in order to be able to pursue them properly, we must first go
back to a time several years before they met.

Sack's, aforementioned excellent patron, the far-sighted
Minister von Heinitz, had already succeeded in 1780 in
warming the 23-year-old Karl Freiherr von und zum Stein
from Nassau on the Lahn, for the state mining and metallurgical industry, which was in a badly depressed state.
This young son of noble parents, who came from an old
Nassau family whose wish it had been to see him enter
into Austrian service, had decided, however, out of sheer
enthusiasm for Frederick the Great, to dedicate his
strength only to this monarch and his state.

This young Karl vom Stein was then employed as a trainee
at the Harz ironworks and repeatedly accompanied the
Minister von Heinitz on his official journeys through East
Frisia, Holland, Westphalia, Saxony, West and East Prussia,
thereby broadening his knowledge extraordinarily and,
with a rare understanding and practical insight, making
himself known as a budding leader.

In 1782, when the minister presented his young protégé
Stein to the King for appointment as State Mining Councillor in Wetter a.d. Ruhr and the King answered that he did
not know anything about the young man, the Minister declared, "Stein has distinguished himself through academic
diligence, on travels through Hungary, Styria and other
German provinces, by examining the mines and iron and
steel works and the steel and iron factories, dealing with
so many important matters in such an outstanding manner

that he must repeat his nomination proposal in order to make sure that this outstandingly competent force remains in Prussian service". On this recommendation the appointment was then carried out and in February 1784 Baron vom Stein was given the management of the Westphalian mining offices and the Minden Mining Commission with the official residence in Wetter a.d. Ruhr. Stein arrived there in May 1784 and was at the same time appointed as voting member of the Cleve-Mörs and Märkische Chamber. In the first period of his life he undertook his business with such single-minded zeal, as he himself had to admit, that, because of his noble character, he soon felt compelled to apologize to his subordinates for often pushing them too hard.

But soon, here in Wetter a. d. Ruhr, the fiercely hot-blooded State Mining Councillor was to recognize in his new young Mining Councillor, as he himself later expressed himself, "such an excellent carrier of all good things" that this was the foundation of a deep friendship based on mutual esteem, which could be steadfastly maintained for a lifetime by both parties. As the most faithful public servants, they were certainly not spared the changeful fates that the fatherland, to which they both clung with the same sacrificial and unselfish love and with the same fervent enthusiasm and veneration, had to endure. Whether working for Prussia's welfare in a common local position or in a separate place of work, they always pursued the same goal and yet the world learned little of it at the time. Each filled his office separately. No one ever referred to the other, they always worked faithfully and quietly in each other's service, since it was always only necessary for both of them to join forces for the good of the King of Prussia and the fatherland.

In 1785, on the advice of Minister Heinitz, Stein was even employed by his great King Frederick II in a delicate political mission. The King deemed it necessary to link the Austrian supremacy with the smaller powers, especially since Emperor Joseph II was eager to take Bavaria in exchange, which had to be prevented. Frederick the Great had only the Archbishop of Trier, the Archbishop of Würzburg and Bamberg, and the Abbot of Fulda on his side, while the Imperial Chancellor, the Archbishop of Mainz and von Dalberg, had already taken the first step towards the Emperor on his own initiative. After long and successful negotiations, first with the Bavarian Agnate for the throne, the childless Duke of Bavaria, who had already been won over by Emperor Joseph for his plans, and by taking an extremely cautious approach with the ambitious and vain Elector of the Church of Mainz, Stein had finally—his old King had already become impatient—succeeded in removing the various obstacles and preparing a brilliant outcome for his mission. The King was extremely happy and satisfied, because the intimate union of the four spiritual rulers and the secular princely houses joining them, which had been achieved by Stein, now formed a solid dam from which the Austrian emperor's ambitious and avaricious intentions receded.

But this splendid success of his mission had made no other impression on Stein than to reinforce his resolute aversion to diplomacy. He was doubly happy to return to his former sphere of activity in Wetter a.d. Ruhr and had turned his attention with renewed zeal to plans already begun for the benefit of the mining and metallurgical works. On October 31, 1786 he was promoted to Privy State Councillor. Soon afterwards he undertook a journey to England, which lasted from November 1786 to August 1787, with the purpose of getting to know the mining industry and the metal factories there, which had been brought to a high degree of perfection. During this time the great Frederick had breathed forth his noble soul and his nephew Frederick Wilhelm II had ascended to the Prussian royal throne.

In November 1787 Stein was transferred away from Wetter, initially as second and on 27 July 1788 as first Chamber Director at the War and Domain Chamber in Cleve and Hamm and soon took up residence in Cleve, as Hamm did not suit him particularly well.

The French Revolution, which broke out in 1789, seemed to be limited to France's interior at first, along with its tumultuous collateral and consequential effects. But when a counter-government to Koblenz was formed among the brothers of the murdered King Louis XVI, who, like all other princes, were preparing to bring about the same end to the Jacobins as the murdered King, and who were diligent to carry their slogan, "War on thrones and palaces, peace to the huts" across the borders, the European rulers took up arms. Their defensive wars began belatedly and not until 1792, when Sack was transferred as legal adviser to the War and Territorial Chamber in Cleve and reunited locally with his patron and friend Stein. One year later, the Chamber Director Stein was appointed President of this chamber, which was based in Hamm, and despite the local separation, a diligent cooperation between master and pupil took place, which Stein used to shape Sack in new fields entirely according to his design.

Stein now set himself the main task of turning his attention to waterway and path construction, making it possible to navigate from the Rhine to the Ruhr. The cooperation between master and student soon succeeded in making the Ruhr navigable and thus in selling the output of the local coal mines directly to Cleve and then to Holland. The salt production from the Westphalian interior also gained profitable importance as a result.

This work of the two, so particularly beneficial for the Lower Rhine, was abruptly interrupted when the threat of war from rebellious France became increasingly threatening for the neighboring countries on the Rhine. The Elector of Mainz, Herr von Dalberg[22], had already capitulated be-

---

22 Karl Theodor Anton Maria von Dalberg (1744-1817) was Prince-Archbishop of Regensburg, Arch-Chancellor of the Holy Roman Empire, Bishop of Constance and Worms, prince-primate of the Confederation of the Rhine and Grand Duke of Frankfurt.
As statesman, Dalberg was distinguished by his patriotic attitude, whether in ecclesiastical matters, in which he leaned to the Febronian view of a German national church, or in his efforts to galvanize the atrophied machinery of the Empire into some sort of effective central government of Germany. Failing in this, he turned to the rising star of Napoleon, believing that he had found in him the only force strong enough to save Germany from dissolution.
Though his political subservience to Napoleon was resented by a later generation in Germany, as a man and prelate he is remembered as amiable, conscientious and large-hearted. Himself a scholar and author, Dalberg was a notable patron of letters, and was the friend of Goethe, Schiller and Wieland.

fore the Jacobins[23], and Stein, in order to secure his own
properties in the next threatened Nassau, hurried first to
Kassel, to confer with his brother. His brother was an envoy at the court of Hesse-Darmstadt, whom it was considered expedient to call on for protection. The further result
was that the King of Prussia himself called on Stein for further similar protective missions with the other Rhine
princes, since he had already successfully worked there
before and was well known.

The Duke of Brunswick, who was in command of the
Prussian defense army, having first advanced victoriously,
was forced to retreat after several successful battles, since
he found all positions in the interior of France occupied by
Jacobins and the inhabitants did not give him the expected
good reception as liberator. Even a second advance of the
Prussian and allied armies was of no avail. The French had
successfully carried out their coup d'état on Mainz, and although Stein had probably initially supported the Rhine
princes with defensive plans, they soon proved to be unwilling to fight and were friendly towards the French. The
Netherlands, Austria, England, and Hanover now waged
the war with greater tenacity and varying degrees of luck
but when the Prussians, who had gone ahead in vain, finally failed to come to any avail, Austria then resolved to
evacuate the Netherlands, having rushed to their aid. Im-

---

23 The Society of the Friends of the Constitution, after 1792 renamed
    Society of the Jacobins, Friends of Freedom and Equality, com-
    monly known as the Jacobin Club or simply the Jacobins, became
    the most influential political club during the French Revolution of
    1789. The period of their political ascendancy includes the Reign
    of Terror, during which time well over ten thousand people were
    put on trial and executed in France, many for political crimes.

mediately the French switched from the defense of their new independence to a war of aggression against all neighboring states. As a result, in 1794, when the French approached the Lower Rhine, the authorities in Cleve, and with them the current State Councillor Sack, had to move to Emmerich on the right side of the Rhine to the fortress of Wesel. In Wesel, the War and Territorial Chamber took its seat, at the same time securing the coffers there. Stein, as president, remained further back in Hamm, Westphalia. Joh. August Sack established the connection between him and the fugitive chamber.

In this extremely difficult war situation, which moreover had quickly brought about the French occupation of the entire left bank of the Rhine, the King, who relied on Stein's advice, knew to choose no more reliable negotiator than the faithful patriot Joh. August Sack for the diplomatic negotiations with the French General Hoche[24] for the necessary clearing of the left bank of the Rhine. It was to

---

24 Louis Lazare Hoche (1768-1797) was a French soldier who rose to be general of the Revolutionary army. He won a victory over Royalist forces in Brittany. His surname is one of the names inscribed under the Arc de Triomphe. Richard Holmes says he was "quick-thinking, stern, and ruthless...a general of real talent whose early death was a loss to France." A famous statement of general Hoche: "*Facta, non verba*" ("acts, no words").
On 22 December 1793 he won the Battle of Froeschwiller, and the representatives of the National Convention with his army at once added the Army of the Rhine to his sphere of command. In the Second Battle of Wissembourg on 26 December 1793, the French drove Dagobert Sigmund von Wurmser's Austrian army from Alsace. Hoche pursued his success, sweeping the enemy before him to the middle Rhine in four days. He then put his troops into winter quarters.

this diplomatically most unpleasant office that the young Sack had to submit from 1794 to 1797.

Even if it meant training this judicial official in a sphere of political thought and patriotic activity that had previously been alien to him, negotiating business with the enemy representative was in itself a most thankless task. For although Sack had succeeded in concluding a treaty with the commanding General Lazare Hoche, the representative of the French, on 12 March 1797 in his headquarters in Cologne. According to this treaty, the 1st Germinal[25] (March 21) of the same year, however, was in reality only a farce on the part of the French, since they already knew then that Prussia, on the basis of secret agreements with the French Directorate, would sooner or later be prepared to cede the left bank of the Rhine in exchange for other territorial compensation.

In 1797 the Prussian King Frederick Wilhelm II was succeeded by his 27-year-old son Frederick Wilhelm III[26], and

---

25 See additional information section at the end of this book regarding the French Republican Calendar.

26 Frederick Wilhelm III (1770-1840) was King of Prussia from 1797 to 1840. He ruled Prussia during the difficult times of the Napoleonic Wars and the end of the Holy Roman Empire. Steering a careful course between France and her enemies, after a major military defeat in 1806, he eventually and reluctantly joined the coalition against Napoleon in the *Befreiungskriege* (Wars of Liberation). Following Napoleon's defeat, he was King of Prussia during the Congress of Vienna, which assembled to settle the political questions arising from the new, post-Napoleonic order in Europe. He was determined to unify the Protestant churches, to homogenize their liturgy, their organization, and even their architecture. The long-term goal was to have fully centralized royal control of all the Protestant churches in the Prussian Union of Churches.

the Peace of Campo Formio[27], as well as the death of the Russian Emperor, had left Prussia in the most impotent of circumstances. Nevertheless, the administration of the Lower Rhine areas was very successful, despite the strong billeting of the Prussian demarcation army for protection against Northern Germany. As early as 1796 Stein had been appointed in recognition as Crown President of Westphalia and by the end of May he had taken up this position, which covered eight landscapes totalling 182 square miles with almost half a million inhabitants. Westphalia was completely cut off from the Prussian state to the east by many foreign parts of territory and therefore had to be governed with the greatest care and attention to the peculiar conditions of the neighboring countries.

In 1797, after Stein had been appointed in 1796 to the office of the Crown President of Westphalia and the conclusion with the French General Hoche, who incidentally died only a few months later, Sack received an appointment from the new King Friedrich Wilhelm III as Privy Finance Councillor to the General Directorate in Berlin as a reward for the liberation of the left bank of the Rhine. For a 35-year-old man, this appointment, indeed was a prestigious and outstanding distinction. In reality, however, this high position meant that Sack had the duty, as the circum-

---

27 The Treaty of Campo Formio (today Campoformido) was signed on 17 October 1797 by Napoleon Bonaparte and Count Philipp von Cobenzl as representatives of the French Republic and the Austrian monarchy, respectively. The treaty followed the armistice of Leoben (18 April 1797), which had been forced on the Habsburgs by Napoleon's victorious campaign in Italy. It ended the War of the First Coalition and left Great Britain fighting alone against revolutionary France.

Karl Theodor Anton Maria von Dalberg

stances demanded, to carry out all the unpleasant financial and business affairs created by the enemy and to bring about the most favorable outcome for Prussia, thanks to his finely controlled, intelligent, just and benevolent compensation.

Stein, having a passionate and fierce disposition, had less of a temperament appropriate for this purpose. He was the far-sighted organizer, whose spirit constantly devised and urged the creation of new plans for improvement but without Sack's clear, deliberate examination and approval, rarely went about their execution.

We will soon realize this when we observe the following cooperation of the two again in the regulation of the difficult secularization of the extensive Westphalian church estates, which in the sad peace of Luneville in 1801 Prussia was forced to accept as compensation for the left bank of the Rhine to France, then to be ceded. This peace took place after the directorate in Paris in 1800 had proclaimed the Citizen General Napoleon Buonaparte as the First Consul and dictator of France, now giving him even more power.

However, shortly after the turn of the century, before this event, which was so profound for Prussia and had such serious consequences for the whole of Europe, which Schiller so aptly illustrated in his poem, we want to turn to the experiences in Sack's private life for a short while, just as the poet turned to his muse.

Where will a place of refuge, noble friend,
For peace and freedom ever open lie!
The century in tempests had its end,
The new one now begins with murder's cry.
Each land-connecting bond is torn away,
Each ancient custom hastens to decline;
Not e'en the ocean can war's tumult stay.
Not e'en the Nile-god, not the hoary Rhine.

Two mighty nations strive, with hostile power,
For undivided mastery of the world;
And, by them, each land's freedom to devour,
The trident brandished is the lightning hurled.

Each country must to them its gold afford,
And, Brennus-like, upon the fatal day,
The Frank now throws his heavy iron sword,
The even scales of justice to o'erweigh.

His merchant-fleets the Briton greedily
Extends, like polyp-limbs, on every side;
And the domain of Amphitrite free
As if his home it were, would fain bestride.

E'en to the south pole's dim, remotest star,
His restless course moves onward, unrestrained;
Each isle he tracks, each coast, however far,
But paradise alone he ne'er has gained!

Although thine eye may every map explore,
Vainly thou'lt seek to find that blissful place,
Where freedom's garden smiles for evermore,
And where in youth still blooms the human race.

Before thy gaze the world extended lies,
The very shipping it can scarce embrace;
And yet upon her back, of boundless size,
E'en for ten happy men there is not space!

Into thy bosom's holy, silent cells,
Thou needs must fly from life's tumultuous throng!
Freedom but in the realm of vision dwells,
And beauty bears no blossoms but in song.

F. Schiller.[28]

---

28 English translation provided by http://www.public-domain-poet-
ry.com/friedrich-schiller/commencement-of-the-new-century-
30653.

Louis Lazare Hoche

Johann August Sack's Family Relationship and Marriage

In December 1791 a brother of Johann August Sack's father died in Glogau in Silesia, who had been revered as a great benefactor among his brothers, nieces and nephews. He ventured fifty years before, as an enthusiastic admirer of the young King from the University of Frankfurt upon Oder, to immediately settle in Glogau as a lawyer when in December 1740, soon after his accession to power, the Great Frederick asserted his rights of inheritance in Silesia and in March 1741, after only a short siege and a quick conquest by the young Prince of Dessau, he had victoriously taken possession of the first fortress of Glogau. His smooth handling of the administration of justice, which was favorable to Prussia, soon attracted the attention of the King and when after the next Silesian wars, especially the so-called Seven Years' War, the great Silesian magnates had to submit to Prussian legislation and the necessary dispute over the landed property required a sharp-thinking mind and a man who believed in justice. Simon Heinrich Sack's reputation rose far beyond the borders. Early afflicted by gout, he remained a bachelor and through thriftiness and frugality, as well as by taking over and repairing dilapidated Austrian estates, he acquired a considerable fortune over the years. As a member of the Royal Commission of Justice he worked out the Prussian Land Law with Carmer29 and set himself the task of educating his many nephews to raise an academically educated higher civil service for the state by supporting them all with study support and also providing his many nieces with endowment funds if they in turn brought academically educated or nobility as spouses into the family. Even if his motivation was primarily to serve the nation of his King, he was also compelled, as he expressed himself in his last will, to "thereby maintain his own kinship (i.e. high)". For this purpose, he had left the major part of his fortune, in addition to all inheritances and legacies, in the form of a family foundation, which he entrusted at that time to the state government of Glogau, with royal consensus, for administration and proper distribution, according to the provisions laid down in his will. The fact that this will, too, drawn up by one of the most outstanding lawyers of the time, had to suffer attacks and legal battles as a result of Prussia's time of severe hardship in the first decade of the new century, should be mentioned here only briefly — because we have not yet unfolded the political background to that extent.

In the last decade of the old century, our Johann August Sack still enjoyed the undisputed blessing which had also fallen to him from this uncle's side, and which now, with the higher position he had achieved in life, made it possible for him and encouraged him to think about founding a permanent household in the capital of the kingdom by his own efforts.

His role model and friend, Baron von Stein, had already married on June 8, 1793, when he received the presidency of the Märkische War and Territorial Chamber with the residence in Hamm. At first, however, he had refused to exchange the first Chamber Director's post for this position of President "because the salary bonus of 134 taler (Thlr.) 17 groschen (Gr.) did not correspond to the new burden and the effort involved". He was then informed that he was to be appointed President of Cleve, which he received on November 25 of the same year with an income of 2,500 Thlr., which was soon increased to 3,000 Thlr. and free lodging in Cleve Castle.

Mrs von Stein was born Countess Walmoden-Gimborn29, of half Hanoverian and half English birth. She was born on June 22, 1772, and already on September 15, 1819, in her 47th year of life, she fell sick after she had been ill for a longer period of time. She died as a victim of an epidemic of dysentery in the valleys of Nassau, which was fatal for her in the burning heat. Stein himself writes in a detailed obituary, which he gives to the immortalized woman, who had been a faithful companion for twenty-six years without, however, fully living up to his hopes, about the first years of her marriage, as follows, "The direction of her whole being was towards domesticity, family life, sociability and rest but it was not her destiny to enjoy them. The content of her life was faith, active through love, from which the virtues that adorned the immortalized were born. Nobility of soul, humility, purity, a high sense of truth and justice, faithfulness as mother and wife, clarity of spirit, correctness of judgment, spoke out throughout her much-tested life and spread blessings to all her circumstances and surroundings. Wife of a husband whose life was severely affected by the storm of time, their wishes and expectations for the enjoyment of the above mentioned were destroyed as soon as they appeared to be favorable, and their whole life was therefore a series of privations, efforts and sacrifices. No sooner had she moved to her new home in Cologne after her marriage in October 1793 than she was forced by the invasion of enemy armies to flee to Wesel, and since this fortress was under fire, in October 1794 she was forced to return to her father's house in Hanover, while her husband's business called him to the Prussian headquarters. The change in public circumstances in northern Germany in April 1795 seemed to give her the pleasure of peace and quiet but did not protect her against the plundering of family property and its occupation by the French armies with the resulting disadvantage for domestic prosperity. As the years passed, the trials became more and more serious, more and more threatening and all her external happiness seemed irretrievably destroyed (especially at the turn of the century!), etc.".

One can well imagine that it was not an easy step, even for Sack, to bind a young woman to his future so closely tied to Stein's personality under the existing and foreseeable circumstances.

The Cleve War and Territorial Chamber together with all the other authorities of the state government administration had already returned from the right bank of the Rhine to the left after negotiations with Hoche had begun and thus the old parental home on the Stechbahn was also ready to receive the dear son from Berlin on a festive occasion when he came home for a visit at Christmas 1798 with the intention of taking his life companion with him from his beloved home town. It seems that the King of Prussia felt especially compelled to reward the hard test of loyalty which his government officials had passed, particularly in the face of this to and fro of jeopardized royal property. For at the time of their return, an astonishing number of the officials of Cleve, who had previously been bourgeois and had been elevated to hereditary nobility, returned to their old positions. From now on we hear and read about the von Rappards, von Schlechtendahls, von Ribbendrops, von Bernuths, and others and it seems quite astonishing, at any rate striking, that Johann August Sack, the Cleve official charged with the most important political mission was on the other hand excluded from this ennoblement. Later, during his time as Governor General of the Lower and Middle Rhine, an explanation is given for this and we read in a reply published in the *Rheinischer Merkur* about the reason for the absence of even the small article "de" before the name of such a powerful man as a Governor General.

In the earlier, more peaceful times on the Lower Rhine, around 1780, in order to put a stop to the gossip that easily developed there, as in every small town, a society, i.e. a closed circle, had formed in Cleve in high society predominantly formed by the civil servants, which wanted to pay homage to a better style of life by means of more noble entertainments — fine concerts, lectures, theatre plays, dancing and the like. An overview of members from the years 1782 to 1800 has been preserved and among the approximately 150 members we find from the very beginning the couple Judicial Councillor Carl A. Sack and soon the grown-up sons employed in Cleve. Also our Johann August, as well as the already several times mentioned neighboring families Focke, Jacobi, Sethe, Bernuth, von Haxthausen, Schlechtendahl, Bölling and Reiman are to be found.

We may therefore assume that there had already been a secret affection between Johann August Sack and Marianne Reiman for some time before he led the daughter of the Privy Councillor, now von Reiman, to the altar on January 5, 1799, she having now matured into an especially beautiful 23-year-old damsel. The last will and testament of the fiancées (attached as no. III in the appendix) shows us how the exact regulation of the mutual financial arrangements down to the smallest detail before such an important event as a marriage was considered necessary among the children of civil servants. This thus fully reflects the way of thinking based on thrift and equitable solidity, not only of the Prussian King, but of his higher civil servants. But that the act of marriage itself (no. IV), which according to French legislation (which had not been repealed on the left bank of the Rhine) was not to be performed before a priest but before the civil registrar, attests that even a 35-year-old civil servant and a 23-year-old damsel still needed the consent of the fathers and the testimony of the court and cathedral preacher Sack of Berlin (presumably in connection with the posting of the bridegroom living in Berlin) in order to be allowed to marry.

Unfortunately, I have not heard of any epithalamium[29] and poems of homage to the bride and groom from the wedding ceremony itself, such as for example, from the wed-

---

29 An epithalamium is a poem written specifically for the bride on the way to her marital chamber. This form continued in popularity through the history of the classical world; the Roman poet Catullus wrote a famous epithalamium, which was translated from or at least inspired by a now-lost work of Sappho. According to Origen, the Song of Songs might be an epithalamium on the marriage of Solomon with Pharaoh's daughter.

ding of Sack's parents in 1757 and their silver wedding anniversary in 1782. From this it can be concluded that in view of the whole political situation, although the peace treaty concluded in Basel in January 1795 should have created calmer times for the Lower Rhine, the wedding can hardly have been a happy and harmonious one, as it was customary in that region. No doubt a new war or some other unfavorable things were already in the air. Already in December 1794, when Stein had requested to cross the Rhine with Sack, who had to go to Cologne, the King decided on the request of the Minister von Heinitz that Stein should not be allowed to cross the Rhine under any circumstances. Sack was hardly left in peace to marry. The whole situation during the winter of 1798 to 1799 is marked by a letter written by Stein on February 15th from Berlin to the young husband who remained in Cleve until mid-February:

Berlin, February 15, 1799.

To the Privy State Councillor of Finance Sack currently in Cleve.[30]

The result of an intrigue sparked in the province and carried out by the High Court Councillor von Rappard and Cabinet Councillor Beyme against the twofold proposal of the responsible minister to appoint R. v. Rappard as Chamber Director:

"He lacks knowledge of the main branches of administration, as entrusted to the Collegio (council), of the provincial locality and of the personality of the civil servants — if, by the way, indirect influence should substitute for the regular way, one would still be satisfied with the choice".

---

30 This letter is a donation of the late Vice Admiral Sack of Berlin (3321 [30/g]), the Privy State Consistorial Councillor Prof. D. Budde of Marburg a./L. (2952 [28/12]) and the Privy State Councillor Justus Budde of Berlin (2972 [28/14]) cf. no. 60 of the *Taube*.*

Several people have applied for this position, and I have suggested that the Mining Judge Boelling be made a Justice Chamberlain and the referendary of Bernuth, a mining judge — the former seems to me to be a good choice, he is a hardworking man who is well acquainted with the Province and its inhabitants through his many and varied employment contracts.

In order to keep peace in the council, to put Müller out of an ailing and tormenting situation which is wearing him down and paralyzing him, I consider it advisable to transfer him to Minden as a councillor and to give him an appropriate department there. The King assures in his cabinet order that he has learned from further inquiries that he is a violent and incompatible man but he would be inclined to entrust him with another directive at another opportunity.

The news from the Rhine is extremely sad, it will be presented to the King by the Minister and tomorrow it will be submitted to the service establishments, approved and the relevant fund granted. When the damage is known and recorded and the cost of restoration is determined, I shall go down with Riedel so that everything is properly dealt with. Meanwhile I have had the *actes ad. reg.* given to me. Now it's thaw weather again. In order to wait for your High Well-Born[31], I will stay until the 14th fut. Hoffbauer is coming here

---

31   In German: *Hochwohlgeboren* (lit. "High Well-Born"; Latin: *magnificus*) is an honorific and manner of address for members of the nobility in some parts of Europe.
This form of address originally had connections with the ability of a *Freiherr* (Baron) to bequeath a family coat of arms and to hold landed property as allodial instead of a fief. The actual address is *Euer Hochwohlgeboren* ("Your High Well-Born") and is the correct form of address not only towards German *Freiherren* but also *Ritter* and *Edle*.
The title should not be confused with *(Euer) Hochgeboren*. This title ranks higher than *Hochwohlgeboren* and is the style of mediate *Grafen* (mediate Counts; immediate counts or *Reichsgrafen* are entitled to the address *Erlaucht*) and those *Freiherren* descending from the mediæval *Uradel*.

in a few days, and I hope to put an end to all the affairs that have brought me here.

I suspect you will be commissioned to give Rappard's introduction so that the Council will no longer be without direction. The appointment of Scholten on August 2nd in Duisburg is quite appropriate and your High Well-Born will probably give the necessary introduction.

The retainer fund is now in Wesel. I hope His Majesty will soon have finished his diplomatic trip and will inform the authorities about the results and the settlement of the trip.

With the well-known friendly and respectful sentiments, I have the honor to be your High Well-Born's

obedient servant and friend

Stein.

In the parental family circle of Johann August Sack of Cleve many things had changed during the last decade in which he had had to leave the city to pursue his career. In 1788 he had lost a blossoming sister to death at the age of 22 and in 1790 his eldest sister Friederike had married a son of the Consistorial Councillor Wilhelm Gillet from the Berlin Reformed French colony. Friedrich Wilhelm Gillet, the son, also served as a pastor in Berlin. After the young pastor's wife had given her husband two daughters, one of whom died very early, she herself was snatched from her husband and daughter by death in 1794 on the day before her 31st birthday. In the year 1795 her 28 year old brother Ernst Wilhelm Sack followed her in death in Cleve,

---

Another honorific title was *(Euer) Wohlgeboren* which ranked lower than *Hochwohlgeboren* and was claimed by Bourgeois notables.

In the 19th century it became customary to address academic and other civil honoraries by this title, e.g., a number of letters to Sigmund Freud are addressed to *"Hochwohlgeboren* Prof. Dr. Sigmund Freud". The terms "High Well-Born, Well-born", etc. have been used in this book.

Judicial Councillor Carl August Sack 1721-1810 died in
Münster on 19 April 1810 at the age of 89

so that the former proud flock of offspring of 11 adults, which had blossomed in the Judicial Councillor's house, had already thinned out by more than one third. In 1796, however, Christoph Sethe, son of the privy councillor at the Cleve Justice Commission, brought the second and this time local son-in-law to the young Privy Councillor. This quite outstanding legal mind, whom the second daughter Philippine chose as her life companion and who later was feared even by Napoleon in Paris and who as Crown President of the Court of Cassation (highest Prussian judicial authority) in Berlin, was decorated by the King with the Order of the Black Eagle. Later he had a successful career. It is a splendid illustration of Cleve affairs, which already soon afterwards in the new century were to bring the whole Sethe's house as well as his father-in-law Sack to Münster in Westphalia. This can be found in Gustav Freytag's "Pictures from the German Past" but it remains to be added that in the meantime, in the shipping and mining industry on the Rhine and Ruhr which Stein und Sack had operated with so much success, a capable successor had grown up in Johann August's younger brother Ernst Heinrich Eberhard Sack, who Stein, when he was director and president in Westphalia, also recognized as a solid pillar in the mentioned mining and metallurgical department. Immediately after graduating from the Joachimthal Gymnasium in Berlin, Ernst Sack attended the School of Mining in Freiberg in Saxony and then the universities of Halle and Erlangen. In 1799, he came to Hamm as a trainee lawyer and then immediately joined the Märkische War- und Domain Chamber under Stein's presidency.

It was just in the year 1799 when the old Judicial Councillor Sack saw his son Johann August happily married and returning to Berlin and knew that his son Ernst in Hamm was well employed in his vicinity, suffered a severe blow through the death of his faithful and cheerful partner Gertrud née Nottemann. After 42 years of an exceedingly happy and delightful marriage, she succumbed in the 64th year to what seems to have been prolonged suffering. This perhaps had an impact on her son Johann August's wedding feast, although she was still present at the marriage. The death certificate, already written completely in French, is printed under the family documents as No. V in the appendix.

For the young, radiant beauty who Sack now introduced to his new home in Berlin, a similarly difficult time immediately began in the same way as Mrs von Stein had experienced in her first years of marriage. However, we may firmly assume that the daughter of a Prussian civil servant, through the last six years in Cleve, was equipped with other experiences and qualities to master a harder existence than a spoiled Hanoverian English Countess, who was also, through her grandmother Countess Yarmouth's love affair, granddaughter of King George II of England.

Sack had undoubtedly chosen a strong, resilient domestic girl's soul as his companion, because during the 32 years of marriage and 20 years of widowhood, Marianne von Reiman remained faithful to him in love and loyalty, created a happy domesticity and even after his death she continued to live and act according to his wishes. The times were no less difficult for this couple, even more difficult than for the people in Styria.

Cleve was soon completely handed over to foreign rule through the Treaty of Luneville in 1801 and Sethe was transferred to the government in Münster in 1803. The elderly 82-year-old father Sack had already concluded a contract of inheritance with his children the year before in which he, enriched by the inheritance of his Glogau brother and his wife, became the owner of 14 different properties acquired over the years. These included three farm estates, three farms, a lot of pastures, farmland and the like. He only retained the right of residence in his previous family home on the Stechbahn and a sixteenth of his income but it was recommended that the lonely man should give up his domicile in Cleve completely and move to Münster in Westphalia with his daughter and son-in-law. Due to Stein's appointment as Westphalia's Crown President and the appointment of his son Johann August at the side of the new minister von Schulenburg of Hildesheim, the old gentleman received a reconciliatory compensation for his difficult farewell from the Cleve home. He had lived in Cleve for more than 50 years. Since the Crown President alternately resided in Hamm and Münster during the years of secularization, the old man often saw his son Johann August whenever Stein met up with him there.

Stein and Sack's Collaboration in Westphalia. Baron von Vincke Joins 1801-1804

This detailed description of the Cleve family, which was inserted here, somewhat jumps ahead in time. It is a characteristic feature of how strong the bond was between the Cleve civil servant families and how this bond affected not only the next but even subsequent generations. We are now again going to follow the development of Sack's activities in more detail.

As we begin the new century with the young couple in Berlin, we hope and wish that they were first granted a brief, albeit peaceful, period of rest and that they were able to devote themselves to the pleasures of domesticity and the many interesting performances in the capital in the free hours remaining to the State Fiscal Councillor—including of course the celebrations of court and other pleasurable diversions for Mrs Marianne's receptive mind.

The restless Stein who in those years—as he expressed himself in letters to his old girlfriend Mrs von Berg, did not find full understanding and the right influence for his impetuous mind from his wife—had occupied himself in 1801 with the sale of his estates on the left bank of the Rhine and a part of his estates on the right bank of the Rhine and in return had acquired a greater dominion of Birnbaum on the Warta in Poznan.

As already mentioned, in 1800 Napoleon Buonaparte succeeded in becoming the first consul in France to be appointed to the head of the directorate. The more he extended his tyranny to neighboring countries, the more he won the admiration of his people at home.

Friedrich Ludwig Wilhelm Philipp Philipp Baron von Vincke 1774-1844)

On February 9, 1801, at the Peace of Luneville, it was openly revealed that the left bank of the Rhine was to be ceded to France and for Prussia this disgrace was compounded by the additional humiliation of having to put up with the interference of foreign neighbors in decisions about German or Prussian interests.

While in Paris, the French ruler began a veritable market operation with barter and money exchange against countries and possessions. Prussia was to be compensated for the left bank of the Rhine with the increase in land etc. achieved through the dissolution of German dioceses, abbeys, free imperial cities etc. ordered by France.

At the end of the year 1801 Stein was called to Berlin to take part in the discussions about Minden's bridge building and to successfully implement all kinds of reductions in business in the chambers of Mark, Cleve and Minden. Stone and Sack once again were together. Cleve had remained Prussian after the occupation of the left bank of the Rhine in its right bank portion and therefore also leaving the War and Domain Chamber as administrative authority for this portion to it. Only in 1803 did the latter merge with the Mark War and Domain Chamber in Hamm. Among his Westphalian officials, Stein had now also renewed his acquaintance with Baron Ludwig von Vincke[32], who he had first met when he met his brother the

---

32 Friedrich Ludwig Wilhelm Philipp Philipp Baron von Vincke 1774-1844) was a Prussian reformer who, among other things, enforced the municipal self-administration of the cities and advocated a new trade code.
After the defeat of Prussia against Napoleon I, Vincke fled to England, where he became acquainted with the local administrative system of self-government. On his return in 1807 he joined the circle of reformers around Baron vom und zum Stein. Until the dismissal of Stein in November 1808, Vincke's decisive reforms included the abolition of serfdom and hereditary servitude, a new trade code and the municipal self-administration of the towns. Af-

envoy in Kassel, in Marburg, where Stein was staying on October 28, 1792. It was in Marburg that he first met Baron Ludwig von Vincke, (who we will also talk about later) and who Vincke had met while still a student. Later he had met Vincke once again at his father-in-law's house, the Field Marshal of Hanover, Count Walmoden, where a paper by Vincke on the inequality of the estates was presented, which immediately met with Stein's lively applause. Stein had not let him out of his sight since then and had turned his particular patronage toward him.

Vincke was a man of petite and small stature, but equipped with an excellent scientific and business education. When Stein introduced his young favorite to King Frederick Wilhelm II, this monarch is said to have remarked: "Do they make children into county councillors here?" to which Stein replied: "Yes, Your Majesty, a young man in years, but an old man in wisdom".

According to a correspondence between the two about Vincke's wish to withdraw from council business and to be allowed to restrict himself to the affairs of the District Administrator. Already Stein had fought for the appointment of Vincke as District Administrator in Westphalia in August 1798 at the almost unbelievable sounding age of 23 years, residing at the offices of Hausberge, Petershagen and Schlüsselburg and having received a seat and a vote in the Council of the War and Domain Chamber in Minden. Stein then suffered from a prolonged disgruntlement, which was later, however, reversed after a more detailed

---

ter Stein's resignation, Vincke became Kurmärk chamber president in Potsdam in 1809 but withdrew to his private estates in 1810.

travel report, which Vincke wrote to Stein from England on the 8th day of his visit. August 1800. After the ongoing changes in the civil service positions in Westphalia, during the soon following secularization, Vincke remained district administrator in Minden, but was appointed president of the East Frisian War and Territorial Chamber on 8 October 1803 replacing Count Schwerin who had been transferred to Magdeburg.

However Vincke was not the only protégé of Stein to be looked by his far-reaching eyes, for in addition, the Princess Luise of Prussia33, who was married to the Prince of Radziwill, and her brother Prince Louis Ferdinand, also placed their trust in him. Stein took great pains to bring this equally beautiful, well-disposed, talented and brave prince, already the idol of the soldiers back to his father and his family. He was barely twenty years old when he was a general at the head of a brigade near Mainz fighting against the French. He was a virtuoso on the piano and of course the idol of the female sex. He had become es-tranged from his family because he was a passionate gam-bler and reckless epicurean and was running the risk of getting further and further away. From birth a high, ide-ally directed nature, thirsting for fame and honor, at-tracted by the great affairs of the state, this boldest horseman and swimmer was at best only able to mock the monarchy, the patriotic weakness and the cabinet regime as well as the scheming army of officials, as Prussia's ruin. But his insights into all departments were only superficial and Stein first sought to bring him back to Minden, where the prince served in garrison, from Hamburg where he had surrendered to the pleasures of the cosmopolitan city.

He wanted to bring him under his personal influence, because he felt a great affection for this rarely attractive princely son. He did succeed in returning him to his family but he did not have the opportunity to tie him to an orderly domesticity and to many other things, such as to balance his noble qualities and his passions.

On May 15, 1802, the "father of mining", Minister of State Friedrich Anton von Heinitz (1725-1802) Sack and Stein's great patron, died, and in his place Count Friedrich Wilhelm von der Schulenburg-Kehnert (1742-1815) was appointed minister and at the same time head of the main organizing commission in Hildesheim, which was charged with the affiliation of the so-called compensation countries in Prussia.

On May 23, 1802, as a result of the Peace of Luneville, provisions were made in Paris regarding Prussian compensation for the loss of the left bank of the Rhine. In Lower Saxony they included the bishoprics of Hildesheim, Quedlinburg and the free imperial cities of Nordhausen, Mühlhausen and Goslar, in Westphalia a large part of the princely-bishopric of Münster and the whole bishopric of Paderborn, Herford, Elten, Essen and Werden, to which Erfurt and Eichsfeld were added from the Mainz property. "To take over all these lands and to put them on Prussian footing, the minister Schulenburg, with the excellent support of the State Councillor of Finance Sack, gave an example of how, by exalting himself above all petty matters, by the greatest fairness and generosity, he managed to remedy and alleviate the inevitable dissatisfaction with such changes at times, paralyzing them here and there, and thus

winning over a significant part of the people", Pertz reports. It was relatively easy to abolish the bishoprics and
church estates in the scattered, predominantly Protestant
cities, which quickly got used to the Prussian government
measures, as Hildesheim in 1813 wished them back. The
situation was different in the Westphalian Catholic area,
such as Münster and Paderborn, which sometimes very reluctantly complied with the minister's orders and sometimes   resisted   them.   Count   Schulenburg   had
commissioned the Crown President Stein to secularize and
take possession of the monasteries and church property
there and appointed him to his post on September 9, 1802.
Stein stayed in the castle, where Count Blücher[33] was living at the same time. He had to disband the troops of the
bishopric of Münster, about 2000 men who mostly went
over to Prussia with him. Stein knew very well that he had
not been given a pleasant duty but since the King wanted
to see the principles of leniency, humanity and justice carried out and since he knew the pious, good-natured sense
of the people of Münster, also knowing his faithful friend
Sack as an intermediary between himself and the minister,
he began his activity without hesitation.

Regarding this Westphalian period of Stein's collaboration
with Sack and the minister Schulenburg-Kehnert, one of
the main sources is present in a correspondence between
Stein and Sack, which has been preserved in Sack's estate,
from which Pertz already drew and from which he inter-

---

33   Gebhard Leberecht von Blücher, Prince of Wahlstatt, 1742–1819),
     Count), later elevated to Prince von Wahlstatt, was a Prussian
     General Field Marshal. He earned his greatest recognition after
     leading his army against Napoleon I at the Battle of the Nations at
     Leipzig in 1813 and the Battle of Waterloo in 1815.

weaved many a particularly characteristic piece in his work: "Stein's Leben". There are thirty-six letters from Stein alone covering the period from March 1802 to March 1804[34], and the Stein archives in Cappenberg and Wiesbaden contain Sack's return letters that are now in the possession of Albrecht Count von Kanitz, Stein's legal successor in the Nassau estate, and which Dr. Bötzenhart recently reorganized there. It would be beyond the scope of this document to include the entire correspondence in its appendix. I shall confine myself to reproducing one or two particularly interesting letters below. Among these is a letter addressed to Stein by the main representative of the church estates, the Cathedral Dean, Count von Spiegel zum Desenberg[35], which he enclosed with his letter.

We see from the mood of the letter writer, which speaks from the postscript, after Sack had meanwhile visited him, how excellently he understood how to silence the most difficult objections of the church princes and to initiate a favorable conclusion.

---

34   Today in the possession of Mrs. Colonel Lieutenant Sack of Berlin.*
35   Count von Spiegel zum Desenberg, Ferdinand August Maria Joseph Anton, Archbishop of Cologne, born on December 25 at Laustein Castle in Westphalia, 1782 Canon of Münster, 1790 Praetor Darius of Osnabrück, 1792 of Hildesheim, 1799 Dean of Münster, was a man of great gifts and noble tolerance.
     After he was later appointed Bishop of Münster by Napoleon in 1813 but was not confirmed by the Pope, he was elected Archbishop of Cologne in 1824. He rendered great service to the peaceful relationship between the denominations and later, in 1834, concluded a secret convention with the Prussian government, according to which he renounced the promise to educate all children in the Catholic Church in the case of mixed marriages. The agreement, which was reached after his death in 1835, provoked the Cologne church dispute.*

Münster the February 2, 1803.

To the Privy Fiscal Counselor Sack, High Well-Born
in Hildesheim.

It is a great pleasure for me to see from the Hon. High Well-Born's very esteemed and friendly letter of 31st March, that Cathedral Deacon v. Sp. also appeared to you to be an esteemed and educated man and I am convinced that his stay in Berlin will be personally useful to him and will give him respect and affection for our state. He is very satisfied with his reception in Hildesheim and with your kind behavior towards him, as you can see from the enclosure. With regard to the contents of his letter, I very much repeat the wish not to meet any general ecclesiastical institutions until you have all been here.

The bishop of Hildesheim is indolent and without energy and his behavior is without all dignity and firmness.

I hope to send you the news about Marienfelde and Liesborn in 14 days to 3 weeks, followed by the news about the Council Judge and the Cathedral Chapter. The news about Abdinghoff and Bodecker will be announced by the Pad. O. Com. Malchus (?) whom I know from his writings and from Hon. High Well-Born's letters would perhaps not be of the benefit he had in Hildesheim at this moment, when the investigation of the ecclesiastical property has already been initiated. I wish he would make an elaboration on the relations of the ecclesiastical authorities, bishop, general vicariate, suffragan, etc. to the Chamber, this is an essential matter. One can read the basic sentences of Riegger's *institutiones jurisprud. Eccles*, especially Part 1. p. 89. 288. 313, Part III. p. 623 IV 151-169. He is a Catholic canonist, in the system of Febronius and Emperor Joseph.

To administrators or actual preceptors of the local domain one will need the previous official pensioners — among them are very reasonable people, e.g. A. M. Geissberg, Reinhardt — partly the Cleves *in specie* Lobbes, Feldmann, Hallensleben. I have engaged Heisselbach for myself, I must have reliable, useful people — Gosebruch, who I have proposed for Cappenberg, is a farmer, field surveyor, and a "hunter" and has general knowledge of hydraulic engineering. He administered my property during the unfortunate war years, sold my products to Cleves and Holland in 1800 and 1801, conducted the surveying in a village belonging to me and carried out the separation, and in 1802 sold almost all of my properties on the left bank of the Rhine. I don't wish to fall in love with him but he is an honest, shrewd and energetic person.

Also, among the local officials who become vacant, there will still be people who can be employed as administrators, because the change that took place in the military, where only 10 officers were taken out of Münster, only allegedly noblemen without any consideration for merit...

(End of sentence missing here.)

I'm busy here with the general plan for the formation of local communities — should the regulations of 1797 and 1798 make the chambers too dependent on the governments and ultimately the Department of Justice? This should be considered as far as possible.

Goldberg seems to be very happy.

The Duke of E...(?) has moved into Rheine. We told him that we would not grant him any other rights to the civil property than if he had attended the previous negotiations of the Dispute Commission.

As Kampfs writes me, one escad. will go to Hildesheim, four to Eichsfeld, two to Münster and one to Paderborn.

Hon. High Well-Born

Your honored friend

Stein.

Attachment to the above letter:

Letter from the Cathedral Dean of Spiegel to Baron von Stein:

Hildesheim, January 28, 1803.

P. P.

Allow me Hon. High Well-Born to use the form of a concise *pro memoria* instead of a formal letter. My fervent admiration for the Crown President von Stein is independent of all formalities — but I am not travelling from here without reporting to Hon. High Well-Born on how I found things here.

The reception of Minister Count von Schulenburg was friendly and good, his open statement about the uncertainty of the fate of the cathedral chapters and the inability of some deputies to obtain something direct from the King. Necessarily and at least very advisable to him, our trip to Berlin seemed to be a characteristic of our most submissive attitude towards the King's Majesty. We are taking letters from Minister Count von Schulenburg to Haugwitz, Hardenberg and Hatzfeld with us. In this respect the Münster travelers enjoy equal treatment with the rest of the cathedral chapters in Hildesheim and Paderborn — the latter (the cathedral dean Count v. Kesselstatt) is still here because of indisposition and fear of the nightly effect of the cold.

The result of the many conversations which I have had with businessmen about the fate of the cathedral and other Mediate Chapters is an urgent, almost inevitable danger of the dissolution of the Cathedral Chapter in Münster and Paderborn — also this one is suppressed but is revived in a rejuvenated form as an episcopal Cathedral Chapter. The heterogeneous selection of the residence at Hildesheim is to blame — the indolent prince-bishop will now, without a substantial increase of his episcopal business, become bishop in Westphalia and other provinces will receive suffragan bishops. Time will teach how great this abuse is and bring about change but some evil will then be incurable. The Mediate Chapters have lost the administration of their property and are dying out. The monastic clergy would gradually become completely lost, the wealthy would be the first to die a political death, the mendicant friars would be used for the time being for pastoral care and the Franciscans, also called observants, would be the most favored.

Count Maximillian von Merveldt

You, dear Mr Crown President, are probably smiling at this horoscope, but essentially time will teach us what needs to be corrected.

The Minister von Schulenburg reveals deep insight and a quick understanding in his remarks and his endeavors to achieve the welfare of the state are the hallmarks of his behavior — seriousness and severity are often regarded as harshness — and the inevitable disturbance of many an individual condition awakens dissatisfied people — I have found many here and may claim with correct conviction that the mood against Prussia is stronger and more lively here than in Münster. Münster's affairs are not yet the order of the day here, so I was not able to obtain proof of the assets of the cathedral chapter. This will remain suspended until the presence of Count v. Schulenburg but as far as the general budget is concerned, which I am taking with me to Berlin, I would ask—in the event that such a work is still required by the Cathedral Chapter of Münster during my absence—to allow a considerable period of time for its submission, so that I can send it over from Berlin. All the assets, however, are indicated in the budgets already submitted.

For the acquaintance I have made with the Privy Councillor of Finance Sack, I am very much obliged to Hon. High Well-Born, as he would have been less accessible if I had not been recommended to him by such a good friend—he seems to be of a lively spirit and of pervasive authority—I have expressed to him the wish that he might get to know Münster, to see the residents and institutions before pronouncing the *anathema* about us.

In Minden I visited the dignified General Lieutenant von Schieden but found him very aged—almost at the edge of the grave, his physical condition is frail and his cheerful spirit and mood have left him. With participation the good old man spoke of Münster and its sad dismemberment. With reverence he spoke of the State President, recognized with me the beneficence of Hon. High Well-Born's presence in Münster but he regretted the removal from Minden.

On Sunday, January 30, I will travel from here to Berlin, where I also like to be but where I will be accompanied by a feeling of gratitude and friendship for my dear conservative friend, Mr State-President von Stein, for whose continuing good will I would recommend.

Spiegel, Cathedral Dean.

Vertatur.

P.S. January 29, 1803.

In the accompanying letters to Berlin is—as I have reliably received—a reference to Hon. High Well-Born about me to Hardenberg—so in Berlin too I will feel the benevolence of your friendship—my feeling of gratitude is like my unlimited admiration.

This morning I had a long conversation with the Privy Fiscal-Councillor Sack about Münsterland and Paderborn's corporate constitution—the more I talk to him, the more he warms to me—his good wishes shall not be lost for me—but my predicament with regard to my travel companion is annoying.[36] Accustomed only to intrigues, his gaze is neither far-sighted nor profound, and his mistrust is unlimited—he is a true Münsterlander and believes that only in Münsterland's moors is mankind happy, something only Münsterlanders can appreciate—he is at the same time an unproclaimed interpreter of my thoughts with his bigoted, hypocritical children of Münster thing and therefore prevents me immensely—but my endeavors in Berlin will be directed toward the unification or rather the establishment of a landscape for Münster and Paderborn to jointly inspire them. Whether the cathedral chapters will be saved in this way, I doubt—I consider the two Westphalian cathedral chapters to be lost. But if a landscape is saved through a consultative vote of the landowners, much is won for the nobility of Westphalia. Much will depend on whether I can have closer contact with the businessmen of Berlin without reference to my narrow-minded con-deputies. The drafting of the memoranda, etc. is up to me anyway, since my companion has no overview of the whole and only ever takes the pawns as the main thing to focus on. That Hon. High Well-Born may prosper is the fervent wish of your admiring friend.

Spiegel, Cathedral Decan.

Stein recommended, in order to gain the basis for a more exact knowledge of the country, to include two excellent businessmen from Münster, the Privy Councillors Druffel and Forkenbeck, in the organization commission, to whom

36   Count Kesselstatt.*

Count Merveldt[37] could still be added in order to win the nobility. He therefore wrote to Sack:

> If one could decide to include a few noble privy councillors, such as Count Merveldt or Herr von Kettler, this would be very useful, they cost us nothing and it proves a liberal, open way of thinking. One should only beware of the hatred against the nobility, which has become fashionable. You know my principles in this connection. One does not think of the nobility as having a monopoly of positions, family trees, and pretenders but rather as the corps of the great landowners who, by their very nature, have influence and are attached to the interests of the country by indissoluble ties.

At the same time he wrote to Sack on October 2:

> First of all I thank you, on behalf of the Münsterland, for the good review of September 11 about the army funds, from which I see that one wants to receive provincial funds and provincial institutes and not draw everything into the General Treasury — the abolition of the estates has caused a great sensation, there is a general feeling of depression, anxiety about the future and the most absurd opinions one can imagine. We really have to do something to win over public opinion and for the time being I would stop at the proposal I have made to include some members of the Privy Council in the Commission.

The remaining letters provide evidence of how difficult it was to come to terms with the small Catholic princes and how important it was to select the right officials for the properties which were now to be transferred to the Prus-

---

37 Maximilian, Count von Merveldt (1764-1815), among the most famous of an illustrious old Westphalian family, entered Habsburg military service, rose to the rank of General of Cavalry, served as Francis II, Holy Roman Emperor's ambassador to Russia, and became special envoy extraordinaire to the Court of St. James's (Great Britain). He fought with distinction in the wars between the Habsburg and the Ottoman empires, the French Revolutionary Wars, and the Napoleonic Wars.

sian administration. Since the King wished to show great leniency in order not to cause bitterness anywhere, it was imperative that the dispute be settled as peacefully as possible and although Stein did not allow himself to be annoyed by the fact that he had to think through the smallest details of the tasks which had fallen to him, especially as regards the utilization of these scattered new possessions, it was uplifting and honorable for Sack to see how Stein did nothing without having received his approbation. Among the men to be newly elected and appointed to higher positions, it is Stein who by the way, also wishes to see Sack's brother called upon, the Mining Councillor Ernst Sack. This is the most beautiful testimony that in these terrible times, when even the world of civil servants only sought to seek their own advantage and many inferior strivers were able to push themselves forward, the purposeful greatest statesman of the century sought to call upon the Clevians he knew and tried and tested.

The disputes with the smaller princes also took place in Münster, where they had sent their deputies. At the beginning of March 1803, Stein was able to send a memorandum on the creation of sources of public income in the Principality of Münster. However, the decision on this question dragged on for a long time as Stein's proposals on taxes and their use and the excise import and transit duties met with great resistance in Berlin. At the beginning of winter the new administration was in place and the new War and Domain Chamber of Münster, Paderborn, Längen and Tecklenburg took over the organization under Stein's chairmanship, whereas he relinquished the presidency of the Minden Chamber. Von Bernuth[38] from Cleve became the president of the Minden Chamber. Vincke was actually supposed to become president but instead became president in East Frisia. Sack had also become acquainted with Vincke during these years and when this small, clever but somewhat difficult official who had just returned from a trip from Spain where he had been purchasing sheep at the request of the minister to improve German sheep breeding. On returning and hearing of Stein's appointment as Fiscal Minister in Berlin and of his desire to see Vincke appointed as his future successor as the Crown President of Westphalia, the latter was not at all pleased. When he expressed this, Stein recommended the position to him, "as one with many means to achieve good and philanthropic ends, whereby he would find in the well-behaved Privy Councillor Sack a zealous patron of all good things". Vincke was appointed President of the War and Domain Chamber by Cabinet Ordnance on November 10, 1804. Stein wrote to him from Berlin, however, only a few weeks later on January 15, "I am only marginally able to take a directly effective part in public affairs in Münster and Westphalia. Meanwhile I have handed over your letter to the active, liberal, insightful and tirelessly interested in Westphalia Privy Councillor Sack in order to give a brief account of the situation of the affairs you have touched on, which he has done in his marginalia. From Stein's next let-

---

38 Karl von Bernuth (1774-1843) was a German lawyer. In 1793 he began studying law at the University of Erlangen, which he continued in Marburg in 1795. After completing his studies he entered the civil service. In 1804 he was Privy Councillor in Münster and in 1809 President of the Tribunal in Dillenburg. In 1815 he returned to Münster, where he became Vice President of the Münster Higher Regional Court in 1824. He held the presidency until 1839.

ter to Vincke, dated February 26, it is clear that, with all the business he is involved in, he is not able to take care of Vincke's chamber department as he would like. "According to the detailed information given to me by Privy Councillor Sack, the Honorable High Well-Born von Spiegel, whom I certainly hold in such high esteem, will now be reassured".

In the spring of 1804, the disputes between Prussia and the church estates in Westphalia were as good as successfully concluded. The English cabinet had declared war on the French consul Buonaparte in 1803 and French soldiers soon moved in. The ruler of Hanover residing in England, George III, who fell ill, had the Elbe and Weser estuaries closed by English ships and gathered around him the loyal and courageous soldiers of the disbanded Hanoverian army, men who, guided by honor and duty, had gloriously carried the flags of the German legion to Spain and Portugal, the Baltic Sea, Sicily and the Netherlands in ten years of war. Field Marshal Count Walmoden, Stein's father-in-law, had first pressed for the reinforcement of the Hanoverian army, but he encountered only weakness and resistance.

Because of the loosening and finally the dissolution of the Imperial Union, the knighthood was hostile and Stein had taken new steps against its destruction by the Duke of Nassau because of his possessions in Nassau, until the Emperor of Austria, as a result of Stein's efforts, took steps to put an end to the princes' predatory intentions and to protect the imperial knighthood in its possession. So the soldiers of Nassau withdrew from Stein's possessions.

In the spring of 1804, a discovered conspiracy had given the first consul in France the pretext to have his rival Pichegru[39] executed in prison, to drive Moreau[40] away to America and to secretly and forcibly remove the Duke of Enghien[41] from German territory and have him murdered in Vincennes under court-martial procedures. These out-

---

39 Jean-Charles Pichegru (1761-1804) was a distinguished French general of the Revolutionary Wars. Under his command, French troops overran Belgium and the Netherlands before fighting on the Rhine front. His royalist positions led to his loss of power and imprisonment in Cayenne, French Guiana during the Coup of 18 Fructidor in 1797. After escaping into exile in London and joining the staff of Alexander Korsakov, he returned to France and planned the Pichegru Conspiracy to remove Napoleon from power, which led to his arrest and death. Despite his defection, his surname is one of the names inscribed under the Arc de Triomphe.

40 Jean Victor Marie Moreau (1763-1813) was a French general who helped Napoleon Bonaparte to power, but later became a rival and was banished to the United States.

His wife collected around her all who were discontented with the aggrandizement of Napoleon. This "Club Moreau" annoyed Napoleon, and encouraged the Royalists, but Moreau, though not unwilling to become a military dictator to restore the republic, would be no party to an intrigue for the restoration of Louis XVIII. All this was well known to Napoleon, who seized the conspirators.

Moreau's condemnation was procured only by great pressure being brought to bear by Bonaparte on the judges. After it was pronounced the First Consul treated him with a pretense of leniency, commuting a sentence of imprisonment to one of banishment. In 1804, Moreau passed through Spain and embarked for America.

Moreau arrived with his wife in New York City, in August 1805. He was received with enthusiasm in the United States, but refusing all offers of service he traveled for some time through the country and settled in 1806 in Pennsylvania, where he bought a villa formerly belonging to Robert Morris near the Delaware River in Morrisville, PA, across the river from Trenton. He lived there till 1813, dividing his time between fishing, hunting, and social intercourse. His abode was the refuge of all political exiles, and repre-

rages aroused a feeling of horror and disgust throughout Europe. Russia and Sweden raised their voices in the German Parliament but German strength had already sunk so low that they silently accepted this violation of their property rights and this deadly insult to the law. In further violation of international law Buonaparte had the papers of the English envoy Drake stolen and printed in Munich and forced the Elector of Bavaria to drive the envoy out of his country himself. Then he took a quick step towards the goal he had long had in mind. He used the republican system to settle the question of his imperial dignity. The French people crawled in humility at his feet, as they had crawled at the feet of Robespierre fifteen years earlier. It was clear that the transformation of the other republics with which France had surrounded itself would now all be inextricably bound to the new empire. The new Emperor had enough brothers and sisters to occupy all of Europe with rulers subservient to him.

On October 27, 1804, Stein was appointed by the King to replace the late minister Karl August von Struensee34 (1735 -1804), who had been appointed to the ministry for

---

sentatives of foreign powers tried to induce him to raise his sword against Napoleon. At the outbreak of the War of 1812, President Madison offered him the command of the U.S. troops. Moreau was willing to accept, but after hearing the news of the destruction of the Grande Armée in Russia in November 1812, he decided to return to Europe.

41 Louis Antoine de Bourbon, Duke of Enghien (1772-1804) was a member of the House of Bourbon of France. More famous for his death than for his life, he was executed on charges of aiding Britain and plotting against France. Royalty across Europe were shocked and dismayed at his execution. Tsar Alexander I of Russia was especially alarmed, and decided to curb Napoleon's power.

Accise, Customs, Commercial and Factory Affairs since 1791 and had now died.

Stein had always been keen to do this because he foresaw his future appointment to Berlin. In his place he wanted to have a suitable man ready to take up his position in Westphalia and to preserve the achievements there in the way he had been doing hitherto. Baron von Vincke was indisputably the right man and Stein had been able to leave Westphalia, which he had grown very fond of, with peace of mind. He found his friend Sack in Berlin, albeit still under Minister Schulenburg.

Regarding the aforementioned Family Foundation of Glogau, one more of Sack's activities could be touched upon here, which, despite all the demands made on him by the state, also required his attention and work on the side.

In the unfortunate period of 1805/06, the increase in capital caused by the accumulation of interest was used by the Minister of Hoym[42] to ask the King to divide the Sack Foundation's capital in favor of the State, which was of course objected to by the family, which unfortunately itself had few rights of veto vis-à-vis the supreme government, despite it being in breach of the founder's testament. From the earliest days of the founder's uncle's retirement, the

---

42 Karl Georg Heinrich Graf von Hoym (1739-1807) was a Prussian statesman.
In 1786, Friedrich Wilhelm II granted him the title of Count and in 1793 also entrusted him with the administration of the newly acquired South Prussia. Here Hoym gave rise to bureaucratic despotism as well as bad administration, self-enrichment and squandering of the state property and thus initiated the Black Book by Hans von Held.

help of the young lawyer of the new generation, Johann August Sack and the preacher of the high court, Sack of Berlin, was called upon from all sides to at least emphasize and represent the moral rights of the family with regard to their foundation. As always willing to do every good deed and altruistic task, Johann August Sack also did his utmost to support these justified wishes and among the family foundation documents there are some submissions which he made in consideration of the just principles always practiced by his uncle Heinrich, in whose spirit he was not going to allow himself to be put off by the King in supporting the family.

Nevertheless, the negotiations, which are recorded in the "Silver Book of the Sack Family", dragged on for a long time due to the ever new counter-attacks of the omnipotent Silesian minister and only after the unfortunate battles of Jena and Auerstädt did Prussia's coffers show very small reserves. Finally, a main comparison—based on totally erroneous calculations by an auditing council—was recommended to the family for approval. It was not in their interest at all, which was to be declared null void and substituted with the rights of the state in favor of the princedoms of Glogau, Liegnitz and Wohlau as agnates[43]. At a time when Prussia's financial power was, as it soon was, completely in the hands of the French victor, there was little left for the family to do but postpone the renewal of its legal position until more favorable patriotic times.

---

43 In law this would be a person descended from the same ancestor or as another specified or implied person (the princedoms in this case).

Stein Finance Minister, Sack Privy Fiscal Councillor

The police authority of the Prussian state, in which the administration of the country was united with the exception of Silesia, as was already mentioned, was under the control of its own minister, the Count of Hoym, consisted of a number of provincial ministers and a few specialized ministers when Stein took over the Ministry of Finance in 1804. Count Schulenburg-Kehnert chaired the Ministry of Finance as Minister of the Treasury and General Controller of Finances. Under his direct supervision were the coffers, stamps, coins, bank, medical services, lottery and post office. Beneath him four ministers administered the provinces: Voss, Mark, Pomerania and South Prussia, Hardenberg Franconia and Neuchâtel, Schroetter East, New East and West Prussia, Angern Lower Saxony and Westphalia. Goltz headed the military department — Minister Struensee had been in charge of excise, customs, stone, salt, factory, manufacture and commercial matters, while Reden was in charge of mining and metallurgy. In addition, there were fifty privy fiscal councillors to deal with financial administration matters, which were prepared by seventy secretaries. Before Stein took up his new position, he had already stated his gratitude in his letter to the King's Majesty, which he had previously given to Cabinet Councillor Beyme for his consideration. He stated that he was basically in favor of the disciplines that had been defined by Struensee and that although he had little previous knowledge, if he nevertheless took up his office and was sworn in, he was committed to the merger of all financial departments and the simplification of business in this way already in the first year, recognizing this as particularly necessary.

Karl Freiherr von und zum Stein 1757-1831
Royal Prussian Minister of Finance from
1804-1808

A number of drafts for streamlining, which Stein had just presented, were soon put on the back burner when, once again, the outbreak of a new war initially thwarted progress.

The continued violent measures of the new French Emperor had already provoked negotiations on armaments at the other courts of Europe. When in September 1805 the King of Prussia also decided to put his army on a war footing, the financial proposals that Stein submitted to Minister Hardenberg were accepted in all parts — after Stein had already taken over the top management of the bank and maritime operations instead of Schulenburg. After the events of the war had turned out to be extremely hopeless for Prussia in the course of the following January 1806, Stein, in a memorandum addressed to the King on April 6, 1806 about the flawed organization of the cabinet and the necessity of forming a ministerial conference, expressed his great concern that with the current closest advisers to the King the state would have to perish. However, the King did not like extraordinary measures and left everything as it was. During the very first campaigns against the French in 1792, he had probably tried to broaden his military viewpoint and had become aware of the shortcomings of his own army. He set a goal for all abuses in the court and treasury administration that had been introduced under his father and in his persistent pursuit of this path he had succeeded in accumulating a new war treasury of 17 million taler by 1805 in the empty war fund he had inherited. But Frederick Wilhelm III had also become aware of the low efficiency of his Prussia and even though he was of a peace-loving, not very energetic character he avoided any independent step. Since, however, in Berlin itself there was already foment, Stein saw himself compelled to join a new petition by the brothers of the King and some other princes, among them Prince Louis Ferdinand, to whom Stein had shown a special benevolence. This was a petition in which, both respectfully and firmly, the dismissal of Minister Haugwitz, who had already had his windows smashed by the people, and of Cabinet Councillors Beyme and Lombard was pressed, because this cabinet government had completely lost sight of the impending danger of war. The King was very upset about this request, which had been dictated only by the imminent danger, expressing his displeasure about it to Stein through General von Pfuel. After the subsequent unfortunate outcome of the campaign in Thuringia, during which Prince Louis Ferdinand heroically fell near Saalfeld, and after the further fatal battles near Jena and Auerstädt, whereupon Lübeck and the surrender of the fortifications, even the bulwark of Magdeburg followed, the governor of Berlin, Count Schulenburg-Kehnert, declared peace as his first civic duty but he himself left the city, leaving behind his son-in-law, Prince Hatzfeld34, as commander. At that time, Berlin had the largest stocks of weapons and powder but Prince Hatzfeld, who later proved to be a friend of the French and an opportunist, did not allow them to be taken away under the pretext of not exposing Berlin to the wrath of Napoleon—the supplies all fell into enemy hands. On the other hand, when Stein, a loyal patriot and caring citizen, received the news of the unfortunate outcome at Jena and Auerstädt, he had already had the substantial supplies brought into the safekeeping of his administration, including the bank and maritime administration and immediately sent them to Stettin (Szczecin) and Königsberg (Kaliningrad), meaning that the King retained funds to continue the war until the peace of Tilsit. One day's delay would even then have resulted in their loss. Stein, who himself had suffered badly from podagra[44], left Berlin and went to Danzig. When the way to Berlin had been cleared for the enemy, the royal family had moved its headquarters to Königsberg.

---

44   Gout of the foot, especially the big toe.

On November 29, the King transferred the Foreign Affairs portfolio to Stein *ad interim* asking him to make proposals for the interim management of his department because, as it was said, the Minister Count v. Haugwitz had gout in his eyes. Since Beyme remained in the Cabinet in place of old Lombard and his son as well as other detrimental creatures in the Foreign Ministry, Stein found the occasion so momentous as to renew his proposal for the elimination of the Cabinet government for the third time, rejecting the royal offer for his person and proposing Baron von Hardenberg, who lived quietly and secludedly in Königsberg, for the office designated for him. The King, embarrassed by Stein's reply, could not decide to exchange Beyme for Hardenberg. A middle course was now attempted. With serious and detailed emphasis that the retention of the present cabinet government in addition to a cabinet ministry with a Council of State attached to it would be highly disadvantageous, a new proposal was submitted to the King by General Rüchel[45] on December 15, after Stein had agreed in a consultation with Rüchel and Hardenberg that only a ministry with a Council of State could work without a cabinet.

But the King was particularly reluctant to recall Minister Hardenberg, who had been in declared hostility to his

---

45 Ernst von Rüchel (1754-1823) was a Prussian general who led an army corps in a crushing defeat by Napoleon at the Battle of Jena on 14 October 1806. He commanded troops from the Kingdom of Prussia in several battles during the French Revolutionary Wars in 1793 and 1794. Afterward he held various appointments as a diplomat and a military inspector. In 1806 during the Napoleonic Wars he held an important army command but has been criticized for his actions at Jena. Wounded, he managed to escape the French pursuit, but never commanded troops in combat again.

CARL GEORGE HEINRICH GRAF VON HOYM

Cabinet Councillor Beyme since his removal in April. But since Beyme, for his part, recommended General von Zastrow to the King as Minister of Foreign Affairs, the King appointed the latter as Minister and ordered Stein, Rüchel and Zastrow to prepare and submit to him, jointly and without delay, the measures to be taken for the good of the State at this most important time.

Zastrow accepted the post of minister, while Rüchel explained that it seemed to him that the King actually wanted to leave the management of the enterprise as it was, so that only those things which were determined by the cabinet should be submitted to the Council of Ministers. Stein also spoke out and concluded his reply with the following sentences: "The ungentle and unfriendly way in which the Minister of State von Hardenberg is now being treated is not very encouraging for me to enter into circumstances which in themselves carry the principles of dissolution and destruction. In addition, my health, which has not yet been restored, leaves it doubtful whether I will be able to fulfil in his time the extensive business duties assigned to me.

For these reasons I must respectfully refuse the position assigned to me by the Council.

December 20, 1806."

Rüchel reported to the King at the same time, "Stein did not want to withdraw from affairs at this critical time but as long as he could be of service to the King, he would be happy to be of assistance to the King to the best of his ability in good fortune and misfortune. Therefore, he would preside over his present duties, express his judgement on everything the King ordered him to do, discuss with other ministers according to the King's orders and appear at the consultations in the presence of the King. He only did not want to give way to the deception as if a real council existed, namely one which regularly dealt with the real affairs of the State as a whole in the personal presence of the King, without intermediaries, so as not to incur a responsibility against the King and the country which he, as a man of honor, could not assume without the means necessary for such an expectation".

By this declaration, the establishment of a Council of Ministers alongside the Cabinet was rejected by the ministers appointed for this purpose, without the King himself seeming to have realized this. For on December 30 he sent a report to Stein through General Köckeritz concerning the reimbursement of costs to Napoleon with reference to the course of business in the Council of Ministers ordered by the Cabinet Order of December 19, and even had the order repeated from Stein's counterstatement.

These growing resentments, which threatened to separate the King from his best adviser in the days of the most serious visitation of Prussia, came to a head in the days of January 1807, when both of them were staying in Königsberg, where the enemies were already threatening to approach. The royal family therefore decided to travel to Memel, where Stein was about to follow them the following night and the situation became so bad that a sudden break was inevitable. That very evening Stein received a letter from the King, written in his own hand and delivered to him by a military police officer, which concluded in gravely offensive terms about Stein's qualities, with the words: "if you are not willing to change your disrespectful and indecent behavior, the state cannot make any great demands on your further services".

Thereupon Stein felt urged to abandon his journey to Memel and to submit his application for resignation on January 3, which was dated January 4, still from Königsberg, which was approved by the King in a form that was tantamount to acceptance of the same. Stein now decided that as soon as his and his seriously ill daughter's state of health would allow it, he would return to Nassau to his own property. His departure was meanwhile lamented by deep expressions of pain from his former employees and subordinates, who now saw Prussia doomed.

On his journey home to Nassau, Stein had visited Sack while saying goodbye to other personal friends in Berlin, and had encouraged him—the rock on which he could firmly build and trust—to persevere in his post after the incident in Königsberg. At the end of March he reached Nassau and here he used his involuntary time of reflection to restore his health. Despite the deep unwillingness to accept the Nassau tyranny and the pain about the unhappy fate of the fatherland, he was busy writing down the results of his experiences here, for the purpose of forming another more appropriate administration in Prussia.

Some time after Stein's removal from Königsberg, the cabinet minister Baron von Hardenberg, who had been removed at Napoleon's request in 1806 and had been quite abandoned, was newly appointed by the King. In the meantime, a meeting between the King and the Russian Emperor Alexander, who appeared at Memel to greet

Napoleon, had lifted the King's spirits, as Alexander promised never to abandon him and encouraged him to remain calm. Alexander honored Hardenberg and recommended him to the King. The latter then left Zastrow, Beyme and Köckeritz in Memel, ordered Hardenberg to accompany him to the army, gave him back the Ministry of Foreign Affairs solely and soon afterwards entrusted him — also instead of Minister von Voss — with the Ministries of the Interior and Finance. In place of Minister von Schrötter, he entrusted him with the provisioning of the army and the other war departments. Hardenberg, supported by the full confidence of Emperor Alexander, in conjunction with General von Blücher, underwent this burden in the hope of soon winning back Stein for the Ministries of Finance and the Interior.

Hardenberg concluded a treaty with the Russian Minister of Foreign Affairs for the continuation of the war, for full cooperation in action and negotiation, in which the foundations of the future state of Europe were laid. By thus resolving the vital question of the present and building for the future, Hardenberg's colleagues endeavored to undermine his influence anew. The ministers Voss and Schrötter, in conjunction with General von Köckeritz, accused Hardenberg of ambitious intentions and there followed violent confrontations with him, after which the former were relieved of their posts as ministers and confined to their provincial departments. Voss took his leave soon after, von Zastrow refused a command in the army and ensured his dismissal. Hardenberg now worked together with Altenstein, Schön, Niebuhr and Stägemann and for three months he had the sole right to speak to the King, whose total confidence he enjoyed. Everything was well under way and Hardenberg soon hoped to share the work with Stein. He had England's trust, he expected an English-Swedish landing in Pomerania and Austria's help to turn the war around when suddenly Russia failed and thus put an abrupt end to its effectiveness. A cabal headed by the Russian Grand Prince Constantine, whose very soul was General Benningsen, had begun to dissolve the Russian army and force the Emperor to make peace with Napoleon. Emperor Alexander, too weak to control the many mistakes and abominations, forgot all his promises and by throwing himself at Napoleon's feet, Russia, instead of the protector of Europe's liberation, became an instrument of Napoleon and Prussia became the victim. On July 9, two days after the conclusion of the Russian-French peace, the Peace of Tilsit[46] was signed between Prussia and

46 The Treaties of Tilsit were two agreements signed by Napoleon I of France in the town of Tilsit in July 1807 in the aftermath of his victory at Friedland. The first was signed on July 7, between Emperor Alexander I of Russia and Napoleon I of France, when they met on a raft in the middle of the Neman River. The second was signed with Prussia on July 9. The treaties were made at the expense of the Prussian King, who had already agreed to a truce on June 25 after the Grande Armée had captured Berlin and pursued him to the easternmost frontier of his realm. In Tilsit, he ceded about half of his pre-war territories.
From those territories, Napoleon had created French sister republics, which were formalized and recognized at Tilsit: the Kingdom of Westphalia, the Duchy of Warsaw and the Free City of Danzig; the other ceded territories were awarded to existing French client states and to Russia.
Napoleon not only cemented his control of Central Europe but also had Russia and the truncated Prussia ally with him against his two remaining enemies, Great Britain and Sweden, triggering the Anglo-Russian and Finnish War. Tilsit also freed French forces for the Peninsular War. Central Europe became a battlefield again in 1809, when Austria and Great Britain engaged France in the War

France. Before any negotiation with Prussia, Napoleon had demanded Hardenberg's dismissal, which he immediately submitted without any decency.

The following day, July 10, 1807, the peace treaty itself was printed in the "Telegraf", a Berlin newspaper devoted to the French. The general horror and the deep depression over this news cannot be depicted. Yet it was still to be surpassed by the horror which the Convention of July 12, 1807, on the evacuation of the country brought about the following day. Everyone, even the French, were shocked by the contents and wondered how Field Marshal von Kalkreuth[47] could have made such a convention and signed it without shame for himself and the whole nation.

In this deep misfortune, which created an impression of desperation in Memel, a saviour was called for.

Now the Queen, the King and with him Hardenberg, Blücher, the Princess Luise v. Radziwill, Schön, Niebuhr and Spalding wrote heart-rending begging letters to Stein that he had to come. He was the only one who was still able to help the fatherland and to free it from the vermin.

---

of the Fifth Coalition. Following the end of the Napoleonic Wars in 1815, the Congress of Vienna would restore many Prussian territories.

47 Friedrich Adolf Graf von Kalckreuth (1737-818) was a Prussian Generalfeldmarschall.
Kalckreuth was defeated in the 1806 Battle of Auerstedt. In 1807 he defended Danzig for 78 days against the French under Marshal Lefebvre, with far greater skill and energy than he had shown in the previous year. He was promoted to field marshal soon afterwards, and conducted many of the negotiations at Tilsit. He died as governor of Berlin in 1818.

Stein himself lay very ill in Nassau, suffering from a Tertian fever that had seized him at the news of the Tilsiter Peace. In his weakness he was not lacking in doubt as to whether he would be able to take over the gigantic task that lay before him. No one was more convinced than he was of the need to help and, to this end, he had quietly and steadily worked out the new reforms of government and state and devoted all his time to these ideas.

In spite of all doubts about his strength, Stein had made up his mind inwardly immediately after receiving the letters and in a message to His Majesty the King, which he had to dictate while still ill because of the continuing weakness of his wife, he declared himself ready, as soon as his health alone would allow it, to take the route via Copenhagen to meet His Majesty to determine how he should work. In this moment of general unhappiness, he would consider it immoral to give credit to his own personality—all the more so since the King himself was providing such high proof of steadfastness.

He made preparation to take up this challenge, to the comfort and joy of all his friends and followers, which meant that his own possessions would now fall entirely to the wretched Rhine Confederation. He also had to experience the collapse of his and Sack's earlier achievements in Münster and Westphalia. The hatred of Prussia had been stirred up there. The lowly clergy had made sure of it in the most disgraceful way, in admiration of Napoleon, and the noble president von Vincke wrote to him desolately about it. Stein's journey went via Berlin, where he arrived on September 19, Sack greeting him. On October 8 he gave the first address to the King in Memel. On October 9, Memel was the first of his new governmental measures to be drafted in Nassau and was the first to receive the Edict on the facilitated possession and free use of property rights. In addition, the personal circumstances of the inhabitants of Memel were also addressed.

During the next period, Stein stayed with the King at his headquarters to discuss his proposals for reform with his monarch in person. As essential requirements Stein describes:

1. A plenary or meeting point of all administrative authorities

2. Distribution of business according to the natural limits of the activities;

3. Complete restructuring of the provincial, district and municipal authorities of the vacated provinces;

4. Temporary employment of the businessmen and as a consequence the reorganization of all departments The dissolution of the Immediate Commission[48] was implemented in late fall 1808. the members of the Immediate Commission were transferred to the Department of Finance and the Police and came under Stein's leadership. In the Cabinet, the Privy Councillors Sack and von Klewitz were entrusted with

48 Immediate Commission—commission that directly (by voting) presents a report to the Prince Regent for a (temporary) administrative task.

the presentation of the financial and legal relationships. When Sack was transferred as the head of the Kurmark, Neumark and Pomerania in November 1808 and returned to Berlin, he was followed by the Chamber of Justice Councillor Albrecht, who then maintained an influential position for years as a Cabinet Councillor Speaker.

The main features of this transitional form in the administration were:

- Abolition of all superfluous authorities, businesses and business forms

- Association of all branches of administration in the Cabinet under the chairmanship of the King

- Immediate handling of all issues affecting the whole state, with the exception of external war and justice matters, under Stein's supervision

- Superior direction of all affairs of State by the Minister and efficient preparation of these by the weekly ordinary and extraordinary conferences

- Simplification of the treasury system

- Certain rules for management in all circles from the highest to the lowest, with free movement and personal responsibility of each person.

In this form, Stein asserted the extraordinary power that the King had given him. This power was also constantly necessary if the transformation was to succeed and Stein followed the ancient lawmakers in their conviction that great deeds must be supported by a widespread conviction that can only be willed and carried out by individuals.

His supreme concern, however, was devoted to the essential improvements, whereby he thought to free the internal forces of the country from its inhibiting fetters, to awaken the independence of the nation and to strengthen and ennoble all ranks by participating in the affairs of the country.

He abolished all monopolies, the thirlage[49], the sales monopoly of the bakers, butchers and hawkers, the buying and selling for the provinces Lithauen and West Prussia and abolished the preferential treatment of the nobilities. He sought to awaken activity, insight and self-confidence in every class, and to create a sense of duty, responsibility, community spirit and everything else for the one great fatherland by invoking public rights.

The peasantry was particularly dear to his heart, the right of ownership was immediately granted to everyone and the right to demand credit for property. They were granted the right to clear wood and forest for pasture and this law, which exerted such a great influence on national prosperity, was immediately submitted to the Chambers and immediately approved. The traces of the long years of

---

49   The right of the owner of a mill to compel tenants to bring all their grain to that mill for milling.

distress under which the farmer had sighed could only gradually be erased. In some cases the municipal constitution could not be granted immediately but Stein's model derives undoubtedly from the very free constitutions in the counties of Mark, Cleve and Geldern, which he had got to know there and which went back to the old Saxons and Franconians and had proved their worth through one thousand years of experience — but did his plan for a new municipal constitution come to fruition? No!

The citizenry could have been rewarded with better results. Centuries of possession of freedom and property could enable the cities to freely exercise greater rights. However, everything had been spoiled over the centuries by the power given only to the magistrate according to the land law, because only its members had the right to vote. The citizenry itself had neither knowledge of the municipal system nor reason to act. Self-reliance, zeal and love and self-sacrifice for their particular town were lost, one only being reprimanded or called upon to make payments.

The need for drastic measures was also evident here. Stein decided to restore the constitution of free and orderly participation of citizens in their affairs. After preparatory work by the minister von Schrötter, who was commissioned to do so, his draft was not recognized as correct and a proposal, which had once been sent to the King anonymously, was now examined by Stein himself and discussed by Schön and others until a city ordinance could be presented to the King. This city ordinance later became the model not only for the Prussian cities but for other German states as well, after it returned to the freer forms of earlier times for city administration. "In the last years of his life, Stein recognized as a mistake the failure to attract the more prosperous and educated inhabitants of a city who were not engaged in trade and who would certainly have been able to be ennobled and elevated as notables and honorary citizens. This is connected with a second change, which could ensure the expediency of the municipal elections, the division of the citizenship not according to localities but according to occupations into a number of related guilds, whose members should be elected as town councillors from the most capable men from their midst as well. The elimination of the more educated class would feed the spirit of dissolution of outsiders and could influence the poorly educated, so that even other people could easily succumb to it, whereas this would not be feared if a city council "united the best of all classes".

(Pertz: „Aus Steins Leben")

Tilsit Meeting of the two emperors in a pavilion set up on a raft in the middle of the Neman River.

Sack, Head of the Immediate Peace Implementation Commission 1807-1809

Before the eventful days in Königsberg shortly before the flight of the royal family to Memel, during the flight from Berlin of the minister Count Schulenburg-Kehnert, who had been appointed governor, and the actions of the French friend of Prince Hatzfeld, the King had already appointed the Privy Councillor of Finance Sack as the present Civil Governor of Berlin. (Regarding the behavior of Minister Schulenburg-Kehnert see the appendix to this section No. VI). Sack immediately followed the call.

What this meant in view of the unheard-of restrictions of public and private life under the rule of the enemy and what vigor of spirit was required to carry one's head high in these surging waters and not to lose courage and thereby prevent or counteract the clash with the enemy rulers in Berlin, standing firm without letting the fateful weakness of one's own government become known, has actually only been fully appreciated after a hundred years. It was only fifty years later, through historiography, after inspection of the files kept in the State Archives, that the written records exchanged between the King and Stein at that time became known. In 1913, the Royal Prussian State Archives, initiated and supported by the Royal Archives Administrator Herman Granier, published the title of a document in the 88th volume: "Reports 1809, from the Berlin French period 1807-1809". Here, for the first time the outstanding unique activity of Sack and its significance gets due attention.

On July 16, seven days after the unfortunate Peace Treaty
of Tilsit, the King also appointed the Privy Councillor of
Finance Sack as a member of the Immediate Peace Implementation Commission. This commission was destined to
conduct negotiations with Napoleon's plenipotentiary,
Count Daru[50], in Berlin. Its main purpose was to clear the
Prussian provinces still occupied after the peace treaty —
all the lands west of the Vistula, West Prussia, Pomerania,
Silesia and Brandenburg — from French troops and thus to
achieve the reinstatement of the Prussian administration.
This withdrawal, however, was made dependent on the
payment of the war contribution, a condition that was as

---

50   Pierre Antoine Noël Mathieu Bruno Daru Count, (1767-1829) was a
     French financier, poet and historian.
     He entered military service at the age of 16 and was war commis-
     sioner when he joined the revolution in 1789. Arrested as a suspect
     in 1793, he did not regain his freedom until 9 Thermidor, but not
     his position. In 1795 he became head of a department in the Min-
     istry of War and soon afterwards head of the Directorate of the
     Danube Army. During this period he completed his translation of
     Horace's *Traduction en vers des poésies d'Horace*, Paris. 1800, 6th ed.
     1823, 2 volumes, which established his literary reputation.
     Napoleon I appointed him to the war administration and increas-
     ingly important business, raised him to the rank of count and ap-
     pointed him minister and plenipotentiary at the peace treaties of
     Pressburg, Tilsit and Vienna. In 1805, 1807 and 1809 he was gen-
     eral director in Prussia and Austria. In 1811 he became Secretary of
     State and fought against Napoleon's plans of conquest in the
     Council of Ministers. After the Restoration, he initially shared the
     lot of the resetting with other supporters of Napoleon, but in 1818
     he was appointed Pair and now voted in the spirit of the moderate
     party. From 1828 he was a member of the Academy of Sciences.
     His brother was: Count Martial Noel Pierre Daru.
     In 1807 he was elected as a foreign member of the Göttingen Acad-
     emy of Sciences.[1] Since 1808 he was a foreign member and since
     1812 honorary member of the Prussian Academy of Sciences. His
     name is on the Arc de Triomphe in Paris.

good as unfulfillable, especially under the provisions of the Königsberg Convention of July 12, 1807, to which Field Marshal Count Kalkreuth had surrendered. The decisive articles of this convention were:

Article IV.

Les disposotions ci-dessus (the withdrawal of Prussia by October 1, the part of Magdeburg on the right bank of the Elbe by November 1, 1807) *auront lieux aux époques déterminées, dans le cas où les contributions frappées sur le pays, seront acquittées bien entendu que les contributions seront censées et acquittées quand des sûretés suffisantes seront reconnues valables par l'Intendant général de l'armée...*[51]

Article V.

Tous les revenus du royaume de Prusse, depuis le jour de l'change des ratifications, seront versés dans les caisses du Roi et pour le compte de S.M. si les contributions, dues et échues depuis le le 1er Novembre 1806, jusqu'au jour de l'échange des ratifications sont acquittées...[52]

---

51 The above provisions (the withdrawal of Prussia by 1 October, the part of Magdeburg on the right bank of the Elbe by November 1, 1807) shall take place at the times determined. In the event of contributions being levied on the country, it being understood that such contributions shall be accepted and paid when sufficient securities are recognized as valid by the Bursar General of the Army.

52 All the income of the Kingdom of Prussia, from the day of the exchange of ratifications, will be paid into the King's coffers and on behalf of H.M. if the contributions, due and matured since November 1, 1806, up to the day of the exchange of ratifications are paid...

From this it can be seen how outrageous the task was that was imposed upon Sack as the Prussian plenipotentiary. On August 6, Sack, until then only a member, was immediately appointed head of the Peace Implementation Commission by the King.

> "In addition to all business and diplomatic skills, it took almost superhuman strength not to succumb here. Behind him the absolute political powerlessness of "his own fatherland, in front of him the certain victory over the Napoleonic Empire, represented by the General Director Daru, who, the more he provoked resentment, even hatred, of his Prussian opponent, the more certain it became that the wise and skilful servant of his lord has to be judged as the punctual executor of a solely decisive will, which would have made all other Prussian men to shun from the task.
>
> All the more highly, however, is the spiritual potency of the man to be appreciated, who under such pressures of the circumstances kept his head high, his soul free and his energy unbroken, whom subjective despair sometimes seized but never the objective, the absolute. This man was Johann August Sack."

These words, which Herman Granier wrote down in the preface to his 573-page presentation of his records publication, are followed by the following observations, based on a brief outline of Sack's life taken from the Silver Book of the Sack family of 1886, which may be familiar to readers:

> "It is this fiery spirit, this impetuous patriot, whose voice we hear in the German documents communicated here that give our publication its real character. They are not political documents, but newspaper reports and diaries, not in a strictly official form but in a lighter narrative presentation, intended to keep the King, who is staying in Memel, informed about the events in his capital. These were all the more important, indeed indispensable, since the Berlin newspapers appearing in print were partly kept under the strictest French censor-

ship, the *Vossische*, the *Haude* and *Spenersche* newspapers, and the specially founded *Telegraph*, were in French pay and championed the French cause without disguise."

Now that the excellent and comprehensive publication of Granier, which covered the days from September 4, 1807, to September 7, 1807, was completed, the work was published in a very short time. Granier's publication, which presents the newspaper reports of the Immediate Peace Implementation Commission, was compiled by Sack. Not only these, but also a considerable number of the reports of Daru and Berthier addressed to Napoleon in the same period of time, taken from the French war archives in Paris, in almost undiminished wording. Therefore only few excerpts directly referring to Sack's person can be found here. Instead, the course of events in that unfortunate epoch of the fatherland, provided in the whole publication render such a faithful picture and also such a splendid documentation of the sincere qualities of our head of the Peace Implementation Commission in the difficult and threatening negotiations with the hard-hearted oppressor that no description of that period can be put on an equal footing with it. Granier himself says:

"The publication of these messages addressed from a prominent position, overlooking the whole and gazing into the individual, to the head of state, opens up a source of most original value for this important period of German history. Whereas we otherwise had to rely on sources of subordinate value, sometimes of a hazy nature, for these inner conditions and moods, memories and memoirs, the inadequacy of which has been confronted by every researcher who has so far dealt with this period in greater depth".

Sack probably did not write these reports himself. The editor of the newspaper reports was Karl Wilhelm Salomon

Semler, a trainee at the Immediate Commission, then at the
State Presidium, who died in 1838 as State Fiscal Councillor, a grandson of the "enlightened" Halle pietist[53] theologian Semler[54], died in 1791, and who himself had literary
inclinations, which he probably expressed in these reports.

But that it was Sack's spirit that filled them is clearly
shown by the dryness that occurred after Sack's departure
in May 1808 reflected in the Immediate Reports, which
were first continued by von Raumer and then taken up by
Minister von Voss, who then became chief, and only after
Sack's return did they regain a fresher life.

They seem to have been a hobby-horse of Sacks altogether,
for, as he wrote to Goethe after the wars of liberation, "I
am allowed to give myself the testimony, during my administration, although now and then under unfavorable
circumstances, never in what could and must have hap-

---

53 Hallischer Pietismus (also known as Hallescher Pietismus) is a
    form of Lutheran pietism that can be traced back to the theologian
    and pedagogue August Hermann Francke. Francke cooperated
    closely with the Prussian state in the development of his school
    city (Francke Foundations) and in the study reform in Halle.

54 Johann Salomo Semler (1725-1791) was a German church historian,
    biblical commentator, and critic of ecclesiastical documents and of
    the history of dogmas. Sometimes known as "the father of German
    rationalism".
    Semler developed a direction of theology that was characterized
    by a distinction between public scientific theology and private liv-
    ing religion: private religiosity is a dogma-free, emotional inner re-
    ligion of the mature individual that does not require a denomina-
    tion. The public religion, on the other hand, is the necessary eccle-
    siastical form, an external religion that adheres to the dogmas and
    traditional confessions. This distinction even enabled the actually
    liberal Semler to agree to the Prussian-conservative so-called Wöll-
    ner's religious edict of 1788.

pened from above and neglecting spiritual things above earthly things but rather to have sought in the former the true center of gravity and support for the latter and to have stimulated the people's sense of patriotic possessions in the field of art and many a higher point of view, which had almost been lost to them during the long French rule."

There are no comments—which Sack himself already lamented—about the reception which these reports received by the King, apart from a rather grumpy warning of literary prolixity[55] from May 1808, when Daru had found out about Sack's reports. While the next report was the last of Sack's for the time being, the royal mood expressed here can be understood. At this particularly critical time far from his people at the outermost border of his empire, the ruler who was beset by serious concerns did not feel the need to write freely, to interweave classical quotations here and there. As the sober King once said, "Poetry—this is too sweet for me now. I must not give in to it either. It makes you soft and does not fit in with what is incumbent upon me in these difficult times".

However, Sack's reports were read at court and by the Prussian state authorities. Count Dohna even later asked for more detailed information. The longing for the return of the royal couple found a resounding echo, expressed time and again in Sack's newspapers,. All the royal birthdays were celebrated in Berlin, despite the absence of the royal couple. The Queen's humble nature was warmly ap-

---

55   The King did not like Latin quotations at all, nor did he like poetic
      encouragement which Sack wove here and there in order to lift the
      King's spirits, unaware that they were just annoying him.*

preciated and prayers were said for her in all the churches and the most heartfelt wishes were conveyed. "Today," Herman Granier continues, "we can say that the King's long absence was a blessing. It may have been caused not only by political considerations but also by the inertia inherent in the King's character. In any case, this spatial distance served to intensively strengthen the loyalty to the King, the authentic royalism of Berlin, which Fedor von Koeppen[56] glorified in the verses:

Wanting not to sacrifice their pride's foundation,
The King, history, glory from the ancestors,
And all that is in the Prussian name......
And because old bonds, misfortune hardens and hallows,
All that is lax in fortune unites in suffering,
All devoted to one another, the hearts of all were joined,
Unanimous, courageous, faithful and steadfast,
The one you trusted, you stood for and fought for,
That One was the King, who suffered for all.[57]

Otto von Bismarck expressed the same thought to the German-American Karl Schurz in pithy prose: "The Prussians are devoted to the dynasty with traditional loyalty to the King. A king can make mistakes, can suffer misfortune or even humiliation, but the traditional loyalty to the King does not diminish. It can be shaken here and there, but it will not perish".[58]

This loyalty to the King, hardened in the fire of misfortune, only began to falter in the minds of individuals such

---

56   Feodor von Koeppen 1830-1904. Poet and military author.
57   This is a very approximate rendering of the original German poem and I have made no attempt here to create an English poem (S.E.).
58   Karl Schurz Lebenserinnerungen. Berlin 1907.*

as Prince Hatzfeld, the Governor of Berlin in 1806, whom the Frenchman Charras described "as one of those rare Prussians who, either out of weakness of mind or lack of courage and character, see the only salvation of their country in its continuing humiliation".

Almost surprisingly, the French war reports and descriptions coincide with the Prussian ones. As a result, Granier's document, which, as already mentioned, follows the foreword on 572 pages, gains at the same time an enhancement and shading that only makes the colour of the painting "From the Berlin French period" more attractive and lively and gives it a closed, rounded structure.

Napoleon Captures Berlin in 1806

When Stein had returned to the King in September 1807 and became the first minister to carry out the reorganization of the whole internal administration, Napoleon was not at all dissatisfied. After all, he saw Stein as the man who, through his previously proven thriftiness in financial matters, gave him the best guarantee of being able to squeeze a great deal out of Prussia. Of course, the procurement of the means of payment was, besides his great reform, also one of the main tasks Stein undertook.

As a result, Napoleon's demands grew monstrously because of Daru, for the emperor's hatred had not been extinguished by the Peace of Tilsit and he initially regarded it as an armistice, leaving the Prussian monarchy to him for destruction at the appropriate moment. The conditions which were again imposed consisted of pledging Silesia, then that Stettin (Stettin) would remain occupied by 6,000 French troops until the monstrous contributions, the fulfilment of which was simply impossible, had been paid. A new commission was appointed, to which the King again appointed the Minister of State von Schulenberg-Kehnert, who rejected the appointment outright, the Privy Councillor of Finance Sack and General von Knobelsdorf. The latter was to travel to Dresden to soften the French Emperor personally but when he got there the Emperor had just left for Paris. Instead of an annual yield of 33 million, Daru was now to demand 150-200 million. Stein set all levers in motion to change the laws immediately, in order to get all provinces, all estates, nobility as well as citizens and peasants, territorial tenants as well as the state as territorial owner to pay tribute, which the Eastern Elbe, Silesians, Neumark and Kurmark despite the leeching pressure of the French occupation causing a state of desperation among the inhabitants. Even the King's brother, Prince Wilhelm with his noble wife Marianne offered themselves as a pledge to Napoleon to give themselves up as prisoners until the contributions were paid. The conscientious Sack had a hard time with Daru, because nothing could be achieved with this monster, who was only willing to serve his emperor without mercy, so that Stein himself offered to go to Napoleon before signing a contract about the amount of contributions that the country could not possibly fulfil. Sack wrote to Stein at that time, "Any legally thinking people cannot finalize anything with prudence until the result of Prince Wilhelm's offer and making use of the Russian Emperor (for which he too had offered his help) is satisfied and agreed. Only General Zastrow wants to blindly throw himself into the arms of the French demands, etc.".

Finally, since nothing helped — even Prince Wilhelm's offer failed to bring about a mitigation — Stein offered to travel to Daru in Berlin, since he had proposed to give away domains worth fifty or a hundred million in the extreme case, which he had been authorized to do by the King, in the form of domains. He also succeeded in getting into a favorable relationship with the French plenipotentiary. The vain Daru objected to Councillor of Finance Sack before the beginning of the negotiations because he was not an Excellency and did not wear a ribbon and also because he (Daru) had been set to one side, in negotiating directly in Paris with Napoleon. He was so embittered that he later, on the occasion of a letter from Sack stated that he did not want to negotiate with Sack anymore. The letter, which stated resistance to having 25,000 men in a French camp close to Berlin because of the famine that already existed in the capital, had traitorously been handed over to Daru. In agreement with Sack, Stein used this opportunity to flatter Daru's self-interest and on March 9, 1808 he succeeded in concluding a contract with Daru according to which, if Napoleon gave his permission, the withdrawal from the country could be expected by the end of April.

It is easy to understand why Sack, as head of the Peace Commission, rebelled when the rumor first appeared that a French camp of 25,000 men was to receive troops in the immediate vicinity of Berlin's cantonments, while he had already been negotiating for over nine months, trying to get the nearest provinces around the capital, in accordance with the peace of Tilsit, evacuated during a widespread famine of the citizens.

The French had demanded money from the estates to build the camps and Sack wrote to the estates to resist this demand. Daru talked about having Sack shot but Stein saved him by promising to pay the sum demanded.

After Sack's departure, Minister of State von Voss was then appointed head of the Immediate Peace Commission.

Sack went directly to the King to answer for his fully justified objection and remained at headquarters for the time being to emphasize the work of Stein and its execution in the homeland. The appointment of Voss as Sack's successor was by no means universally approved, e.g. Hardenberg remarks on this in his diary: *Quod vale improbandum.*

That this simple and natural course of action of Sack's stirred up a lot of dust in Berlin and Paris between the new chief and the Prussian envoy Brockhausen as well as Prince Wilhelm, only testifies to the terrible dependence and servitude under which Prussia found itself. See corre-spondence on this in Appendix No. VII.

In the course of the summer of 1808, the increasingly mea-gre reports of the Immediate Enforcement Commission usually only reported on the intolerability of the French camps and the lack of bread supply in Berlin as well as the shortage of money for the city and the estates. Almost all the reports deal with the same problems, except that at the end of July the King is told of Austrian armaments and Spanish unrest.

In the meantime, Napoleon, busy with Spain, was growing irritable with the Prussian envoy in Paris, Herr von Brock-hausen, and suspected him of sending news of Napoleon's impotence and of great dissatisfaction in France to Berlin. Brockhausen had to be recalled at the end of the year.

On August 13, General Victor received Napoleon's order to march his First Corps from Berlin to Mainz to partici-pate in the Spanish campaign. There had already been a catastrophe in Andalusia, which made the fastest-possible march of the First Corps necessary. On August 6th he was also ordered to have the whole infantry ready to march off without arousing suspicion in Berlin about the real reason. In addition to the First Corps, the Sixth Corps (Ney) and soon also the Fifth Corps were pulled from Germany to Spain. Marshal Davout was transferred from Warsaw to Breslau to command in Silesia and Poland, and Marshal Soult from Stettin to Berlin, with the instruction that his command should extend to Küstrin and the rest of Prussia, with a total of 120,000 men remaining on the other side of the Rhine. In Prussia the agitation for armaments for the liberation grew secretly, which were already being prepared by Scharnhorst at the headquarters in Königsberg.

The certainty of the departure of the First Corps was the most joyful news for all the inhabitants of Berlin and a means to revive the hope of all patriots. In the last days of August the fateful incident occurred. Stein wrote a letter to Prince Wittgenstein zu Doberan in Mecklenburg-Schwerin in which he advised him to do everything possible to carry on the agitation in Westphalia as well. He entrusted this letter to an official, the assessor Koppe, who had often been used as a mediator of important letters. Wittgenstein defends himself immediately from Hamburg when the contents of the letter became known that he did not understand von Stein's inexplicable letter and that he had never known the arrested Koppe in question.

Marshal Soult found it only opportune to report back from Charlottenburg to Napoleon on September 19 about Stein's intercepted letter. In the meantime Napoleon's attention had been directed completely to Spain. Prussia had been pushed into the background, therefore armament could be continued by Scharnhorst, Blücher and Gneisenau in secret. Scharnhorst wrote a memorandum, dated Königsberg, September 1 under the title "Our political situation" and Stein presented the King with a memorandum on September 14th. He showed the course of the negotiations, the blatant injustice of renewed demands of the French and the clear impossibility of satisfying them even with the ruin of Prussia. He encouraged the King to persevere in view of the recent liberation of Portugal, the advancing war of Spain, the participation of Russia and Austria and suggested to reject new proposals, to delay the March treaty and to recall Prince Wilhelm. Then, however, Napoleon suddenly arrived in Erfurt again and Emperor Alexander, on his way to visit him there, arrived in Königsberg in the same September days on his way to Erfurt. Stein immediately used this opportunity to acquaint Alexander with Scharnhorst's memorandum on the political situation and his own assessment. He even concluded his own written statement with an urgent appeal to the Russian emperor as follows:

It is necessary in the present circumstances

a) for Russia to take measures to be able to use its armed forces for the great purpose of liberating Europe,

b) that Russia, Austria and Prussia enter into a precise agreement to attack France, while it is busy with Spain, in order to liberate Germany and

c) that in Erfurt the most advantageous way of vacating Prussia and fulfilling the Peace of Tilsit should be concluded.

Stein's ideas probably made a deep impression on Alexander but he recommended the King to be patient again and promised only to work for a reduction of the French demands in Erfurt if Stein followed him there to finally bring the negotiations to a favorable conclusion.

On the morning of the day designated for Stein's departure from Königsberg, the *Moniteur* of September 8, 1808, brought the letter to Prince Wittgenstein—other papers, such as the Berlin Telegraph, had already printed it with the threat that Stein, who had exchanged the monastery property of Cappenberg in Westphalia for his Birnbaum estate, was a subject of the King of Westphalia and would lose his possessions there.

Stein immediately realized that the King must first hear this from his mouth and went to his monarch to demand his dismissal. The King declared that he could not spare him for the time being under the still unfavorable patriotic conditions and in any case did not want to decide until Emperor Alexander had returned and sent the minister of foreign affairs, Count Goltz, to Erfurt.

Stein himself immediately wrote to the Russian emperor that it was a letter from a Prussian official to another, which the French should not have confiscated, and immediately informed him that, after Count Goltz's return, he would refuse to take any control of internal affairs in order to appease Napoleon's bitterness, who mistakenly considered him a subject of the ceded Prussian provinces. The King was still not ready to make a decision.

Meanwhile the noblest men, including Sack, united to preserve Stein. But among the French, Stein was now described as the center of a great conspiracy and from Erfurt it was advised that Stein wanted to resign his position in order to make Napoleon more favorable, since, as the Minister of Foreign Affairs, Count Goltz, wrote, he was raging against him. During this waiting period, Stein was busy finalizing the basic rules of his new constitution so that he could leave them as a guideline for the King and in it he gave a detailed presentation of the main principles for the administration of the provincial authorities, in which he stated that the creation of the Crown Presidents for each province was an important link between them and the central authority. The domains, the officials in general and also the Jews were given special sections but Stein also laid down firm ground rules about the court and would have liked to see the King and his family now returning. The King approved the new administrative plan on November 24, at the same time with a heavy heart together with Stein's farewell. However, as if that were not enough, Napoleon hurled a proscription (banishment) order to the minister on December 16th and with it, Stein's fate to have to stay away from home for years was sealed.

At the same time however, all plans for armament had receded into the background — the King resigned himself to the new test of patience imposed on him by the loss of Stein and decided to visit Petersburg, although Stein had always advised against it.

On December 3, 1808 the French troops finally marched off, after they had committed themselves in Erfurt to pay 30 million taler in 30 months. In Berlin, hopes for the King's return were stronger, which however did not happen so soon. The minister von Voss had already been recalled by the King in October. The Immediate Peace Implementation Commission was dissolved by the cabinet order of December 16, 1808 and on December 17, Sack was appointed as Crown President of the now liberated parts of the country: Kurmark, the three Magdeburg districts right of the Elbe, the Neumark and Pomerania. For Berlin a special Crown President was planned. However, it did not come to this and instead this position was also assigned to Sack. Thus the latter exchanged Königsberg for Berlin and again took over the office from the King's Majesty to Petersburg and Königsberg to return to his old accustomed newspapers about the capital including all incidents in it and in the surrounding area. Most of the reports were now sent to Count Dohna, Minister of the Interior and their full imprint can still be found in the publication by Herman Granier.

In the appendix to this document there are only the excerpts from the Paris War Archives by and about Sack in 1807 and 1808.

Stein's Escape. Sack's Effectiveness as Privy State Councilor and Crown President of the Kurmark — including Berlin, the Neumark and Pomerania, Governor of the Territories between Elbe and Oder

The Proscription Order for Stein contained the following wording:

Imperial Order

1. The name of Stein (ce nommé Stein), which seeks to stir up unrest in Germany, is declared an enemy of France and the Rhine Confederation.

2. The properties which the said Stein may possess in France or in the countries of the Rhine Confederation shall be seized. The said Stein will be personally detained wherever he is accessible by our or our allies' troops.

In our Imperial camp in Madrid,

December 16, 1808 (signed) Napoleon.

Napoleon's hatred hereby described a single powerless man as an adversary in life and death. Innumerable people who read this proscription order, which was posted on every street corner, heard Stein's name for the first time but the ostracism immediately enveloped him in the holy splendor of the martyr. The hearts that were longing for liberation in all parts of Germany had found their vibrant focus. Stein became a political power and the expectations and hopes of the downtrodden people began to look beyond Prussia's borders.

The decision to leave had to be taken quickly. Stein made arrangements with his friends Sack and Knuth to save a part of his fortune. He reported the persecution he had suffered to the King, asked him to seek protection from the Emperor of Russia and indicated that he was leaving for the Bohemian border, awaiting his orders from General von Scharnhorst. He had already left Berlin in the night of January 5. On January 9 he surprisingly arrived at Buchwald near Hirschberg in Silesia at the Count and Countess Reden[59], who took the best care of his accommodation. He travelled as Karl Frücht (since Frücht[60] belonged to his Nassau estates). On January 10 he received letters from

---

59 Friedrich Wilhelm von Reden (1752-1815) was a German pioneer in mining and metallurgy. He was born in Hamelin in the Electorate of Hanover and died in Schloss Buchwald in Prussian Silesia.

Reden was knighted by Friedrich Wilhelm II. Following the Napoleonic occupation of Prussia, he remained in office as the Minister of Mines to prevent the plundering of the mines by the French. Because of speeches on November 9, 1806, on the French occupying power, he was sacked from his ministry by Frederick William III, on 9 July 1807.

In the evening of his life, Reden retired to the Hirschberger Tal (Kotlina Jeleniogórska), at the well situated Buchwald (Bukowiec), which he had acquired in 1785. In 1802, he married Friederike Riedesel, Freiin zu Eisenbach, daughter of Friedrich Adolf Riedesel and Frederika Charlotte Riedesel, but the marriage remained childless.

One can see a common interest and fate of Stein and Reden from the above.

60 Frücht was first mentioned in 1159 as Wruhte. Until 1613 Frücht belonged to the county of Nassau and was then sold to Johann Gottfried vom Stein. Together with Schweighausen, Frücht belonged to the imperial direct dominion of vom Stein, whose last owner was Heinrich Friedrich Karl vom und zum Stein. In 1804/06 his dominion was annexed to the Duchy of Nassau, to which it belonged until 1866.

Berlin. Mrs von Stein, in her fear for him, had obtained a passport for him from the Austrian envoy and sent it with the urgent request to cross the border as soon as possible. Sack implored him to follow the advice of his wife, who thought and acted only for him. She and the children would follow him wherever he went.

Stein was pleased with his wife's noble decision and asked Count Arnim himself, in case Austria denied him permission to stay, for a passport on Karl Frücht to England, taking leave of Prussian soil on January 12. Finally in Prague he received the longed-for news from Vienna: the Emperor of Austria would gladly grant him a stay in Prague — where too many foreigners were staying and where he would not be safe. Stein might therefore choose the capital of Moravia, Brno, for his stay. Sack had also written to him that the Chamber Assessor Eichhorn[61] (No. 3420 mar. silver book [33/3!]) himself had left for the Prince-Primate of Dalberg to obtain mitigations for Stein's possessions in Nassau. On the first of March, Stein was reunited with his family.

---

61 Eichhorn, Albrecht Friedrich, born 2 March 1779, died 3 May 1852, voluntarily followed the King's call in 1813 in the vicinity of General von Gneisenau, a close friend of his, as a councilor of the Supreme Court. The Minister vom Stein appointed him as a lecturer in the central government of the powers allied against France. 1817 Privy Councillor, 1831 Director of the Ministry of Foreign Affairs, 1840 Minister of Culture, was married in 1812 to Amalie, the fourth daughter of Bishop Sack. His son Hermann, District President of Minden, was ennobled in memory of his father's merits in 1856 - Hermann v. E.'s son was Prussian, who was murdered in Kiev on July 30, 1918. Field marshal Hermann von Eichhorn.*

The answer of his King was:

> My dear Baron von Stein, I had already been informed of the
> measure taken against you by Emperor Napoleon when I re-
> ceived your letter of the fifth of this month. I had also asked
> the Emperor of Russia to intervene on your behalf with Em-
> peror Napoleon. The former promised me to do all that was
> possible for you under the circumstances and I have now re-
> peated this request, sincerely hoping that things will turn out
> well. It is very important to me that you have decided to
> leave my countries immediately, so that no compromise and
> bad consequences can continue to arise. I must ask you to re-
> main faithful to this decision in the future as well, since no
> other course of action is compatible with your personal
> safety due to the circumstances which are so distressing to
> me.
>
> St. Petersburg, January 16, 1809
>
> signed Friedrich Wilhelm.

This letter, written in Scharnhorst's hand, was appended
by the King himself:

> The emperor would very much like to grant you asylum in
> his states but wishes you to travel through Galicia to the Rus-
> sian Empire.

Scharnhorst wrote at the same time:

> Hon. Excellency, I send here with the most heartfelt emotion
> the King's reply to your letter. I have been instructed to add
> that not only your pension is to be paid out but that the King
> would also seek in every way to give you proof of his grati-
> tude. Should Hon. Excellency need anything, such as money,
> etc., please let me know but I would advise caution with re-
> gard to the coat of arms.
>
> With the deepest feelings of gratitude and eternal veneration
> I remain Hon. Excellency's most obedient servant
>
> v. Scharnhorst.

p.p. I will seek a passport from the Emperor of Russia for Hon. Excellency.

Crown President Sack and Privy Councillor Knuth in Berlin provided everything possible to ease Stein's fate with true friendship, while a German church prince, Baron von Dalberg, betrayed the hope built on him.

As we know, Eichhorn, an assessor of the Court of Appeal, had hurried to the Rhine in order to obtain a mitigation of the confiscation of Stein's property, which was pronounced in Napoleon's letter of condemnation. The government of Nassau showed a very willing inclination to grant the feudal authority referred to by Mrs von Stein from her husband's estates. Eichhorn then travelled to Frankfurt a. M. to make a personal appeal to the Prince-Primate who was staying there. At first Dalberg did not want to accept Stein's letter at all and was reluctant to accept Eichhorn's idea that Stein would not send him a letter through the bearer, which could compromise His Majesty in any way. He took the letter, broke the seal and read it on the spot. Then he said to Eichhorn: "You didn't tell me who this man was, I don't want to and am not allowed to name him—whatever I can do I will gladly do, I will send for you and give you an answer. He hurried into an adjoining room and left Eichhorn alone. Eichhorn visited all the assembled, stepping in their way everywhere, but no reply was forthcoming. So Eichhorn asked once again for a private audience. He received an invitation to a public audience and when it was over, the church prince brushed against Eichhorn in passing and said, "You have brought me a letter. You can easily imagine that I can do nothing." When Stein later sent a transcript of his letters and Eichhorn handed him the leaf in Aschaffenburg, he was initially reluctant to accept it. After he had read it he said, "First of all I am Prince-Primate and as such I have duties that are most sacred to me. If these do not come into conflict, then the friend is the most highly regarded for me. They can easily imagine that I can do very little, as I have told them several times before — one has to wait for the right moment. And without even giving him the opportunity to answer, the prince declared that he wanted to be alone and Eichhorn had to go home empty-handed. Stein, instead of a shepherd's crook and a German man, he had only found a wavering reed in this religious friend. The best consolation was given to the disappointed Sack by the old Minister von Heinitz who said, "Prudence is watchful and when adverse events occur, we only need to marvel at their ways and not judge them" A few years later and the fate of Prince Primate was in Stein's hands which gave him what he had deserved in the service of Germany.

After Stein's departure a number of the best men saw the whole country doomed. Niebuhr, an excellent financial expert from Memel who, just in 1806, had been appointed bank director of the Maritime Administration by Stein, wrote about his destroyed hopes and about his intention to leave the Prussian state after only a short time of endurance. He did not consider it the worst lot for him to be driven to Russia as an emigrant.

Nevertheless, on the whole it was beneficial for Stein to spend the tranquil time in Brno, detached from all business — only delighted by the faithful reverential letters of Prince and Princess Wilhelm and Luise and his many faithful admirers — in the charming but otherwise spiritually uninspiring city and to settle down to the most frugal things in a foreign country.

Even when Napoleon went to war with the Austrian emperor in 1809 and was victorious, Stein stayed calmly in Brno and devoted himself to the education of his two daughters. One can imagine his feelings and those of his friends at home when Emperor Franz bowed so deeply to the Corsicans that he gave Napoleon his daughter as a wife. It was no wonder that Frederick Wilhelm, now abandoned by Austria and only ever mollified by Russia, could still congratulate himself on not having followed the advice of the Prussian patriots and taken part in a war at Austria's side.

After Stein's departure, the new ministers Altenstein and Dohna presented the King with their proposals for the implementation of Stein's new decrees and the associated appointments. However, just one week was enough to give this tightly-knit structure a different complexion. Among the appointments proposed by Stein, Sack and Graf Reden were kept out of the ministry, instead of being appointed, and replaced by subordinate officials.

In June 1810, the royal decree was issued which dissolved the previous ministry after a period of eighteen months and transferred to the State Chancellor Baron von Hardenberg the top management of all state affairs, which remained with him for twelve years until his death in fall 1822. The end of Altenstein's ministry was received with great satisfaction by the Prussian population but no consensus was reached quickly about the successor.

In any case, Stein, had recommended Hardenberg to the King instead of himself and like Stein, Sack tried to come to an understanding with his measures, especially as long as Hardenberg respected and consulted his master Stein.

Sack wrote to Stein:

"Lord von Hardenberg is strong and industrious and heaven grant that it remain so. He has not surrounded himself well everywhere but we must now do what we can to support him. For the examination of the new financial plan, which essentially consists of the creation of fundable assets by a direct contribution, the extension of the Accise to the lowlands, the funding of the cash depository bills and all national debts and the establishment of a National Bank. A commission consisting of von Heydebreck, Ladenberg, von Raumer, Benth, von Beguelin and others has been set up. The Council of State is to be introduced immediately, the previous organizational plan you have drawn up is to be kept firmly in place and completed and representation is to be improved.

When the Chancellor of State communicated his provisional budget to the Privy Councillor Niebuhr for examination, the latter declared himself unconditionally opposed to it, so much so that he felt obliged to present it to the King and requested that it be submitted. The monarch sent Niebuhr's report to Hardenberg, who, furious at Niebuhr's step, appointed von Schön and a number of other councillors of state and sent his plan to Stein by State Councillor Knuth at the beginning of July. The latter delivered letters from Sack, Schön, Count Arnim and Spalding, who, the new administration and their obedient attitude towards France were of very different opinions.

Stein then commented in great detail on his dissenting opinion. Hardenberg accepted Stein's changes to his financial plan and in the need to discuss the matter in more detail with him, he had Sack propose a meeting on the

Silesian border. As the current president of the Kurmark, Sack wrote: "A part of the Kurmark Adels had offered everything to hinder the improvement of the state and only recently managed to get Count Dohna, the minister, to abolish the reasonable plans for an improved constitution of the estates, which proposed to impose equal burdens on all classes, and to suspend the whole thing for two years. The nobility wanted to remove all burdens from themselves and let other classes suffer under them, to perpetuate all the differences of the provinces and castes". Hardenberg was of the opinion that this evil should be eliminated immediately but he wished to proceed with extreme caution. Since Stein was in the main the creator of all these measures but otherwise felt a lively satisfaction with the Chancellor of State's plans, he accepted the proposal of the meeting. This meeting had to be concealed with the most profound secrecy. The slightest imprudence could bring Napoleon's wrath down upon Stein, Hardenberg and the whole Prussian state. On September 12, Hardenberg sent him the files of the first financial plan for preliminary information, which was to be followed on September 13 by the overview of the various schemes and outlines of the financial plan as now intended by the State Chancellor.

The examination of the papers submitted determined Stein to make substantial amendments to his earlier findings and set out five basic requirements.

The place and hour of the meeting, which Sack arranged for the two of them, have not been reliably determined. The two statesmen probably met on September 16 in a lonely residence on the other side of the mountain ridge.

It was in Hardenberg's character, however, that what he might have heard as powerful and grand from Stein, was often only half executed and spoiled or paralyzed by the addition of outside help, like the advice, "Form an understandable, respectable ministry and remove the old women, organize the Council of State into a point of unification which the president and first ministers direct", in its first part remained without effect. Hardenberg did not understand how to keep the noblest and most capable men. He put his trust sometimes in this and sometimes that subordinate, so it was no wonder that he was served accordingly.

Stein left the Chancellor of State at that time with the hope that the effectiveness of this intelligent and noble man would bring unity back into affairs. The picture Stein received soon afterwards of the King's promised adherence to the advice he had worked out was not very pleasing. Sack confirmed Stein's steadfast loyalty under the unfavorable circumstances which seemed to him to be caused by the King's prolonged absence and who had stayed in Königsberg with his ministers throughout 1809. He continued his regular immediate reports in his detailed manner as the Cown President of the parts of the country liberated from French occupation and as governor of Berlin, sympathized with all those who continued to promote the armaments of war and with his straight and unswerving sense of purpose helped Stein to carry out his reforms quietly and steadfastly in the parts of the country he now administered.

Since Westphalia became a French kingdom, Vincke had been President of the government of Potsdam and had been at his side in the most diligent manner. This resulted in a warmer relationship between the two of them, so closely linked by their love of Westphalia's red earth and by their loyalty to their fatherland and their exiled first minister. The archives in Münster i. Westf. contain between twenty and thirty letters by Sack from Vincke's estate from the period 1803-1816.[62]

The 290 documents in the Granier publication were only completed at the end of December 1809, when Sack had agreed on the preparations for the entry of the returning royal family and all necessary steps for their reception in Königsberg. Letter No. 288 contains the list of authorities and deputies to be received by His Majesty the King, handed over on December 26, 1809. There are twelve authorities represented by twenty-three persons, including seven clergymen. From the Court and Cathedral Ministry are listed: The State Consistory Councilor and Court Preacher Sack (3388 [33]) and the preacher Gillet (mar. 1223 [10!]), brother-in-law Joh. August Sacks, as representatives of the Reformed congregation. Letter No. 289 is a letter of thanks from the King, which was sent in writing to Crown President Sack on December 28th, who had fi-

---

62 According to a statement by Dr. Kochendörffer, Director of the State Archives in Münster i. Westf., who published it there under the title "Der Briefwechsel Steins und Vinckes" ("The Correspondence of Stein and Vincke") in the publishing house of Aschendorff'sche Buchhandlung. With the permission of the Governor of Münster, the portraits of Stein and Vincke in this publication are also taken from this work.*

nally returned to Berlin at the end of December. The letter of thanks read:

"The intimacy and tranquility which welcomed me here on my return are a great Honour to the inhabitants of Berlin and the police institutions. Today I am testifying to this to the local magistrate and police president Grüner and I am happy to feel obliged to express my special satisfaction to you as

Your well-favored King

Friedrich Wilhelm."

Princess Luise v. Radziwill

On her return, the loyal Berliners had donated a covered carriage to Queen Louise, which she boarded at the gates and in which she then made her entrance into the jubilant capital.

Sack as Crown President of Berlin and the Kurmark welcomed the royal couple and was happy to see the success of his never silent pleas to have the high couple back among their loyal "Kurmarkers" in Berlin.

Not only during those years, when the King took residence in Königsberg, did the care of the capital Berlin and the state of Prussia rest on Sack's shoulders amidst the imminent violence and presence of the enemy but also after the King's return when it was necessary to bring the badly battered capital and the surrounding provinces back into strict order, rendering extraordinary services to the severely tested kingdom and royal house. Since, after the King's return, the daily private journal reports to Königsberg which had been taken up again by him, despite the continuing unflattering reports by agents to Paris, ceased to be published. Since Sack's time and effectiveness could be used and developed more freely and more intervening, he kept all the strings secretly in his hand to diligently and faithfully keep his friend Stein up to date. These connections reached him from the few men who worked quietly and steadily on the liberation of the fatherland, such as Scharnhorst, Gneisenau, Blücher, Schön, Niebuhr, Knuth, Privy Councillor Albrecht, Count Götzen, some of them on secret missions. Even the hope for better times in Prussia was something he himself could only nurture and maintain in his deepest being. The King, in all his nobility and in his fatherly care for his subjects, was only able to approve of that high flight of thought of the still unbowed civil servants but not to promote it at present nor to give his sanction to an assessment of the terrible French yoke, to the satisfaction of the cruel tyrant. When in the year

1810 his beloved Queen Louise, who was loved by him as
well as by the whole people, descended into the grave, it
was his only endeavor to find consolation in the memory
of her and her humiliation by Napoleon, quietly and in-
tensely in his daily duty before God. The feeling of powerlessness had, as twenty years ago, once again gained a
crippling power over him and it required the complete re-
straint of their feelings on the part of the courageous and
liberating band of men who remained, to avoid bringing
about the opposite of what they so desperately longed for.

In the following years Sack worked diligently under the
leadership of Scharnhorst to formulate his military code
and to transform the mercenary army, cleaning up the aristocratic officer corps, into a people's army and introducing
universal conscription. Some letters from Sack's estate
written by the men quietly preparing an uprising from the
time before liberation are included in the appendix. The
letter[63] included here shows Sack's tireless efforts to promote civic life through literary undertakings, which we
will encounter several times.

> Sigl. to send a copy of *brevi mani* to each of the directors and
> councillors of the Upper Chamber of Accounts.

Berlin, November 26, 1812.

Schlabrendorf.

I intend, with the permission of His Majesty the King, to
publish a journal to promote business in the Prussian state.

---

63 Property of State Railway Councillor Dr. Eduard Sack of Marienburg i. Westpr.*

Friedrich Schleiermacher

Hon. High Well-Born I recommend this enterprise to the benevolent promotion of the same by initiating a collection of subscriptions and take the liberty of publishing thirty copies of the announcement for Hon. High Well-Born himself and the Royal High Chamber of Auditors here, whereby I note that in the subscription collection amongst the audience the individual is at liberty to sign for several copies, or also for a higher contribution than that stated in the announcement, calculated exactly according to the minimum costs of 3 rths for printing and 3 rths, 12 sg. on writing paper, to be more interesting and thus to contribute to the perfecting of the work inside and outside. Please send me the subscription list.

Berlin, the December 19, 1812.

Sack.

pd. November 26.

The internal administrative measures taken by Hardenberg in the last months of 1810 and those of the following
year caused a great stir in all parts of the Prussian state.
This led the State Chancellor to convene an assembly of
deputies from the provinces remaining to the King. The
deputies did not fail to come forward with their com-
plaints. In a third such assembly the Chancellor of State
declared that he could not change his system. Stein was a
stranger to all the arrangements that Hardenberg had met
to remedy his disapproval. In particular, he disapproved
of the agricultural laws as a disastrous upheaval to the
peasantry in its internal family relations, which was later
confirmed by experience to the full extent. Schleiermacher
wrote, "It cannot be denied that the present administration
has completely abandoned its course". At length and full
of bitter resentment Gneisenau expressed himself, "Things
were bad when Hon. Excellency left us, now they are atro-
cious".

At that time, Prussia's situation between to be and not to
be seemed desolate under the exhausting pressure of the
French war payments, which robbed the country of its precious metals and under the pressure of the continuous
French occupation of the three Oder fortresses and the
threatening French troop movements, as well as the trade
blockade against England. Only the feeling of sharing all
the misfortune with one's own ancestral royal house and
knowing that it was constantly laying and nurturing the
seeds for a better future remained a comfort to the Prussian people — but the terrible tyrant in France did not rest.

His ambition to seize and defeat the English, unable to meet them on their island kingdom, by waging a land war in the East Indies, gave him the idea of overpowering Russia first.

As early as the winter of 1811, at the age of 12, Emperor Alexander sensed the danger that threatened him and began preparations to counter this challenge. While Frederick Wilhelm was feeling compelled to bury all hopes of liberating his Prussia and to conclude a humiliating alliance treaty against Russia with France, even to have to leave his capital and to restrict himself personally to Breslau, a French governor returned to the city of Berlin. Sack again had the difficult task of having to open up the parts of the country he administered to Napoleon's troops which were living in and devastating it worse than if they had been enemies, while Prussia had had to ally itself with its Emperor. Stein was summoned by the Emperor of Russia in March and met him in Vilnius on June 12.

Alexander received him very graciously and in a long conversation explained to him the reasons that had forced him to make peace in Tilsit. At the same time he expressed his unshakable determination to wage war with the greatest perseverance and to bear all the consequences rather than enter into an insulting peace. Stein, on the other hand, reserved the right to assist the Emperor only on his own terms, inasmuch as he would be able to bring about the liberation of the German fatherland through Russian power. In the summer of 1912 he presented the Russian Emperor with a memorandum which clearly described the means to be employed by Russia in order to make the forces of Germany effective not for France but in favor of Russia. How Stein and Alexander succeeded in bringing together these two peoples, and how, step by step, the Russian campaign became a war of liberation for Prussia and the whole of Germany, is too great and well-known a historical event for it to be necessary to go beyond the scope of this publication. In 1813, immediately after the Battle of Leipzig, the King appointed Sack as Civil Governor (the "Crown Presidents" created by Stein were sacrificed but the old title of Civil Governor was reinstated) of the land between Oder and Elbe and here he found a new opportunity as the unbendingly loyal support of his monarch, to bring the reforms of his friend Stein to bear in their original form in the reestablishment of the liberated parts of the fatherland. It was not long of course before his purposeful work came to benefit this region. After the first Paris Peace Treaty and Napoleon's exile to Elba, in 1814 the allies appointed him Governor General of the abandoned territories on the Lower and Middle Rhine, based in Aachen and in 1815, after Napoleon's second final exile to St. Helena, King Frederick Wilhelm III appointed Sack as the head of the Rhine Province, which had been granted to him at the Congress of Vienna. However, the second half of this book will report in more detail on this and Sack's subsequent activities.

This first section of my compilation will conclude with the letter that Stein was able to write from Paris to his wife on April 10, 1814. Behind him lay the magnificent work of liberation which he had initiated and carried out with the help of Emperor Alexander of Russia and his troops, who had been so successfully influenced by him, as well as the Prussian People's Army created by Scharnhorst and its leaders. These were all the phases of hope and disappointment, of discouragement and enthusiastic joy which Sack experienced during the years of separation from his friends who were staying and working in Russia, as a fighter with the Dohna-Altenstein ministry and under the State Chancellor who was increasingly distanced from Stein's great administrative work—a situation which he was able to master. The fact that Sack had to bear the brunt of his own constant and unchanging legacy and that he was able to develop and assert his administrative principles with ever more independence and vigor not only preserved his friend's old esteem and love but also preserved the affection and confidence of his King, who, in full appreciation of Sack, possessed a rare strength of character and purity. The letter accurately reflects the mood of 1814, it read:

Paris, April 10.

I have been here in Paris since yesterday, the anniversary of my arrival in Dresden—what events since, what abyss of misfortune from which we are saved. Thanks to Providence, the Emperor Alexander and his brave comrades in arms, Russians and Germans! To what degree of happiness, of independence, of peace we have come—we finally dare to surrender to the pleasure of the feelings that this situation instils and return in peace to the fold of our family, the lot of those of whom it is composed, secured against the misfortune that threatened to destroy them. Only when I compare the feeling that spreads throughout my entire existence with the pressure and suffering that gripped me for nine years, only this comparison enables me to appreciate the full extent of my present happiness, the magnitude of my previous suffering.

The tyrant ended like a coward. As long as it only mattered to spill the blood of others, he was wasteful with it but he does not dare to die in order to at least end up bravely. He accepts a reward of clemency, he returns to nothingness, he negotiates in order to keep his life and to prolong a shameful existence. Suwaroff wrote to me recently that in Bonaparte's story there is a mixture of oddity and greatness, of Tamerlaine and Gil Blas[64] but there is a third legacy in the horrible, deformed combination which forms his character, that is meanness—he is a monster. It was manifested in his escape from the army in Russia, in his treatment of those whom he had persecuted and oppressed, in his dealings, in his speeches and presently in his conduct in misfortune—it goes as far as meanness, fear for his life—cowardice.

The noble, generous, benevolent behavior of Emperor Alexander captures all hearts, tearing them away from the tyrant by force, making the French forgotten and, above all, the fact that foreigners were ruling their capital.

They feel humiliated however, to have had twenty years full of horrors of inconsistency and lies in their history and to have passed through the horrors of the revolution to lawlessness to be defeated by the foreigners who were at the same time their liberators instead of acting as avengers of the shame they suffered.

The emperor conducted the negotiations on account of the interior according to the purest and most sublime principles. He let the great state authorities act, he did not prescribe anything, did not force anything—he let it happen, protected but did not speak as Lord—you will find a rare combination

---

64 *Tamerlano* is an opera in three acts by George Frideric Handel. It takes up the legends of the Ottoman Sultan Bayezid I, who was captured by the Mongolian commander Timur Lenk (1336-1405) in 1402 during a devastating battle and probably committed suicide. Timur Lenk is also called *Tamerlan*, Italian *Tamerlano*.
Gil Blas was written between 1700 and 1730 by Alain-Rene Le Sage. Despite being set in Spain it is basically a French tale. The hero starts as a sly servant to landed gentry and even goes to prison, sometimes regretting his actions.

of wisdom, nobility, courage and sublimity of the soul in this procedure. This impure, impudent and lecherous French race is already abusing its magnanimity, it wants to be ruled by an iron scepter. It is disgusting to see, after having covered itself with crimes, it speaks of its common decency, its goodness, its magnanimity, as if it were not she who covered Europe with blood and sorrow, who murdered three kings in two centuries and who showed the most repulsive greed in all relations.

The city is not beautiful, some areas are, but the biggest part consists of dirty, narrow, smelly streets etc. In short my dear friend, I will thank heaven when I can return to Germany.

Napoleon hunted on the 9th. He thinks only of his usual pleasures. The same lack of spiritual uplift that prompted him to flee Russia, leaving his army to all the horrors of hunger and cold, now makes a shameful existence bearable for him — the archduchess returns to her father, Gerome goes to Stuttgart, Joseph to Switzerland and so all this scum is brought down.

Stein.

Appendix 1

Family Documents

I. Marriage certificate of the Judicial Councillor Carl A. Sack

Carl August Sack married on January 30, 1757. His wife Gertrud was a daughter of the registrar Rottemann from Cleve and his wife née Hermessen from Gennep.

The entry in the marriage register of the reformed community of Cleve is verbatim:

1757 Den 30. Januarius
im Hause copuliert
De Heer Criminal-Raat, mits-gaders
Regeerings-Advocaat en Schepen der Stadt Cleve
Carl August Sack J. G.
met
Mademoiselle Margareta Gertrud Notemann J. D.
Beiden woonachtig allhier

According to the transcript the priest must have been a Dutchman, mits-gaders means "at the same time also", Schepen = lay judge, J. G. = bachelor, J. D. = maiden.

According to the documents in the Cleve City Archive, Carl August Sack was sworn in as a lay judge on May 6, 1755.

His wife was baptized according to the baptismal register of the Reformed parish of Cleve on May 27, 1736, her birthday was May 23. The entry reads literally:

Christened

Of Gerhard Nottemann and Charlotta Sophia Mechjilt Hermessen the child Margaritha Gertruyd. Godfather Mr Johan Dittmar onder (second) Mayor Schmitz,

Godmother Mrs Privy Councillor de Beyer born Romswinkel.

II. Baptismal Registrations of the Children of the Sack Couple with their Birthdays

The twelve children of Carl August Sack were baptized according to the baptismal register of the Reformed community of Cleve:

1. Friedrich Gerhard on May 15, 1758.
2. Carl Heinrich Theodor on July 15, 1759.
3. Charlotta Luise Gertrud on September 11, 1760.
4. Cornelius Christian August on October 29, 1761.
5. Friederica Sophia Christina on May 12, 1763, born May 10.
6. Johann August on October 11, 1764.
7. Dorothea Wilhelmine Louise on February 2, 1766.
8. Ernst Wilhelm on June 28, 1767.
9. Ferdinand Johann Arnold on May 27, 1770.
10. Henrietta Philippine Helena on January 5, 1772.
11. Ernst Heinrich Everhard Sigismund on January 29, 1775, born on January 26.
12. Justus Leopold Maximilian on July 18, 1776, born on July 14.

Where the birthdays of the children are not indicated above, the baptismal register does not contain any mention of them.

As godparents are listed:
Child 1   Preacher Sack in Hecklingen and Frau Administrator von Renesse.

Child 2   Mrs District Administrator Elsner, preacher
          Hermsen zu Gennep, Judicial Counsellor and
          Government Advocate Sack of Gross-Glogau.
Child 3   Lady Privy Councillor Lucanus of Halberstadt,
          Mrs Widow Rotemann and Judicial Councillor
          and Government Advocate Sack of Breslau.
Child 4   Mademoiselle Schürmans and Christian Sack of
          Lübeck,
Child 5   Friederica Sophia Sack of Hecklingen and Ad-
          ministrator von Renesse.
Child 6   Widowed Mrs Lerett and Privy Court Councillor
          Lucanus.
Child 7   Mrs Widow Preacher Sack of Hecklingen, Court
          Preacher Sack of Berlin and "spouse" Mr Privy
          Postal Secretary Resay of Berlin,
Child 8   Commission Councillor Einicke of Erdeborn in
          the county of Mansfeld and Mrs Privy Council-
          lor Sack in Breslau,
Child 9   Military Councillor Resay of Halberstadt, Ad-
          ministrator von Renesse and Crown Govern-
          ment Secretary Sack of Glogau.
Child 10 Mrs Henriette Lucan (probably should be Lu-
          canus) of Halberstadt, Mademoiselle Catrin He-
          lene von Renesse and Lieutenant Philipp
          Wilhelm Sack.
Child 11 Crown Government Councillor Lucanus of Glo-
          gau, Justice Councillor Lucanus of the same
          place, Preacher Sack of Hecklingen and Made-
          moiselle Sack of Pasewalk.
Child 12 Preacher Sack in Magdeburg, Crown Councillor
          Heyen of Alsleben, Mr Luffneii of Utrecht,
          Mademoiselle von Erpens of Gennep "Auch ona

Dem. Verschow a. Nymegen" (i.e., one also has
Demoiselle Verschow of Nymegen, which apparently means that she was not present at the
baptism).

III. Joh. August and Marianne von Reiman's Testament as Engaged Couple

Stamp omitted here because of the time circumstances and French occupation.

It is hereby declared and made known that the following marriage contract has been established between the Royal Privy Crown Financial Councillor Johann August Sack and Miss Marianne Gertrude Johanna von Reiman, the youngest daughter of Mr Privy Councillor and Land Administrator von Reiman, with the accession of both parents.

1.

Since the prospective spouses are engaged with the consent of both parents and have already been proclaimed and since their marriage is to be consummated by legal assent at the earliest opportunity, they promise to behave towards each other in this state as befits a righteous spouse, so that the ultimate goal of a happy, prosperous and blessed marriage may be attained.

2.

Both fiancées bring into the marriage all their present and during the marriage accrued assets of all kinds.

3.

In particular, the bridegroom already now brings in what he has acquired from the inheritance of his uncle who died in Glogau and otherwise during his well-paid years of service, as well as the bride brings in what she has already accrued through inheritance cases and otherwise. Both, however, contribute without distinction everything that might in any way fall to them.

4.

And since the parents of the bridegroom have promised to give the same as their other children, the sum of three thousand Reichstaler Berl. Court. now to his establishment, the parents promise the Mademoiselle Bride *pro dote* (as a dowry) a quantum of three thousand Reichstaler Clev. Court., in addition to a reasonable supply of clothes, linen and underwear into the marriage.

5.

In consideration of the total of the assets now contributed and those to be contributed in the future, a community of good will is constituted for the complete unification of the mutual interest, in such a way that both the acquisition and the substance of the assets shall be common.

6.

During the marriage, therefore, the entire property is regarded as joint property, in such a way that although it is legally administered by the husband, both spouses have undivided ownership and the principles of general marital property community prescribed by general state law are to apply.

7.

After a separation of the marriage, however, and if there may then be children from the marriage, the surviving spouse retains the usufruct of the entire property until the spouse either moves on to another marriage, or the children marry or start an establishment, in which case the surviving spouse is obligated to return to each child *fuo sua rate* (respectively), who marries or establishes himself with his consent, a third part of the property as determined in § 8. On the other hand, the children of the surviving spouse shall be brought up in accordance with their status from this usufruct, the sons shall be given the instruction necessary for their advancement but the daughters shall receive the necessary instruction in the parental home until they are married and, in the case of marriage, the property defined in § 7 shall serve *loco dotis* (as a dowry).

8.

In such a case the substance of the property is divided between the surviving spouse and the children in such a way that the former receive one half and the latter the other half in their own right.

9.

At the end the surviving spouse shall be obliged to draw up an inventory immediately after the death of the other and, in the case of the children who are minors or under-age, to hand it over closed to the court of wards and to hand over an open copy of it to the next of kin of the deceased spouse. The surviving spouse, on the other hand, shall be dispensed from all accounting expressly and for as long as divorce and division must be established in accordance with § 6.

If the mother remains the longest survivor, she will be the guardian of the children who have not yet reached adulthood but she will choose an assistant from among the deceased husband's closest relatives, with whom she will jointly consider the upbringing of the children and any changes to be made to the property.

10.

If, however, contrary to hope, this marriage would not be blessed with children, then half of the deceased spouse, if not otherwise disposed of in any other way, shall go to the closest relative of the same and shall be held in accordance with the laws of the place where the death occurs. However, both spouses reserve the right to dispose of the property both in the case of childlessness as well as when there are children, *salva legitima*.

11.

In the case of childlessness and unless otherwise disposed of, half of the property is returned to the deceased's next of kin but only after the death of both spouses on the basis of an inventory of the property drawn up by the surviving spouse, since the survivor is entitled to the usufruct thereof for the rest of his life. However, if one spouse may dispose of his or her property for the benefit of the other, the parents of the other spouse shall make use of the other spouse's legitimate rights.

In all cases, however, the survivor is deprived of the choice to keep the moveable property, linen and for the extrajudicial valuation to be made by a sworn appraiser at the death of the other spouse. Just as the fiancées of both spouses recognize the inclined declarations of their parents, especially the promises of their parents regarding the gift with due gratitude, so these spouses are in mutual trust with the parents of both fiancées and the brother of the Mademoiselle Bride, Chamber Assessor von Reiman, as her assistant, and expressly stated that it should be considered as valid everywhere, whether before the Prussian or French courts, and that it should be attached to all the pieces, which is why such pieces were also made in triplicate and signed and sealed by all the interested parties mentioned above.

Accordingly in Cleve on January 3, 1799.

Johann August Sack - Marianne Gertrude Reiman Carl Sack (Father)

Gertrude Sack geb. Notemann (Mother) Johann Reinhard Peter von Reiman (Father)

Maria Godfred Reiman née von Forell (Mother) Georg
Johann August Gerhard von Reiman (Brother).

IV.   Marriage Certificate

Today, the sixteenth day of the month of Nivose[65] in the seventh year of the Frankish Republic, at six o'clock in the evening, Joseph Weygand Swaaters, assistant to the Municipal Agent of the Community of Cleve, appeared in the municipal hall to make a marriage covenant: a marriage covenant between Johann August Sack. Privy Crown Fiscal Councillor in the service of the King of Prussia, four and thirty years old, living in Berlin, son of Carl August Sack, a citizen here in the Commune, and of Magaretha Gertruda Noteman, otherwise Marianne Gertruda Johanna Reiman three and twenty years old, Daughter of Johann Reinhard Peter Reiman, citizen here in the Commune and of Maria Gertruda Forell who were accompanied by both future spouses, by the intended mutual fathers, recently Carl August Sack aged seven and

---

65   i.e. the fourth month of the French Republican calendar which was a calendar created and implemented during the French Revolution, and used by the French government for about 12 years from late 1793 to 1805, and for 18 days by the Paris Commune in 1871. The revolutionary system was designed in part to remove all religious and royalist influences from the calendar, and was part of a larger attempt at decimalisation in France (which also included decimal time of day, decimalisation of currency, and metrication). It was used in government records in France and other areas under French rule, including Belgium, Luxembourg, and parts of the Netherlands, Germany, Switzerland, Malta, and Italy.
There were twelve months, each divided into three ten-day weeks called décades. The tenth day, décadi, replaced Sunday as the day of rest and festivity. The five or six extra days needed to approximate the solar or tropical year were placed after the months at the end of each year and called complementary days. This arrangement was an almost exact copy of the calendar used by the Ancient Egyptians, though in their case the beginning of the year was marked by summer solstice rather than autumn equinox.

seventy, citizen here in the Commune, and Johann Reinhard Peter Reiman, also seven and seventy years old and citizen here in the Commune, also by Georg Johann Gerhard August Reiman, six and twenty years old, Assessor at the Prussian War and Domain Chamber at Wesel, brother of Marianne Gertruda Johanna Reiman, and of Ferdinand Johann Arnold Sack, aged eight and twenty, assistant with the Prussian government at Emmerich, brother of the Privy Crown Finance Councillor Sack.

I Joseph Weygand Swaaters after the present fathers of both parties have now given their consent to this marriage orally, having read out in the presence of the parties and the witnesses, first, the Act of Proclamation of the marriage promise between the future spouses, drawn up by the President of the Municipal Administration of the Canton of Cleve on the fourteenth of the current month of Nivose and posted on the door of the Municipal House of Cleve on the same day, and then, secondly, the testimony of the Royal Court and Cathedral Preacher Sack *sub dato* Berlin on the seventeenth of December one thousand seven hundred eight and ninety and which was there three times—on the second, ninth, and sixteenth of December One thousand seven hundred eight and ninety. After Johann August Sack and Marianne Gertruda Johanna Reiman also declared in a loud voice that they would take each other in marriage, I have pronounced in the name of the law that Johann August Sack and Marianne Gertruda Johanna Reiman are joined in matrimony and have drawn up the present agreement, which the parties and the witnesses have signed with me. Done in the parish house of Cleve on the day, month and year as above.

signed Johann August Sack. Marianne Gertrude Reiman.
signed C. Sack. Reiman. Reiman. Sack,
signed Swaaters.

V. Death Certificate von Gertrude Sack née Nottemann

(In this section italics denote translation from the original in French)

Year Eight of the French Republic.

Today in the year eight of the French Republic on the fifteenth day of Frimaire[66] at half past eleven, before me Henri Forstner, President of the municipal administration of the Canton of Cleves, appeared in the public hall of the commune house of Cleves the citizen Henri Thoma, sixty years old, pensioner, and Jean Henrichs, sixty-seven years old, carpenter, both residing in this Commune in a street named Steckbahn, neighbours of citizen Margarethe Gertrud Notemann, married to citizen Charles August Sack, pensioner, also residing in this Commune, have declared to me, that the relative Margarethe Gertrud Notemans died yesterday at six o'clock in the evening in her home number three hundred and four at the age of sixty-three years six months thirteen days. According to this declaration I immediately went to the place of residence, I ascertained the death of the said Citizen Margaretha Gertrude Notemans. I have drawn up the present deed, which Henri Thoma und Jean Henrichs signed with me in the Commune house of Cleves on the above day, month and year.

signed Thoma.   signed Henrichs.   signed Forstner.

---

66   Third month of the French Republican Calendar.

Excerpts from Granier's Work from the Privy State Archives in Berlin and the Parisian State Archives

VI. About the Prussian Minister von Schulenberg-Kehnert

On August 1, 1807, General Clarke, who during the war was the Governor General of all conquered Prussian territories that were divided into four departments and also Governor of Berlin, reported to the Emperor Napoleon:

"The King of Prussia had instructed a Mr Le Coq to deliver to Mr de Schulenburg, Ex-Minister of Lutzow and Zack [Sack] the orders of the King, who appointed them his commissioners for the arrangements to be made, to which Napoleon answers to Clark: *"I see with pleasure that Mr Schulenburg did not accept the mission of the King of Prussia."* (italics original in French).

As early as August 18, 1807, the Prussian minister Count Schulenburg-Kehnert wrote to his daughter, Princess Hatzfeld: *"I am perfectly willing for you to accept it",* She had been offered the position of Crown Court Mistress with the wife of Jerome, the King of Westphalia. At the same time he wrote to his son-in-law: *"The Emperor only reaches out once in his life and a refusal is an offence. Prussia can only be unhappy, you are not Prussian, you were even mistreated there, so think of yourself."* (And that was written by a Prussian minister!)

On May 10, 1803, Count Schulenburg-Kehnert himself, who had been a Prussian general of the cavalry since 1798, transferred to the French and was admitted as divisional general with Jerome, (as it is shamefully called). Count Schulenburg himself wrote to his son-in-law Hatzfeld on May 11 about this:

"In this moment I have received a letter from Cassel announcing that I am appointed Major General and President of the War Section of the Conseil d'Etat. I shall arrive as soon as possible".

VII. Concerning the Demands of the French

Sack to General von Knobelsdorf:

Berlin, Sept. 22, 1807.

Mr Daru refuses to accept our liquidations and has positively stated that he cannot withdraw any of his claims, adding that this is not a matter of arithmetic but of politics....

In September 1807, when the demands of the French exceeded all proportion, Sack also wrote to the Prussian Envoy Baron von Brockhausen and Knobelsdorf, who was responsible for military matters, answered Sack personally on October 7, 1807:

"Even though I do not have the honour of knowing that your work is devoted solely to the service of the State, you have earned the admiration of all Prussians and may your sorrows be rewarded by success!

And further Brockhausen wrote:

Paris, Nov 10, 1807.

For President Sack was on his own. Word has been going around that Sr. Daru was being recalled. His many enemies hope so and were working accordingly. Our plight finds many sympathizers, but it does not do us much good. The Russian Ambassador, whose extreme astonishment marked his first talks on the request for the five fortresses has caused these terms to be modified, is absolutely of the opinion that no fortresses should be granted, that the article of the transfer of the Domains should be evaded and that they should be offered at most as a mortgage. However, he wants this opinion to remain secret and that he has nothing to do with it...

Then Brockhausen writes to Sack:

From Paris, Nov. 12.

With true admiration I saw Hon. High Well-Born's firmness. It is no small thing to get along with Daru, who is praised here as an honest man but is generally hated because of his harshness.

VIII. About Sack's Refusal to Grant a French Camp around Berlin

The note of the French Minister of Foreign Affairs Champagny to the Prussian envoy in Paris, Baron von Brockhausen, dated May 21, 1808, was about Sack's behavior after his departure:

Monsieur le Baron. His Majesty the Emperor and King knew that a letter had been written to the States of the electoral campaign to incite them to oppose with all their means the execution of a project that had been manifested by the Intendant-General of Tannée Françoise. There was no fear of provoking the members of the States to resistance, by presenting it as a duty. Their honour as men and as faithful subjects is at stake. They are threatened with the curse of the people and the vengeance of their sovereign if they decide to favour the views of the French Government. I say enough, Mr Baron, to ensure that the author of such a manifest provocation to revolt cannot remain unknown to your court.

His Majesty Emperor and King could not learn without regret that a person enjoying the confidence of His Majesty the King of Prussia had allowed himself to take a step which was so obviously aimed at breaking the union of the two States.

He is not the only Prussian agent who shows himself to be animated by feelings opposed to those your court has assured. Here he forbids a Mr Roux to stay in France and continues:

It is to be desired Mr le Baron, it is even of the highest interest, that all agents employed by the Prussian court be strictly con-

tained within the rules of their duty. Provocations similar to those which have just taken place in a country still occupied by the French troops, might bring things to such a point that His Imperial Majesty, justly offended, would regard the Treaty of Tilsit as broken. What responsibility would then be borne by those who would once again call war and all the evils that follow from it upon their country.

I have the honour to renew to you, Mr le Baron, the assurance of my highest consideration.

Brockhausen answers this note with a letter of apology to Champagny. The Immediate Commission i.e. Sack — only remonstrated and in no way provoked the resistance (la révolte) of the estates. That would have been completely contrary to the will of the King:

nothing more sincere and solemn than the King's wish to set aside everything that might give offence to the Emperor and to leave no stone unturned in order to revive in His heart feelings of trust and friendship from which he finally awaits happier days.

The King had prescribed his negotiators:

"to put, in their public and private conduct, that discretion, that moderation, that dignity befitting misfortune... But can the unfortunate Monarch be responsible indiscriminately for the conduct of all persons in his service?"

This submissiveness was very much to the liking of Minister Voss with his limp disavowal of the brave Sack. Of course, at that time, outward bravery in Prussia was of no use any more, only the imposed resignation here should not have been so lacking in dignity.

Brockhausen writes about it himself to Sack:

"Daru makes himself incredibly hated here because of his methods known in Berlin. He has an infinite number of enemies working against him. The (Russian envoy) Count Tolstoy was also very upset about the idea of a convention given by Daru because of military communications between the French Corps in Warsaw and those who remain in northern Germany.

Correspondence of the Minister of State von Voss with the envoy Baron von Brockhausen and with Prince Wilhelm of Prussia in Paris Concerning Sack's Dismissal:

Voss to Brockhausen June 9, 1808.

You have done, Mr Baron, all that could be done to destroy the unfortunate impression that Mr Sack's departure may have left in the mind of His Imperial Majesty. The efforts of V.E. are worthy of dislodgement and will undoubtedly have achieved the most satisfactory results. I have immediately made known to the King the letter which she addressed to the Count de Champagny, as well as the reply of the Minister of Foreign Affairs. It seems that this unfortunate affair is over and that the French authorities in Berlin are not still resentful of it, for they do not speak to me about it and, on the contrary, show me a great deal of confidence. I hope that Monsieur de Champagny will also confine himself to the letter he wrote to V. E., and that there will no longer be any question of an unfortunate event which could so adversely affect our affairs....

Voss to Prince Wilhelm: Berlin, June 10.

I dare to hope that the incidents which last occurred both in Berlin and in Paris will not have such unfortunate consequences as V. A. R. appears to have apprehended him. At least I can assure You, Monsignor, that the impression which Mr Sack's affair may have produced seems entirely destroyed in the minds of the influential persons here and one will probably limit oneself to the stern letter which Mr de Champagny has just written to Mr de Brockhausen, unless one keeps a closer watch on the opinions and actions of the King's employees.

Brockhausen to Voss Paris, June 23, 1808.

I am delighted to see by the last letter that the French authorities have shown such well-deserved confidence in V. E.. It appears that there will be no more talk of the small dispute produced by the parties. Perhaps even the camp project will not be carried out and humanity will be touched by the profound misery which is crushing us.

Prince Wilhelm to Voss. Paris, June 27 with the Prince's handwritten signature: *Your very devoted friend Wilhelm, Prince of Prussia.*

The letter that V. E. was kind enough to write to me on the 10th of this month has been delivered to me and I am very pleased to learn that the French authorities have given You, Mr le Baron, the marks of confidence and esteem that You so rightly deserve.

Minister of State von Voss to Prince Wilhelm, Berlin, July 1, 1808: ... *Mr Sack currently only finds cases that involve our courts of law and every eight days he reports to H. M. in person. He has no involvement in political and administrative matters.*

IX. After the Nomination of Sack to the Crown Presidency

On November 23, Marshal Davoust writes to N.: *"The choices the King makes are proof to the public of this prince's feelings, or his advice to France. He has just thanked the Earl of Woss (Voss) who only spoke to him of his true interests and of the necessity of not giving umbrage to the French. He has replaced him by a Mr de Zach (Sack) who has no other title to his benevolence than that of having been dismissed by Mr Daru, six to seven months ago, for having written to all the authorities of the country a circular enjoining them to oppose by all means the establishment of the camps and to refuse all the requests of the French authorities. All sensible people are dismayed by this conduct, as well as by the plans, which are being manifested to imitate Austria.* And on the same subject Daru reported Berlin, November 20, 1808 to Napoleon: *The King of Prussia has just withdrawn his authority from his Minister of State, Count de Voss, who was his plenipotentiary here. He replaces him by Mr Sack, a creation of Mr de Stein, who had already compromised himself with us, until he was forced to confess a letter which provoked the resistance of the local administrations to the French authority"*. (Paris National Archives).

Davoust wrote to Clarke from Erfurt on January 1, 1809, about Sack's recall:

"This Mr de Zach was dismissed from Berlin by Count Daru as preaching, at the instigation of Mr de Stein, rebellion against the French authorities". (Paris War Archives).

About Stein and Sack's influence in Westphalia:

Berlin, October 7, 1808

The public is more uncertain than ever about the fate of Prussia, because thoughtful people cannot reconcile the King's current policy, which distinguishes Stein and Sack and the friends and creations of the former more than ever, at a time when he wants to obtain a pardon from Emperor Napoleon. It's good to know that Stein has been Crown President of the once Prussian Chambers of Estates of Westphalia for 10 years and that he has many people in this country who owe their existence to him and who look to him and Sack for great benefits if they are able to bring about a revolution.

Agent report to Marshal Davoust in Erfurt without signature:

Extract from the secret correspondence Berlin, February 11, 1809

Sack is hated for his harshness and arbitrary conduct, he sets new impositions, demanding the old ones with the utmost rigour even from the poor. The magistrate persisted in presenting at the expense of the poor bourgeois a carriage to the King with 8 horses, which will cost 11 thousand ECU.

Berlin, February 10, 1809.

We are here in a veritable interregnum, one might even say in complete anarchy. Neither the officers nor the soldiers obey their superiors, nor do the civil authorities obey their leaders. No justice is administered, the soldiers receive no pay and there is general confusion.

They complain about old man l'Estocq and laugh out loud at the commander and his aides de camp, they despise President Sack without obeying him and they allow themselves violence against the police. If the King were to remain absent for another four weeks, the revolution would break out on its own in this town, for all spirits have risen to the highest degree.

Letters to Sack from the Years Before the Liberation. Taken from his Papers

To

the Royal President of the Crown Nechen Chamber Mr v. Schlabrendorff High Well-Born.

To fulfill my promise I send you by the younger v. Modceveis that folder that I have received this moment from P. Estaffette from Silesia, from all my heart

your own Blücher.
Stargard, October 16, 1809.
Transcription.

High Well-Born Count,

Particularly esteemed General of the Cavalry.

With the greatest attention I have seen from Hon. Excellency's Letter of May 8 which steps you have taken to bring His Majesty the King to one of your as well as my, as well as to those of all of us who are faithful, desired conclusions. If this request does not bear fruit either, it is likely that what the High one feared will happen. However, it is then our duty to leave a glorious memory and a good example to our descendants. I at least hope to be allowed to act in such a way, for my mandates ordered me to do so in the most definite way. I am to defend Silesia and its fortresses against any enemy attack and to use all means to

achieve this end. I have been appointed supreme commander of all military power in Silesia and all civil authorities.
In addition, the Lieutenant Generals of Gravert and L'Es-
toy are instructed to support me in this task with all their
strength.

The peace has indeed already been concluded, but Emperor Franz will only sign it if Russia guarantees it. An
Austrian general has therefore been sent to Petersburg to
ask Emperor Alexander for his guarantee. Although it is
almost foolish to count on reason in Russian politics, it is
still possible that Emperor Alexander will finally become
aware of the abyss on the edge of which he stands. In any
case, I will give Hon. Excellency all the important news.

With the greatest affection and veneration I have the honor
to be Hon. Excellency's most obedient

Glatz, Oct. 13, 1809 Gr. v. Goetzen.[67]

Unfortunately, my health is not yet as good as I would like
it to be able to take such a gracious condolence from Hon.
Excellency, but I believe that the cause lies more in the
outer circumstances than in the body and I hope that if it
should come to drawing the sword against the general enemy, the forces to lead it will also find themselves and I

---

67 Count Friedrich Wilhelm von Goetzen, born in 1767, later 1806
    Gereral Governor of Silesia, to whom the militarising of this prov-
    ince is attributed. Through his steadfastness he contributed much
    to the fact that Silesia was preserved for the King of Prussia in the
    Tilsit Peace. In 1807 he wrote a memorandum on the organisation
    of the cavalry. In 1808 he was appointed chief of the 9th Hussar
    Regiment. In 1809 he negotiated extensively in secret.*

will have the opportunity to show myself worthy of Your Excellency's trust.

G. v. G.

On the envelope it states:

The Royal Prussian Privy Councillor and Crown President
                                    Mr von Sack
(Siegel)   High Well-Born
Royal General Government of Stettin
of the Provinces of Pommern and Neumark.

Transcript Berlin Oct. 10.

Unfortunately, I have received the most unfavourable news from a certain source about a disgraceful peace which has probably already been concluded between Austria and France, so that there is no longer any doubt about it. Our fate will be decided as a direct result of this peace and it seems to me that far-reaching prospects are emerging. I have therefore felt compelled to send Major von Lohsan to the King and to ask him to give me certain orders of conduct for all cases, of which I have tried to inform your High Well-Born under the seal of secrecy.

Since His Majesty the King has made it my strictest duty to secure Colberg, especially on several occasions, its supplying with all the requirements for the event of a siege would have to be our main concern, just as it would be necessary to keep all the money that could be raised ready for such a case. For this reason, as well as for many other items, I would like to be able to talk to you in person very soon. Since your High Well-born, as I have heard externally, decided to travel to Stettin on the fifteenth of this month, the circumstances mentioned above cause me to make a sincere request for you to possibly go to Stettin via Stargard and not first come here from there, as you may have intended.

Stargard, October 8, 1809   Blücher.

To the Royal Privy State Councillor... x. x.
Mr Sack
High Well-Born of Berlin

October 8 to the long distance post *Cito* for personal opening Red seal	On the addition to the address

October 8 to the long
distance post   } On the envelope, in ad-
Cito for personal opening   dition to the address
Red seal

(Only the signature of this letter is handwritten)

Berlin, October 10.

I am informed that the Hon. High Well-Born intended to arrive in Stettin on the 15th. Please arrange your journey in such a way that you come to Stargard first and then go from here to Stettin, since you will have many things to talk about since I received the unfortunate news that Oestreich has concluded a sad peace from a squadron from Glatz this night. The French Emperor expressed himself that we had not paid our contribution and that he wanted to collect it himself and that the lot of Hesse[68] was intended for us. Even today I am sending Major v. Lohsow to the King as a courier and demand certain instructions and conduct as to whether I should reinforce the garrisons of Stettin and Kostrzyn. By the way, I reserve the right to speak orally about our unfortunate situation with Hon. High Well-Born Privy State Councillor von Heidebrecht who is with me at this moment.

Stargard, October 8, 1809
Blücher.

To the Royal Privy
State Councillor and   This letter is completely written
Crown President Herrn v.   in the persona handwriting of
Sack   Blücher.
High Well-Born of Berlin

By another hand on the letterhead with the seal of the
Commanding General von Blücher.

Venerable friend,

The old secretary Councillor v. Worsig is in an oppressed situation, since he lost his income from various branches, I

---

68 Hesse-Darmstadt was a member of Napoleon's Confederation of the Rhine during the Napoleonic Wars. Rapidly expanding during the mediatizations, Hesse-Darmstadt became an amalgamation of smaller German states, such as the Electorate of Cologne. The legal patchwork of the state culminated in a decree issued on October 1, 1806 by Louis I. The old territorial estates were abolished, which altered Hesse-Darmstadt "from a mosaic of patrimonial fragments into a centralized, absolute monarchy."

need not mention anything about his usefulness, if you can help him in your sphere of activity to a position next to his own, which will increase his income by about one hundred percent, you will certainly receive his heartfelt gratitude.

Faithfully,   Blücher.

Stargard, March 15, 1811

A few days ago I received a letter from our mutual friend v. Stein, he is well and content.

B.
Handwritten letter
(Nothing on the envelope)

Well, my venerable friend,

I have to take advantage of a great friendship. I leave Berlin after the State Chancellor has given his hand and word of honor to arrange for Delitz to stay in the Lachowa administration and to agree with my wish that wherever he thinks the King might be inclined to do something for me, it is now all about my getting something to do as soon as possible in order to forget the ingratitude with which I am treated and my agitated annoyance. I therefore ask you to be my trustee and to bring the matter to a speedy conclusion. I can't imagine that the King would want to make me a pitiful wretch on this occasion, as he knows that I don't own a foot of earth as my own property and that half my salary will be deducted to pay my debts of 2200 rthlr. I will lose 2200 rthlr. every year by confiscation of my prebende[69], I cannot survive if I am not reasonably compensated. If they wanted to give me the Delitz estate without leaving the forest with it, I would not be able to make use of this favor. I am relying on you to talk to Hardenberg. It would be best if President v. Brauschitch gets the order to arrange the matter with me, since both of you are here, one shouldn't push an old favorite away. Who can guarantee that there aren't cases where such an old offshoot is still useful. I think Schoverweber asked for the matter to be taken into consideration. If they push this a

---

69 Prebende was originally used to indicate the income of a chapter of canons (choristers) that was intended for the livelihood of these clergy. In church law, the word prebende only occurs in this sense, in everyday parlance it is an indication of ecclesiastical income, which are called benefits and also vicaries.

The prebende must be brought up by a diocese, parish, monastery or by the founders of the individual vicaries. The earnings of the ladies of the Theresia-Order and a commandery of the Teutonic Knights were also called prebenden.

Under the ancien régime, absolutist Europe before the French Revolution, the princes and kings divided the income of monasteries and dioceses among their friends, family and relations. A clergyman could draw income from several dioceses and monasteries and did not even have to perform his office.

This construction was called a Preende sine cura (animarum), Latin for "money without (soul) care". The Dutch word sinecure derives its existence from this. The prebends were enjoyed and the clergy controlled the goods.

Since the Middle Ages, the well-intentioned gifts to churches, monasteries, prebends and vicars continued. This capital was withdrawn from society and in fact—whether or not willingly—it was an increasing economic power. This was followed by a power-political struggle between church and state. Ecclesiastical goods and monastic goods and prebends were nationalized in several countries, such as Russia, Austria, France and the Netherlands. This culminated in the nationalization of ecclesiastical goods and secularization in the period after the French Revolution of 1789.

little, it will be fine. Because completely inactive life is ruinous, I would not be to just sit back. So if I cannot bring this to a satisfactory conclusion, then I must myself approach Berlin again, however reluctantly. Farewell and do not neglect that which you have devoted yourself to with all your heart.

Blücher.

Stargard, December 13, 1811.

Yesterday, the magistrate Friederici read me an alleged plan about the Kurmark debt, according to which the wretchedness of the author's unauthorized handling of such matters would only cause annoyance over lost time, if the prevailing opinion in it were less dishonorable. In fact, all we are talking about is to leave the bonds without interest payment, to order tenders according to the principles of the past and to use the money raised to buy up the securities which have been deliberately rendered even more worthless. But he does not stop there, he wants to play dirty. Partly the acquired bonds are to be sold again and in addition, with the help of a competent conductor, two merchants are to be employed as consultants, one Jewish and one baptized.

Hon. High Well-Born, to say anything about the senselessness and dishonorableness of this project would be very superfluous. You too will be outraged by it—if similar things had not already happened too much in the past—and you too will be convinced that such ideas, if they were to become known even as belonging to the people, would not only bring disgrace but also obvious ruin to the province by exposing it to infamy (which, thank God, is unthinkable).

Mr Friderici, however, claims to have submitted his project to Mr v. Pomeritz, and I therefore ask you very much to make him understand the abomination of such ideas. In the drafting of the minutes of the conference, the estates make the acceptance of the plan communicated to them as a salutary council dependent on the state assuming their bill debt, as if they were showing a great favor! The state cannot take over anything straight—except what, after very careful consideration, could not be granted at the moment with regard to the Altmark and similar points—it can and will hopefully do so indirectly and without attracting attention. The plan is certainly to arrange the bill debt, if one would be quits, the rest could be arranged without special arrangements. Furthermore, Stägemann and I are credited with several proposals that came from the other side—even a new tendering procedure, which I would have never thought worth mentioning again. It's bad enough and not my fault that the income tax regulations have been delayed for so long but why don't we raise the tax for the time being according to the versions proposed by Hon. High Well-Born already in November? Now the regulations should be adopted more simply and everything possible should be done to speed up the collection. According to the experience in East Prussia, two or three months at the most are sufficient if everyone wants to follow the example of strength and activity you give, even if only to a small degree. I hope that the unlimited repetition of the levying of this tax will convince me that only a real levy can provide the yardstick for the budget, so it must be accelerated. Suggestions for improvements and remedies will always be found afterwards and will be heeded. The burden of the province has to be limited and determined if it is not to go under but you will never get out of this chaos if you do not even make a serious start. If this seriousness is shown, then the state is obliged to do everything possible — if only God wanted that, it would be more than can be imagined! Until then, he cannot answer for any help given. I commend myself to your friendship with the highest esteem.

Niebuhr[70], January 8, 1810.

Do not take it as negligence, dearest friend, if I have left your letter from the day before yesterday unanswered until now. On the contrary, believe that I have enjoyed the friendly trust that has been invested in it and that I am very grateful to you for giving it to me. It is, however, urgently necessary that in the case of the Section a completely different extension of the organization than hitherto must occur if it is to become something useful and even if individual considerations have already been taken into account for the time being, the circle is not yet complete in this case.

---

70 Niebuhr, Berthold Georg, born 27 August in Copenhagen as son of the great traveller Karsten N. Historian and bank director in Danish service since 1800, was used in 1806 at the invitation of Frhrn. v. Stein in the Prussian civil service for extraordinary financial transactions and was also appointed Privy Councillor of State. He gained great recognition in all his official positions through his conscientiousness and incorruptible love of truth, but lasting fame is linked to his literary achievements.*

I have seen Government Councillor Jacobi in East Prussia and know all the more how important it was for our eternally revered minister Ernst to grant him a beneficial position, since I myself drafted the ministerial letter which was issued to him and Mr v. Rohr and which contains the assurance for him and, in case of an accident, for his family. You know yourself that, to our shame, this is not a favourable recommendation at this time but you also know that any thought of this kind is as sacred to me as it is to you. So it would be doubly painful for me if the Minister were to refuse a proposal which I – like you – do not misunderstand, as you believe I do – would be bound to do to your judgment, as it might well be done. I therefore believe I must prevent this annoyance by ensuring that the Minister receives the proposal in writing in a combined plan. Perhaps the relationship between the sections and the ministers will soon be completely different, however difficult this or that minister may find it. But now a question. But now a question. Where is there quite a decent man who would not be afraid to clean out a mess which is necessary – that is the bank, which is now a hidden pitiful evil in the state. The knowledge of the accounting business, which is primarily the issue here, belongs to Mr. R. R. Jacobi, but he seems to me to be a very gentle and good man, so would he be able to bear to go to a beast like Reichert to reveal his wiles to him?

If he is too gentle with this vile business, would you know another one who would like to take a crack at it? Would you like to think about it? I will visit you at the beginning of next week and talk to you about it – until then let us both remain silent about our ideas. Nothing will happen for the moment.

Leon tells me that he has organized his assignments in Münster. Let me commend myself to your friendship, which I respectfully ask you for. I thank you once again for giving me the opportunity to at least prove to you my desire to contribute to something pleasant for you, if only it would not be withheld from us.

Niebuhr, April 13.

Please receive my most sincere thanks for your kind disposition regarding the salaries to be paid here. The Kurmark government or Mr von ?? will probably give us official news of the same, which will please all interested parties.

However, I take the most sincere and spirited interest in the new evidence of the satisfaction and great honourable confidence given to you by the transmission of the vast important business circle of His Majesty the King, and I thank you for having had the goodness to confirm to me what I had heard only by means of an uncertain rumour. May God grant you the rare strength and vigour of spirit and the good health that have made it possible for you to manage so many important and difficult matters with so many successes.

By the way, it will probably remain your motto: *ne cede malis, sed contra audentior ito.*

With regard to the happy delivery of sister-in-law Susanne Jacobi, née von Reiman, my whole house sincerely wishes her the best of happiness and I ask you to show our support and our best recommendation to your wife, the woman in childbed and her husband.

Cousin, I do not know whether I have already sent you the translation of Eulius which I have published and which I intended to send to you. If I have, please dispose of the enclosed copy, or send it to your brother-in-law Gillet some time.

The letter from Mr Dürr, which you kindly shared, is hereby returned.

Sack, November 10, 1810

(Crown Consistory Councillor, Crown Court Preacher and later Bishop).

von Gneisenau

to Privy State Councillor Sack.

Once again, I take the liberty of reminding Hon. High Well-Born of the Government Auditor Laar of Colberg, to congratulate him at starting a new position. He has trained in the field of justice as well as in the economic and police fields and is therefore ideally suited for a position in which a thorough knowledge of these three branches of administration is required. He was employed as a magistrate in Landsberg a. W. when he was transferred to Prussia after the unhappy October days. He spent the time there happily and did not refuse to take over an auditor position with his recruits. So he came to Colberg and since the government auditor there was happy to give up his business, I entrusted him with all his services and he has clothed them to my great satisfaction. Since then the earnings of his post have fallen to 20 rthl. a month. Such a man cannot survive on that and it is therefore very important to me to improve his situation. May this man be commended to Hon. High Well-Born.

Things are not good for us, as luck would have it. We do not want to make ourselves worthy of it. Let us grieve, because we cannot do anything to change the situation and if only there were thousands of men like you.

Vale ad fave tuo

N. v. G.

pd. 15. Dec. 11.   E. 15./12. 11

August Neid Hardt v. Gneisenau

pd. 25. Febr. 13.
City 27. Febr. 13.

My dear friend, I have received your first as well as the 2nd letter of the 15th correctly. No one is happier than when patriotic men quietly and vigorously pursue their careers to work good. I owe you a special thanks for the hints and suggestions you have given me, I will follow everything you have advised me. I am pleased that the second or third stand, as you want to call it, is so well-behaved and patriotic. The achievement of our independence requires the unification of all, a hard struggle and luck. Nothing can be achieved by ordinary means. The bearer of this letter will tell you many things in detail. Warmly and sincerely your adoring friend.

Scharnhorst, Lieutenant General.

Breslau, February 20, 13.

Second Section

Sack, Governor General of the Lower and Middle Rhine, then Crown President of the Rhine Province

Johann August Sack Royal Prussian Privy State Councillor Head of the Department of Trade and Industry in the Ministry of the Interior, Knight of the Order of the Red Eagle.

When, in 1810, the "Crown Presidents" that Stein's proposals had created were revoked by Hardenberg's[71] re-

71 In Stein's own notes from his life, von Hardenberg says, "He had the good-naturedness and kindness of sanguine pleasure-loving people, a mind that was easy to grasp, industriousness and an advantageous appearance. But his character lacked a moral religious base as well as greatness, intense strength and firmness, his mind lacked depth and his knowledge lacked thoroughness. Hence his weakness, his exuberance in happiness, his tearful softness in adversity, his superficiality, which was guided by his sensuality,

forms, Privy Councillor Sack had been given the department of general police in the Ministry of the Interior but in
1812, at the instigation of the French, he had had to exchange it for the Department of Trade and Industry.

When, in 1813, before he became Civil Governor of the
newly liberated lands between the Elbe and the Oder and
distinguished himself by his eminent effectiveness, by
quickly lifting and reorganizing these areas, which had
been badly affected. The ministries were then newly occupied, his friends, among them Stein, expected that he
would now be given the ministerial post of the Interior,
which had already been intended for him by Stein. However, this expectation was not fulfilled.

When in 1814 Sack received the appointment by the allies
to the General Government of the Lower Rhine, which had
been ordered in Basel on January 12, 1814, in Berlin his
soul rejoiced in a way he had hardly ever thought possible
to feel again in his life. So it was to be his destiny, after all
the terribly hard years of struggle here in the East of the
kingdom, to be allowed to breathe the heart-thrilling, free

---

pride and falsehood, caused so much evil. He removed all capable
people, surrounded himself only with mediocre, often wretched
people who abused him and treated him shamefully. His favorite
entertainment was lewd talk. The intimate association with unworthy women, which contrasted with his gray hair, his pride and
his dignity, made him even more contemptible. He undermined
the old Prussian spirit of thrift and obedience and when he died he
left the finances shattered and the affairs of state in the hands of a
host of badly chosen officials. He did not strive for the great and
good for the sake of the greater good but rather as a means to his
own fame. Thus he did not understand this and departed, not respected, not mourned."*

air of his beloved homeland and to serve it! Was this not the fulfillment of his deepest and innermost heart's desire, which he had always kept locked away in his pious and unselfish soul but which he had learned to reject as all too desirable and forever far out of reach? And now the call met him quite unprepared and unexpectedly, in the midst of the most outgoing care for those areas which had been so deeply stricken and sucked dry by the enemy. These areas were just beginning to regain the courage to live and the love of life again, under his understanding and benevolent consideration of the trials they had gone through together. When he thought of the fact that he had just begun to experience the first traces of a favourable change here and now had to leave them and entrust them to another hand, it was like guilt weighing upon his compassionate mind. Had he then been the one who had desired this change? No! It was again friend Stein who had proposed his person to the allied powers, for he, Stein, had now been granted the central administration of the parts of the country that had been abandoned and reclaimed and so he was allowed to assume that there were at present much more important tasks to be solved there than the reconstruction work being done here. Nevertheless, he could not leave the latter in the lurch so quickly and had to ask first of all that he be given time before taking up his new position. After all, it was the entire capital and the most important of all administrative districts in the kingdom so far that he had presided over for almost seven years and for which he had been the intrepid head in 1807-09. It was only in 1812-13 that he had been the dauntless head again, due to misery and death. What awaited him today at home in return? A militarily occupied borderland whose

fate was still unknown. Without treating it as enemy territory, the lost spirit of the majority of the inhabitants, who
had turned to the new Napoleonic sun, was to warm the
minds of the now victoriously allied states and, by hoping
for a better future, to make the sacrifices of the moment
bearable for them. This was the truth of the situation in his
homeland, the homeland he so fervently loved, which he
had left 15 years ago as a young husband, full of hope and
confidence. Nor was he to find a dear parental home in
Cleve. In 1810, his mother, who was soon to be lost, followed his aged father of 89 years old who was far away in
Münster and, separated from his mother who was then on
French soil on the Lower Rhine, had to find his resting
place there in French Westphalia. However, the sister
Philippine Sethe, who had looked after the precious old
man until the end, had followed her husband, who had
been transferred to the Düsseldorf Higher Regional Court
as president. This family circle and his brother Ernst followed, whose career had also been forced to move under
foreign rule, had to offer him a replacement in his homeland for the trusted relatives who, through Marianne's sister Jacobi in Potsdam and with the families of the court
preachers Sack, Gillet and Spalding, had gathered around
Sack's house in Berlin.

Nevertheless, despite these beloved people, both of them
had never made Berlin their home. Alone the conceited
bureaucracy, which had made itself so unpleasantly widespread in the ministries and among the obedient souls of
the officials was as unsympathetic and alien to Stein, the
fiery spirit of the Rhineland, as it was to his own being. In
confidential hours the two friends, Stein like he, had had

to admit to each other that Prussia in its eastern provinces was far behind the much freer and more independent West, not only in its far-flung population but also in the measures taken by the government. Even many points which Stein had included in far-reaching new principles of administration had been familiar to both of them, as they had long since proven themselves in their Rhenish and Westphalian official functions. It was therefore a completely different field of work on the Rhine and in view of this, Sack, with an almost intoxicated joy, promised himself together with his friend that he would perhaps be able to crown their life's work there and in any case to restore their homeland anew..

Stein was still in Paris when Sack had finally freed himself in March to take up his new post with his residence in the old imperial city of Aachen. With a powerful speech that he had published in the newspaper, he greeted the inhabitants of his Lower Rhine General Government as "his own beloved first fatherland, to which he himself owes his first education and his earlier effectiveness. That it was now granted to him to be allowed to give back and strengthen religion, independence, freedom and honour to the population after the long worn foreign yoke, fills him with unspeakably happy feelings" and when he assures "that he is seeking justice, security, truth and order as the foundations of the German constitution and will be strict and honest, always speaking up for both high and low" we still feel in the echoes of these words today that it was the really deepest soul of this excellent man that made itself known in simple speech. (Read, on the other hand, the pompous, lengthy proclamations which the French had showered down on the inhabitants for 20 years!).

He immediately embarked on the process of reorganization. First of all, prefects and sub-prefects were replaced by commissioners and county directors, and four governorates alone were formed in the Lower Rhine. What a miracle that soon after Sack's take-over we again met at their head, bearers of the well-known Cleve Names. Even that Assessor Koppe, the unfortunate bearer of the Stein letter to Witgenstein, who had been exiled since 1808, was employed here as commissioner of the Lower Meuse governorate. The French tax system was initially maintained with regard to direct taxes and since before the imposition of new, urgently necessary taxes of four million francs, necessitated by the immediate abolition of the hated Douanen and the French *Droits réunis*[72], deputies were immediately elected and summoned from among the country's residents now convincing themselves of the necessity of the new burden. The confidence shown in this

---

72   The *Régie Nationale de l'Enregistrement des Domaines et Droits réunis* was the first State financial administration created by the French Revolution.
     Its roots are to be found in the imposition of legal acts dating back to the *Ancien Régime*. It was managed by the *Ferme Générale* and then, from 1780, by an independent body, the *Administration générale des Domaines et Droits domaniaux*, initiated by Necker and implemented by a decree of January 9, 1780. It was the culmination of a slow and complex evolution. By a decree of February 7, 1791, the Legislative Assembly pronounced the abolition of the administration of the Domains. The decree of the following May 18, sanctioned on the 27th of the same month, created the *Régie nationale*. It had been preceded by a major tax reform, notably of registration and stamp duties, aimed at putting an end to the complexity of the duty rules of the *Ancien Régime*.

way was reciprocated with equal coin and the residents submitted to the payment of the new burden with willingness and without grumbling.

Yet, all over the place sad deficiencies were revealing themselves! As Sack now looked at his Rhine province, which had been so exemplary to him as he was in the East, he was certainly asking himself what become of the solid, orderly administrative district of the Lower Rhine. The old, solid foundations of the Duchy of Berg still stood out like indestructible cornerstones but in the industrial area around his new residence, the proud imperial city of Aachen, things were looking bleak, especially the basic foundation for an orderly state structure and its progress in the demands of culture. Under the rule of the war-raving Buonaparte, the school system had experienced far more inhibitions than support. In the case of the elementary schools it was particularly evident that not much more was taught than educating in order to keep the people incapable of judgment. Therefore, even in the Lizeums and colleges normal classes were supposed to be established for the special training of elementary school teachers but in the whole General Government no such institution was even found. In fact Sack found everything here had sunken desperately low! School supervision proved to be extremely deficient, being led by academy inspectors who, having no knowledge of German, could not be supervisors of German schools nor advisers to German teachers. They usually played a more than ridiculous role during their annual school inspections. In addition, there was the lack of knowledge about the progress in pedagogy that Germany had made.

In the factory districts where the machine and earning a living alone dominate people's minds — recorded in Jülich-Bergisch's own home district — he found children who as physically and morally crippled creatures from the age of 6 were already being employed in factory facilities.

He found the Scholars' Schools[73] in an almost equally sad state. Whereas these were formerly run by monks and operated in a one-sided ecclesiastical and monastic manner, they instead cultivated a one-sided Napoleonic spirit directed towards the universal world domination of the great French Empire.

Worse than the educational institutions, however, Sack felt the lack of educational drive in the existing academies that had replaced the abolished universities of Cologne, Bonn and Trier, namely those of Liège, Metz and Mainz. Those who could only do arithmetic and writing had found good employment with the French bureaucracy. The only people who were required to have a scholarly education, the judges, were the worst paid in the country.

Thus the Governor General found public education desperately neglected which was going to contrast his achievements in his short two-year term of government in terms of raising standards, all the more brilliant. He appointed the Consistorial Councillor Grashof as Director of Public Education in the northern part of his territory, as he had already found the School Council Dr. Görres in the

---

73 *Gelehrtenschulen* (lit. Scholars' Schools) were secondary schools in Protestant areas which, since the time of the Reformation, had been run either by a town or a sovereign.

southern part. The statistics initially collected by these gentlemen produced downright alarming results. One third of the communities had no elementary schools at all and of all school-age children only two-fifths attended any school at all. In order to control this dreadful state of affairs, Sack had a commission of understanding educators and clergymen of both denominations under the chairmanship of director Grashof draw up a plan of reorganization. As a result, in every parish a local school board was established by decree and given precise instructions. The fact that the participation of the clergy was consulted was highly successful. Teacher training colleges were established in several places, whereby the commercial school in Brühl and the Pestalozzi school in Koblenz offered the most public-spirited help. The Natorp[74] singing method, which had not even been known by name before, was introduced and the maintenance of the teachers was provided for by a revision of the municipal budget.

Sack gave the same attention to the Scholars' Schools. Fully-fledged grammar schools were established in Aachen and Cologne, only the lack of well-trained Catholic teachers caused difficulties. He supported these institutions with particular liberality and not only from state funds. He also knew how to reclaim and usefully apply the funds of the former University of Cologne, which had grown to millions and had been confiscated by the French. Sack was however unable to replace the lack of a

---

74 German music teachers debated about the right method for singing instruction which focused on numerals instead of syllables. The most influential method with numerals in opposition to Pfeiffer and Naegeli was developed by Natorp (1813). (Bresler, Liora (2007) International Handbook of Research in Arts Education).

university in his short time but prepared everything for a university in Bonn and approved a propaedeutic course in Cologne, for which some scholars had offered to give lectures.

In the same way, the medical sector and the building trade were also promoted – the construction of roads, which had been badly damaged by the troop marches, had to be thoroughly improved. The forestry sector, which had been impoverished by constant deforestation, was now in dire straits. He had hunting and fishing taken into new custody and care by a comprehensive hunting regulation of August 1, 1814 and on the same date a new forestry administration with a special forestry directorate came into effect.

The mining industry, which Sack had found to be without any administration since the flight of the French chief engineer, was given three trained mining commissioners, who had to administer it for the time being according to the French mining regulations until new legislation could override the previous one.

Sack's work for the poor also received considerable attention and improvement. He recommended the country poor houses at Brauweiler and Trier, which were not fortunate like Frankenthal to have a special director, to the clergy for supervision and tried to find suitable charity funds to strengthen them.

The extraordinary needs of the war hospitals required an appeal for charitable and voluntary contributions, which was accompanied by excellent results and was further enhanced by the establishment of women's associations. Wife Marianne immediately took over the leadership of one such association in Aachen and Philippine Sethe, as founder of the same, became its president in Düsseldorf. The results of this blessed institution, first established in Berlin by Sack and now also transplanted here, were beyond all expectations.

The four governorates, the Roer, the Ourthe, the Niedermaas and the Niederrhein, had been taken into the firm hands of Privy Councillor Sack during the short period of the first three months. On June 15, 1814 the counties of the Middle Rhine between Sambre and Maas, on the Saar and Moselle, as well as the Department of Forests were additionally put under his control. New government commissioners had to be appointed as his auxiliary officers. In addition, the assessor Koppe, whose right arm had been shattered in the battle of Leipzig, had not yet been able to take up his office. Among these new officials of the Governor General, the Government Councillor Ernst Sack was entrusted with the provisional administration of the Rhine-Moselle Departments and took up his seat in Koblenz. The entire government of the territories, which had been increased by the new but still shifting borders, was now governed according to the provisions of the Treaty of Paris of May 31, 1814, now on behalf of the Royal Prussian Government and thus took on a character quite different from that of the first period, which had been carried out on behalf of the allies. Thus whilst at first it had only been talked about, it was now already ordering and guiding — indeed, predetermining — in view of the fact that these areas would, in all probability, later fall entirely into the hands of the King of Prussia.

Although the arrival of the allied armies on the right bank of the Rhine had spread general enthusiasm, the inhabitants of the left bank of the Rhine shared these feelings of new confidence only where they had already been Prussian in the past. The transformation after the long period of French rule was considered too sudden and the power of Buonaparte too great for the new order of things to be trusted. This was influenced moreover by the fear of losing the free and profitable sales of factory industrial goods enabled by access to the French market. Sack's concern was therefore first of all to show the people that, in contrast to the many French unkept promises, keeping one's word had not disappeared from German culture. Taking a lively interest in the factories, he issued reassuring assurances about the French Douane and immediately concluded a contract with the Belgian General Government for the free export of its own Rhenish products on June 18, 1814 with the most profitable consequences and soon bringing millions to the industries. In this way they reached a level which they had never enjoyed before but which, unfortunately, like so many of Sack's caring steps for the whole of the people, could not be allowed to continue undisturbed and was later curtailed again by stricter legislation.

Since most of the left bank of the Rhine, which had been enlarged since June 15, was devoted to the Catholic religion, Sack had to focus his attention on calming the popular spirit so that complete freedom of conscience and public worship would be an unalterable guideline of the new government.

A particularly delicate matter was the church system, on which so much depended in this blatantly Catholic country and where the clergy always sought to influence their confessors politically. According to the instructions received, the constitution still had to be applied in the reconquered countries. Thus, for the General Government the Concordat for the Catholics was decisive — for the Old Catholics the law of 15th Germinal Xll and March 17, 1808.

The small number of Protestants who had only attained unrestricted freedom of religion through the revolution, since Napoleon's fall saw this threatened once again by the status quo of the majority. The Jews, on the other hand, whose equality before the law of Napoleon had been shaken by extremely strict credit laws, held great hopes from the far more liberal legislation, as their fellow believers in Prussia indeed enjoyed. In the handling of the existing constitution it was now important to instill in all parties that, without preference for any religious denomination, the King of Prussia was a thoroughly mild and just ruler. At the same time, the old law must first retain its validity and therefore any insolence which violated it would be punished. Despite all the religious questions that arose, Sack took the trouble to establish in the minds of the inhabitants the firm conviction that his government regarded religion as the highest and most venerable purpose of human life, whereas Napoleon had always regarded it as only a positive or negative tool for his state purposes. These principles filled the fearful with confidence, the more stable with new security and everywhere there was a pleasant feeling of a new peaceful development. In the Diocese of Lüttich, where the visit of a confirming bishop had been lacking for a long time, Sack immediately provided for this possibility by giving the bishop of New York who happened to be present there, the order to administer the sacrament. He resolutely opposed attempts to restore the flagellant processions of both rites, burying the dead in churches, incantations of devils, collections for religious orders, controversial sermons and all those things that were intended to stir up the church and increase its influence. Other processions, such as the pilgrimages to Kevelar and Echternach and the processions on Corpus Christi Day, to which the population was very attached, were tolerated in silence. That the fruits of the victories, in which the General Government included the return of looted church art treasures, such as Rubens' altarpiece to St. Peter's Church in Cologne, Diepenbeck's paintings to St. Nicholas' Church in Aachen, to the cathedral there its Egyptian garnet and porphyry columns, to the Church at Sinzig the mummified Corpse of the Holy Bailiff[75], which was so precious to them, was an extremely effective moment of highest satisfaction for the Catholic Church and

---

75   Baron von Stein assumed that the bailiff was an ancestor of a branch of his house that had been located on the Landskron, which is said to have had its hereditary grave in the church at Sinzig. Arndt recounts in his "Rhein- und Ahrwanderungen", "Soon after the return of the holy bailiff from Paris I saw the Minister von Stein in Nassau who jokingly and laughingly said to me: 'Do you know what kind of salvation has been granted me? I can now never perish, I now have a Catholic saint and intercessor in my house, an old ancestor and bailiff of Landskron, who was perhaps during his lifetime a drunkard and ruffian and did not dream that he would one day be called among the saints!

contributed favorably to the veneration and esteem of Prussia.

In the very first weeks of his activity on the Rhine, the small town of Büderich near Wesel had to be rebuilt in April 1814. The French had simply razed it to the ground in order to build another stronghold for the fortress of Wesel in its place. This had to be done under the demands of the building the bulwark, which was renamed Fort Blücher. Sack's call for gifts of help on the left side of the Rhine was so heartwarming that the Prussian government received considerable funds within a short time so that the new Büderich, with its church and school, as well as all its farms and peasantry, was soon able to rise far more spaciously and beautifully than ever before. Sack, like a caring father of the country, took care of all the needs of the homeless inhabitants and his praise and appreciation were always closely linked to the restoration of Büderich.

The Protestant Church was administered by the Reformed and Lutheran Consistories, both wishing to restore the former synodal constitution. The entire Protestant clergy was characterized by their joyfully living spirit for the good German cause and everywhere they welcomed the freedom of spiritual pursuit, which seemed to be guaranteed by the regained Germanity.

As far as the military administration is concerned, it was no longer provided by the Governor General alone, as in the first period, but most of it fell to the Royal General Army Command since the enlargement of the borders. It was transferred again before the end of a year, along with

the arming and the conscription of the inhabitants of the
country, when the return of Napoleon called the armies
back into the field and the strength of an already popular,
purposeful head such as the Governor General was required here above all else.

Initially, however, for the second half of 1814, Sack only
had the task of exercising civilian government and was
now able to do this all the more calmly. After moving into
Paris at the beginning of April the Allies had partly already agreed in May on the great issues of the victories
and soon decided to meet again in Vienna in September to
give this understanding a more definite form.

As early as the late fall of 1813 after the battle of Leipzig,
when the Rhine Confederation princes had flocked to the
headquarters of the allied victorious powers and vied to
renounce their traitorous cause, the Duke of Nassau had
lifted the confiscation of the Stein estates and returned
them to their owner along with the income retained from
the previous years. Blücher had provided them with a security guard. Since Stein himself could not take them over
as he was absolutely indispensable, they had been entrusted by him to the administration of his sister Marianne.

Stein had already contacted Emperor Alexander in April
1814 with the request for his dismissal. The emperor expressed his regret that Stein did not want to accompany
him and asked urgently what he could do for Stein. He
thanked the Emperor and asked only for the continuation
of his mercy and protection. Alexander allowed him to go

to Germany but on condition that he come to Vienna for the forthcoming congress. At the same time he made Stein promise to write to him and accept his orders. On June 2, when the Emperor was certain that the essential provisions of the new constitution had been accepted by Louis XVIII, he himself left Paris and the following day Stein returned to Germany.

The King of Prussia publicly thanked his army on that June 3, raised the State Chancellor Hardenberg to the rank of prince, Field Marshal Count Blücher became Prince von Wahlstatt-Jork, Kleist, Bülow and Tauentzien and they received together with the title of count the bynames of the scenes of their main deeds. Also Gneisenau became a count.

Stein's return journey to his homeland went via Meaux, Chalons, Luxembourg, Trier to Koblenz. He arrived in Nassau at night on June 10. The late hour had not kept his friends, including Sack, from welcoming him. All the inhabitants around him had not missed the opportunity to receive their "Great Countryman" in a festive manner. Two Cossacks on the Lahn, wearing long false beards and long lances — a reminiscence of the excellent Cossack Guard, which the Emperor of Russia had always assigned to him for his personal protection and service — waited for his carriage by the road, escorting him from then on. On the "Stein (Stone)", the rock from which the family took its name, bonfires blazed towards the sky, under the ringing of all the bells and the cheers of the inhabitants who had illuminated their houses. He entered the city as foot soldiers formed a guard of honor all the way up to his castle — all

evidence of the faithful devotion of his homeland, which
moved him deeply. What a change since he, barely conva-
lescent, went to his King in Memel seven years ago to save
Prussia! To commemorate his happy and glorious return
home, Nassau's inhabitants decided to celebrate an annual
Schützenfest (Marksmen's Festival) on June 10, with a procession and target shooting, for which Stein himself offered a capital of one thousand taler to award prizes and
medals.

After he had given orders to a master builder in Koblenz
to thoroughly restore the barely habitable living quarters
that he had given to his wife, he left Nassau after four
days to take up residence in Frankfurt. On June 15 he immediately sent Sack decrees about the Rhine shipping and
the warehouses in Cologne and Mainz, in order to be able
to put it on a firm footing at the forthcoming congress in
Vienna to the advantage of German trade and to in order
to claim benefits. Stein held out the greatest hope for a better future for Germany and Sack, imbued with his personal greatest achievements in recent months down on the
Rhine, was thus capable of nothing but strengthening him
in this joyful confidence. Insight, education, morality, true
piety, rather than being devoid of reason and without regard for the importance of work which was widespread
among the people, replaced with moderate claims to that
self-determination of common affairs that seemed to have
been lost through the alienation of the nation, were now
rescued by strong, determined intervention. Sack's assurances already granted the possibility of being able to count
on the free discussion of public affairs with equal rights
and equal duties among the people. This soon promised to

create a permanent state of affairs which ensured that every effort would have its natural sphere of action and led all to the common promotion of the common good under a generous, far-sighted government.

Stein was determined to meet the just demands of the well-meaning among the peoples who had their eyes set on him more than anyone else. As "Germany's liberator", welcomed by princes and peoples, in his high morality and inner modesty he did not feel worthy of a merit for which Providence had chosen for him as its most eminent instrument. Now he prepared everything to secure the future of the Fatherland at the forthcoming Congresses. To this end, Stein also had prepared public opinion in Germany. Not only did he have a small paper published by Arndt, his assistant who had already been successfully employed in Russia, entitled *Ueber künftige, ständische Verfassungen* (On Future Constitutions of the Estates) but he also turned to the newspapers. Among these it was mainly the *Rheinischer Merkur*, which had come into being in Koblenz in January 1814 and which was the fruit of the national euphoria triggered by the struggle for freedom in Germany. From then on, the articles in this paper were directly influenced by Stein, and even during the Congress of Vienna they became the mouthpiece of Stein's reticent views and disappointments.

The *Rheinischer Merkur*, headed by the school professor Joseph Görres[76], who lived quietly in Koblenz, was pub-

76 Johann Joseph Görres, since 1839 von Görres (1776-1848), was a German writer, philosopher, theologian, historian and journalist.
    In 1813 he again took up the cause of national independence, and in the following year founded Der *Rheinischer Merkur*. The outspo-

lished by the printer Pauli from 1811 onwards as the continuation of an insignificant local paper *Mercure du Rhin*
but now resurrected as the first and, for a long time to
come, only independent daily newspaper. As such it
wanted to win public opinion for the allies first by making
the people aware of their German affiliation again and by
thoroughly eradicating the gallophilia[77] that was still rampant here and there. Görres himself a Catholic, had been a
young hot-tempered Jacobin in the days of the French Revolution, which he happily forgot, and had welcomed the
French as liberators in sympathetic fraternity celebrations.
At that time he founded a magazine "Das rote Blatt" ("The
Red Paper") in order to wean the people from their sense
of slavery, which had become second nature to them. He
advocated a free Rhenish Republic as close as possible to
the French. The ideals of the first storm and stress period

kenness of its hostility to Napoleon made it influential, and
Napoleon himself called it "a fifth power". It campaigned for a
united Germany, with a representative government but under an
emperor, Görres having abandoned his earlier advocacy of repub-
licanism. When Napoleon was at Elba, Görres wrote an ironic
imaginary proclamation issued by him to the people. He criticised
the second peace of Paris (1815), declaring that Alsace and Lor-
raine should have been demanded back from France.

Stein used the Merkur at the time of the meeting of the congress of
Vienna to give expression to his hopes. But Hardenberg, in May
1815, warned Görres to remember that he was not to arouse hostility against France, but only against Napoleon. There was also in
the *Merkur* an antipathy to Prussia, expression of the desire that an
Austrian prince should assume the imperial title and also a tendency to liberalism—all distasteful to Hardenberg and to his master Friedrich Wilhelm III. Görres disregarded warnings sent to him
by the censorship, so that the *Merkur* was suppressed early in 1816
at the instance of the Prussian government and soon afterwards
Görres was dismissed from his teaching post.

77 The love or admiration for the country, culture, language or people
of France.

had long since been buried during the Napoleonic consulate and he had come to study German history and the German soul through philosophy and literature. In Heidelberg in 1806, he had met with Brentano and Arnim for that round table of German patriots to which the brothers Grimm and Savigny were also close and which had set itself the task of reviving and warming up the contemporary world that had frozen into national lifelessness and lack of conviction. The year 1813/1814 had proven what this thinking and striving of the young minds had achieved—Stein himself once said about it, "In Heidelberg, a considerable share of the German fire was ignited which later consumed the French" and this testimony of honor had been valid above all for the Germanity of the past nurtured there. Görres himself gave lectures on old German literature and published the "Lohengrin" from these studies, simply because he found in it a faithful connection to German nature and German sentiments. His aim was to lift the German people up from their depths to self-confidence and pride in their special character and to strengthen their unity through a common love for their government, in which a legal attitude and justice set the standards with which the prince and the people were chained together for the prosperity of the state and its citizens. He also aimed to instill this political will in the German people who until then had only existed in the upper classes and to raise political principles and political and patriotic opinion in the general public. To educate the Germans in the importance of the freedom of the press, which Niebuhr had already striven for in his *Preussischer Korrespondent* (Prussian Correspondent), having tried to influence the Prussians, always felt the pressure of the censorship as a bitter fog. Görres made the freedom of the press as his first condition and above all he treasured the freedom of the word.

The *Rheinischer Merkur* served Stein to help all those who used their senses and endeavors to protect German interests at the Congress of Vienna and whose aspiration was to free themselves from French paternalism asserted through Russian magnanimity, the lust for power in Austria and the presumption of Talleyrand[78], to make clear the necessary self-confidence and the firm feeling of belonging to the Germans of the West. It also seemed to be on the

---

78   Charles-Maurice de Talleyrand-Périgord (1754-1838), first Prince of Benevento, then Prince of Talleyrand, was a French politician and diplomat.
He was Napoleon's chief diplomat during the years when French military victories brought one European state after another under French hegemony. However, most of the time, Talleyrand worked for peace so as to consolidate France's gains. He succeeded in obtaining peace with Austria through the 1801 Treaty of Luneville and with Britain in the 1802 Treaty of Amiens. He could not prevent the renewal of war in 1803 but by 1805, he opposed his emperor's renewed wars against Austria, Prussia, and Russia. He resigned as foreign minister in August 1807, but retained the trust of Napoleon and conspired to undermine the emperor's plans through secret dealings with Tsar Alexander of Russia and Austrian minister Metternich. Talleyrand sought a negotiated secure peace so as to perpetuate the gains of the French revolution. Napoleon rejected peace and, when he fell in 1814, Talleyrand eased the Bourbon restoration decided by the Allies. He played a major role at the Congress of Vienna in 1814–1815, where he negotiated a favourable settlement for France and played a role in decisions regarding the undoing of Napoleon's conquests.
Talleyrand polarizes scholarly opinion. Some regard him as one of the most versatile, skilled and influential diplomats in European history, and some believe that he was a traitor, betraying in turn the Ancien Régime, the French Revolution, Napoleon, and the Restoration.

best way to succeed, since the *Rheinische Merkur,* thought to be the voice of the people, soon had the largest number of subscribers. A series of fortunate circumstances united to secure Görres two years of what was then an unprecedented freedom of speech! First there was still the victorious mood of war and the order of the government to foment a second time against Napoleon in 1815. Then there was the trust and friendship of Gruner, who even used the *Merkur* as an official organ for a while. Later, Sack's affection and the esteem and sympathy that Stein, Gneisenau and other leading men showed to the *Merkur* had led to a closer relationship between Sack and Gneisenau, which in time grew into a lifelong friendship.

The state chancellor Hardenberg was far from cutting the wings of *Merkur* at that time. In October 1814, he merely sent a confidential reminder to Görres through the Crown President Sack to moderate his language a little but otherwise assured him of his freedom of speech, saying, "It would be contrary to the spirit of our government to subject this newspaper to such censorship which would suppress all charitable freedom of thought, disrupt the exchange of ideas about matters of the common good and stifle the public voice against public injustice and disorderly arbitrariness. Görres expressed his thanks in a letter where he happily stood up for his beliefs of November 1, 1814, in which he said, among other things:

"It is not given to me to move spiritually under compulsion and consideration. If I can no longer follow my convictions and if I have to question a judge other than my feelings and my tact, then the spirit departs from me and I can hardly do even the simplest task. I would then have to ask His Serene Highness to forbid me to continue to publish the paper as being out of keeping with the times, so that I can justify myself to the world with such bans that my resignation in the present crisis was not out of cowardice. I would then be happy to retire to the quiet solitude into which I have retreated for 13 years since Napoleon came to power and from which I have only left because I hoped that my active intervention at that time would be of some benefit to my country".[79]

Supported by such an absolutely German-minded press, Sack was able to fill the large number of inhabitants with confidence in the Prussian future. If these people were still somewhat perturbed, it was now only due to the long delay in Vienna about the final decision of their fate. Among other things, Stein had strongly recommended the German imperial regimen in Vienna, while Hardenberg, in opposition to Stein's memorandum on the subject and his oral presentation had Humboldt, who together with the State Chancellor was the Prussian representative at the Congress, prepare a paper against it.

Then suddenly Buonaparte reappeared in March 1815, and everything immediately took on a different form, even the administration in Sack's hands.

As already mentioned, the civil service had to be combined with military service again, the latter being predominant and new burdens, new efforts and new sacrifices

---

79 The paragraph about Görres is taken from: "Der deutsche Staatsgedanke" by Arno Duch, Drei-Masken-Verlag, Munich.*

became necessary. But the mood among the inhabitants was already much too firmly established to cause any further difficulties for their Governor General. On March 24, Sack issued a proclamation clarifying the situation:

To the good people of the Lower and Middle Rhine!

The capital of France had sworn to stand up in strong defense of the throne and constitution against the onslaught of the scorned robber. The capital of France had lied, like France itself. Napoleon Buonaparte occupied Paris without a single stroke of the sword.

Thus the renegade has become usurper again for a short time and an armed Europe must, by extermination, deserve the thanks of its fellow men and posterity, which France has spurned.

The great allied powers have expressed their firm decision in this respect in Vienna by the Declaration of the 13th of this month. The victors of Moscow, Leipzig, Wittoria and Paris are already rushing in all directions to give emphasis to that declaration. A great woe is being wrought upon the wicked man who, contrary to all law and human trust, has thrown the torch of war anew among us. If it were necessary, the people of all Europe would throw themselves upon France to smother the fiend in the blood and tears of its own people but that will not happen. Perhaps Heaven has already granted the brave Prussians, Englishmen, Hanoverians and Belgians who were at the vanguard between the Rhine and France the glory of becoming executors of its justice!

You can and you shall contribute to it, good inhabitants of the Lower and Middle Rhine! The good and noble of all classes must firmly join together to build a wall of iron against malice and betrayal. May the strong young people come here to dedicate their arms and their courage to the just cause and the fatherland. For Germany is your fatherland and will remain so at all costs. May the strong men and patriarchs of all ranks also arm themselves under your banner of

*Gebhard Leberecht von Blücher. Artist
unknown, copying Paul Ernst Gebauer.*

the citizen militia, not for wars of aggression but for the protection of their own hearth against enemies and traitors! The fatherland entrusts you with the weapons, you good and young men of the Rhine, Moselle, Roer and Meuse. I myself have become your guarantor that you will lead them with German loyalty and strength.

In this way you will gain a fair share of the triumph of a just cause and you will turn away from the curse which would weigh upon you from your children and your children's children, if your inertia or indifference were to blame for the fact that the whole of Europe's war power should burst across your corridors like a devastating torrent against the common enemy.

Aachen, March 24, 1815,

The Governor General of the Lower and Middle Rhine:

Sack.

Sack also immediately ordered a ban against France, issued strict orders against any disturbers of the peace and

"The Crucifixion of Peter" by Peter Paul Rubens

called on all military personnel in French service to return
immediately. Similarly, those natives who had previously
been in French service and had already returned were ordered to report within twenty-four hours, after which they
were incorporated into the Royal Regiment.

Since Count Dohna, the Councillor of State, who had been provided with state funds by the Minister of Finance, was unable to raise the sum estimated at 6 million francs needed for the war needs that had been put out to tender, Sack had to try to raise this sum again by means of a general money loan from his own Rhine lands. In order to make it easier to obtain the necessary funds, he came up with the idea of giving the districts the freedom to supply money or supplies of all kinds. The Chambers of Commerce provided essential services in this respect by quickly bringing in clothing, grain, forage, horses, cattle, fittings and fixtures, brandy and wine, so that in a short time all this was brought together in a quite unexpectedly fast way. The governor general then had the deputies of the country meet again in a spirit of trust, presented the budget for the main needs openly to them, discussed with them the ways of obtaining cash, left the supervision of the war-chest to them and handed over the minutes of the meetings to the public by printing them.

The women's associations immediately took up work again for the provisioning and construction of military hospitals.

Sack used all possible means to direct this tension to the great purpose and wisely calculated on the common sense of the population. This was all published in the official journal of the Lower and Middle Rhine. He had this very powerful statement printed with great effect by the already generally highly celebrated Görres in the *Merkur* and had a common French proclamation for comparison made afterwards.

It was at this critical time that the official possession of these lands in the name of the King of Prussia took place and which was immediately published with the decree on the wearing of the Prussian National Cockade[80]. The officials, the gendarmerie and the citizen militia swore Sack to the new sovereign without long hesitation. It seemed to him the most appropriate thing to do now. It was not only the moment itself that demanded it but also the certainty of success, which was achieved by urging officials and inhabitants to act with equal speed by diminishing the time for every hesitation and criticism of the measures taken.

---

80 A cockade is a knot of ribbons, or other circular- or oval-shaped symbol of distinctive colors which is usually worn on a hat. The armies of Napoleon brought the blue-white-red cockade to all of Europe. During the wars of liberation Napoleon's opponents used cockades in their national colours as a military identification mark, and Prussia chose black and white. The royal proclamation read:
   Ordinance Requiring the of Wearing the Prussian National Cockade dated February 22, 1813.
   We Frederick William, by the grace of God, King of Prussia etc. etc. Considering that the heart-raising general expression of faithful love of the Fatherland demands an outward sign for all citizens, decree: that
   1. except for military service, by all men who have completed their twentieth year, the Prussian National Cockade of known form, black and white on the hat, shall be worn if this honour has not been forfeited by them.
   2. The cockade shall be worn by all those who were born in Our State or who have acquired the rights of Our subjects by settling or entering Our service.
   3. The right to wear the cockade shall be forfeited, by cowardice before the enemy, by the provisions of the present law on avoidance of military service and by imprisonment in a fortress or penitentiary combined with penal labour. The ever-present symbol of the banner of the fatherland must doubly satisfy everyone who wears it in the cockade with the remembrance of his most sacred duties.
   Given at Wroclaw, February 22, 1813.

Immediately after the proclaimed seizure, the oath of alle-
giance was declared at Pentecost on May 15 in Aachen. At
the same time the national army was mobilised and armed
and equipped with restless zeal. In the first days of May, a
punishable insurrection of the Saxon troops took place in
Liège. It is well known that in the Kingdom of Saxony,
even before the Battle of Leipzig, the central government
of Stein had had to take its first steps, since the King of
Saxony was expelled from his country as an ally of
Napoleon and still shared the same fate as the Rhine Confederation princes, whose landed property was subject
only to the decision of the Congress of Vienna. The inhabitants of Liège and the surrounding area however, gave a
commendable proof of loyalty and prudent obedience on
this occasion as did the city of Aachen. In the latter city
there was no garrison left when one of the rebellious bat-
talions passed by so the citizens themselves immediately
took up the guard, occupied the gates, patrolled the city
and behaved so excellently that it could not have been
done better by the King's oldest provinces. On May 15,
1815, the royal celebration of hereditary homage[81] took
place in Aachen through the Governor General and the
General of the Infantry, Count von Gneisenau, who the
King had appointed to receive the guests in his place.

The enemy, however, was already so close again that
Gneisenau was indispensable in the field and had taken it
upon himself to postpone the ceremony. The governor
general, however, found predominant reasons for the strict

---

81 Instead of a coronation as such the King here is installed as King of
    Prussia by a ceremony known as an *Erbhuldigung* with the heredi-
    tary right to rule.

observance of the festival in a border area where public opinion might still be wavering in secret and the belief in Napoleon's genius had not yet been extinguished. Not even the slightest hint could remain that the happy outcome of the new battle was in doubt and so the preparations continued and in all public papers the announcement of the tribute ceremonies and oaths of the not yet sworn-in officials was made the day before. In the evening the bells rang. Again on the 15th early in the morning the bells were rung, the church service *Tedeum* and the the new sovereign was included in church prayers and a solemn procession passed through the city from the city hall to the throne room where the homage ceremony took place. All the marshals in black velvet clothing with swords accompanied the governor general. Walking in front of him were the government councillors Carl Focke (1107 [9/1!]) and Count Merveldt[82], who also had to stand beside him on

---

82 Maximilian, Count von Merveldt (1764-1815), among the most famous of an illustrious old Westphalian family, entered Habsburg military service, rose to the rank of General of Cavalry, served as Francis II, Holy Roman Emperor's ambassador to Russia, and became special envoy extraordinaire to the Court of St. James's (Great Britain). He fought with distinction in the wars between the Habsburg and the Ottoman empires, the French Revolutionary Wars, and the Napoleonic Wars.

Maximilian entered the military as a young man, and acquired his first combat experiences the Habsburg wars with the Ottoman Empire. Following his experience in the Balkans, he retreated to the cloister at Bonn, where he spent a year as a novice in the Teutonic Order. At the outbreak of war between the Habsburg Monarchy and France in 1792, he returned to military service, and proved an intrepid and enterprising cavalry field officer. His role in the Habsburg victory at Neerwinden in 1793 earned him the honor of conveying the news to the Emperor in Vienna.

In the War of the Second Coalition, Maximilian served in Swabia and northern Italy and Switzerland. In subsequent wars between

both sides of the throne. Later there was a table with a toast by Sack to the sovereign accompanied by trumpets, trombones and cannon shots. From 2-3 o'clock the hospitals and the school children in the poor houses received a festive meal. After the banquet was finished at 7 o'clock, there was a play in the theatre. At 9 o'clock fireworks in front of the Albertstor and at 10 o'clock a ball on the Redoute. "The city was most certainly 'enlightened'."

In the following month of 1815, the third epoch began for the Rhineland, in which Sack now had to administer the Royal Rhine Province as "Crown President of the King of Prussia". This beginning of his third term of office was marked not only by new responsibilities and sacrifices but also by no less important events. After the Battle of Ligny[83] the inhabitants behaved exemplarily and it could be convincingly observed on all sides that they no longer wanted to come under the French yoke. Thus their joy was sincere and profound when the ever memorable day of Belle-Alliance put an end to the war. Since in Belgium they had not

---

France and the Habsburg Monarchy, his role on the battlefield often meant the difference between defeat and victory. He was wounded and captured at the Battle of Leipzig and, as a condition of release, he agreed not to bear arms against France again. He was subsequently appointed as an envoy to Britain, where he died in 1815.

83 The Battle of Ligny was fought on 16 June 1815, in which French troops of the Armée du Nord under the command of Napoleon I defeated part of a Prussian army under Field Marshal Blücher, near Ligny in present-day Belgium. The battle resulted in a tactical victory for the French, but the bulk of the Prussian army survived the battle in good order and played a pivotal role two days later at the Battle of Waterloo, having been reinforced by Prussian troops who had not participated at Ligny. The battle of Ligny was the last victory in Napoleon's military career.

taken steps to receive the wounded, it was touching to see how they gave everything they had here in the new Prussian province to enable the Women's Association in Aachen and its daughters' associations in the provincial towns to cope with the first mass demands.

On August 1, Sack was then able to publish in the *Bergisch Government Gazette* in Düsseldorf the aforementioned "Announcement concerning the restitution of art treasures stolen by the French". It had the following contents:

"By an official letter from the King's General Director of the Army of the Lower Rhine, Privy Councillor Nibbentrop, d. d. Paris, dated July 15, I am informed that immediately after the capture of Paris, Field Marshal Prince von Blücher-Wahlstatt, Serene Highness, has resolved to order the seizure of all the art and literature treasures which were formerly stolen from the Royal Prussian States by the French and to return them to the places from which they were stolen. In order to carry out this order, a special commission has been set up in Paris under the direction of the General Director and at the same time a command line has been organized from Paris to the Rhine. The first transport departed from Paris on the 16th of the month. With it, among other things, was the priceless image of St. Peter, with which Rubens venerated his hometown of Cologne and which was stolen from the sacred and classical soil by the sacrilegious hand of our foe.[84]

---

84 At the time of the author it had been reclaimed by the Treaty of Versailles in 1919 and returned to Paris.*
The history to date is as follows: "In 1794 the painting was taken to the Louvre in Paris on the orders of the French occupation. It was not until 1815 that it was returned to St. Peter's, with great

The order had also already been given to dismantle the magnificent granite and porphyry columns[85], which the same sacrilegious hand had stolen from the sanctuary of our cathedral in Aachen and exhibited in the Parisian Hall of Antiquities as the support for the vault, and to return them to Aachen. I had asked our noble field marshal for both of these objects immediately after the conquest of Paris. He immediately fulfilled this wish and thereby rendered outstanding service to the cities of Aachen and Cologne.

Look at Prussia on the Rhine! The State, whose youngest children you have become, has not forgotten to let you share in the fruits of its victories at the first opportunity. With grateful rejoicing your cities will celebrate the day when the looted property of your fathers, taken away from the predatory enemy, will return to their walls by the strong hand of your King and his commanders.

------

sympathy from the population of Cologne. Two further times the painting was removed from the church. In 1941 it was evacuated to Schloss Pommersfelden near Bamberg before the Allied bombing and returned to the rebuilt church in 1961. In 1997 it was brought to Cologne Cathedral together with the painting by Cornelis Schut for the time of the renovation of St. Peter's. In March 2002 the paintings returned again, where they were alternately displayed on a revolving wall behind the cross altar by Eduardo Chillida. Since 2004, the "Crucifixion of Peter" has again been hanging on the front wall of the southern side aisle, where it had hung for several years since 1988". (https://www.sankt-peter-koeln.de/wp/raum-2/rubensbild/—translated).

85   The church was built over the remains of a Roman thermal bath with building material from many parts of the Frankish Empire and was perfected by means of the reuse of such things as the ancient columns, and Roman building material from the region.

Lithograph of Joseph Görres as a young man by
August Strixner, after a painting by Peter von
Cornelius

As far as my knowledge of the art and literary treasures dragged from the Royal Rhine Provinces to France was sufficient, I have already sent the list of these treasures to the Restitution Commission. I would therefore ask any friend of art and of the fatherland who possesses a note that does not come to my attention through publicity or through reports from the authorities, and which may concern a work of art of the brush or of sculpture, jewels or relics, documents, manuscripts, incunables or other treasures, to inform me of it as soon as possible for further consideration. The moment is favorable and we must seize it. Our children's children would accuse us before God and posterity if we had not done something about it.Aachen,   July   21,   1815. The Privy Councillor of State and Supreme President of the   Royal   Prussia   Provinces   on   the   Rhine Sack."Schiller had already written in 1800 about the outrageous French robbery in just indignation:

That which Grecian art created,
Let the Frank, with joy elated,
Bear to Seine's triumphant strand,
And in his museums glorious
Show the trophies all-victorious
To his wondering fatherland.

They to him are silent ever,
Into life's fresh circle never
From their pedestals come down.
He alone e'er holds the Muses
Through whose breast their power diffuses,--
To the Vandal they're but stone!

It is thanks to the lively use of the Prussian statesmen, including Humboldt and Eichhorn (3420 [33/5]) that a part of the Palatine Library, which had come to Rome from Bavaria by Tilly and Maximilian, was also given to the University of Heidelberg on this occasion and now became accessible to German scholars again. At the beginning of August, when Sack was held up by the Nassau-Oranian Commissioners due to delays in their annexation, he had to call on the help of the State Chancellor, who threatened to have the country occupied immediately, which did not fail to have an effect.

Initially Stein was still receiving support from the central administration but when he resigned from his post as head of the administration in Paris on June 15, 1815, the ministries in Berlin granted the Governor General a helping hand to cope with the increased tasks resulting from the Prussian take-over. Some of them, however, had volunteered to help him gratuitously, such as his two brothers-in-law, the Privy Councillor von Reimann and the Privy Auditing Councillor Jacobi. The latter, however, was soon recalled and replaced by the Privy Councillor Delius, as well as the Assistant Chamberlain Koppe, the Estates Councillor von Bandemer, Assistant Chamberlain Focke, the District Director Neigebaur, Captain and Adjutant von Hansen, later replaced by the Commander of Aachen, Captain Hardt and finally Count Merveldt. Also the then Consistorial President Jacobi[86] (son of the philosopher and friend of Goethe, Jacobi), as well as the government trainee Freiherr von Schenkendorf and the former Secretary General at the Prefecture of Osnabrück Heuberger were temporarily employed by him.

The same ceremony of homage to the then sole authorized Governor General Sack then took place in Koblenz on August 8, 1815. Everything went smoothly and quietly there

---

86 Johann Friedrich Jacobi (1765-1831) was a German cloth manufacturer and politician.
    With the end of the French period in 1814 Jacobi lost his posts as President of the Consistory General and in the corps législatif and returned to the now Prussian Rhineland. From 1815 onwards, he took over the office of auditor of the entire tax and customs system for the Prussian Rhine province and a little later became head of the Central Commission for Navigation on the Rhine, based in Mainz. After his retirement he spent the rest of his life in Bonn. Until his death in 1831 he was mainly active in literature.

as well. On both occasions a more harmonious and cordial celebration could not have been imagined, it was as if the danger and its conquest had only served to bring the new subjects closer to their Prussian ruler. When commemorating the occasion in Koblenz, it was Sack's brother, Ernst, who as the commissioner of the government there had led the preparations and the celebration himself. The following dinner took place at his residence but Sack painfully missed his friend Stein, with whom he had hoped to celebrate the reunification of his home province with the rest of his fatherland, the crowning glory of the great work of liberation. However, Stein was staying in Paris again where, increasingly entangled and disagreeable the prospects for his Prussian fatherland, which were closest to his great heart, were shaping up before his eyes.

Such was the sting that Sack felt bitterly in spite of all his own successes and not without the same disappointment as the brave Görres, who voiced them ever louder in his *Merkur*, while Sack, as royal official, had to transcend them silently.

As early as June 1815, the King, who had come under the increasing influence of the reaction that had emerged in Vienna, to the delight of Metternich and Talleyrand, had issued a cabinet order to Sack, which energetically demanded an immediate restriction of the freedom of the press.

Sack had immediately ordered Görres to do so and had then had him repeatedly warned and threatened with punishment by his brother if he spoke too openly, whilst he initially withdrew from him completely.

The Congress of Vienna had come to an end at the end of May 1815 — the King of Prussia had left Vienna on the 26th, Emperor Franz on the 27th. Stein returned home immediately after their departure but already at the end of July he received an urgent request from the State Chancellor to come to Paris as soon as possible. In July he had received Goethe's visit to Nassau and had visited the Lower Rhine in his company. Arndt, who saw the two of them at that time, compared their journey with that of the iron and clay pot. He told of the attentive and careful tenderness with which the worthy old gentlemen walked next to each other without bumping into each other. Goethe had shown a kind of astonished awe of Stein but Stein had been unusually gentle and mild "He held his bold and fickle breath and restrained the lion so that he never peeked out". After receiving Hardenberg's letter, Stein decided on the spot to immediately leave for Paris. The Emperor Alexander received him very warmly and embraced him but on the whole expressed great disapproval of the negotiations conducted so far in order to reach an overall satisfactory conclusion in Paris. Stein returned to Nassau on September 16 after leaving the parties in Paris in the utmost agitation towards each other. The formal conclusion of the peace finally took place on November 20.

The insight of the outcome from this last year of European settlements in Vienna and Paris that the great statesman had taken home with him was, "For Germany, the dearly bought lesson from these struggles and negotiations is that none of the European powers sincerely desires its salvation, its security and its strength. That each of them is ready to wage war with German blood and German arms under all circumstances, that the German mighty both great and small are sought and celebrated in their hour of need and encouraged to devote themselves with the most succinct promises but despite the fact that German armies have won the victory and the common enemy has been defeated, no German authority great or small may count on just compensation. Instead it can only expect the other powers to join hands over Germany's losses. Germany must place as little hope in England as it does in Russia or France. It must count on no one but itself. Only when no German may humiliate himself as a foreigner's pawn, when all small passions, all subordinate considerations are silenced in the face of national feeling and when a strong will of Germany's destiny directs Germany's fortunes as a result of a unified attitude, will Germany once again stand strong, proud and feared in Europe, as in its earlier great times. Until then it must tolerate and remain silent". (Pertz: "Aus Steins Leben," 1815).

After the end of the war the military administration had returned to General von Dobschütz, and Sack now had to devote himself to the redivision of his province into certain administrative districts. They are almost still maintained at the time of writing with the exception that in Berlin there were then two Upper Presidential Districts, A with the administrative districts of Koblenz, Aachen and Trier, B with those of Cologne, Düsseldorf and Cleve. In the first district, the Count of Solms[87] was to reside in Koblenz as president, in the second district, with the city of Düsseldorf, Sack was to remain as president.

On October 7, the people of Aachen insisted on celebrating the birthday of their Crown President in a particularly solemn manner.

The play "Bürgerglück" ("Citizens' Joy") was performed in the city theatre, followed by an epilogue spoken by Mrs Heuberger, on this and in Sack's honor. Secretary General Heuberger had written it in the name of the administration staff.

> You saw, revered ones, this picture
> The happiness of citizens in most beautiful light,
> For civic virtue stood at his side
> And domesticity joined the alliance.
>
> But there are virtues of a higher order
> To charity she sacrifices her own fortune
> Independence, to go far around
> Restlessly striving to establish civil well-being.
> She stands magnanimously at the source itself,
> But draws them only to dispense again.
>
> The man who has the reputation of a wise king
> In the midst of a whole nation,
> To practise law, to establish order
> And the organ of royal clemency

87 Friedrich Ludwig Christian Count zu Solms-Laubach (1769-1822) was initially a member of the Imperial Court Council in Vienna. Later he became a Prussian civil servant. He was the first—and only—Crown President of the Province of Jülich-Kleve-Berg, which was united with the Province of the Grand Duchy of the Lower Rhine bordering to the south to form the Rhine Province in 1824 shortly after his death.

An 1815 caricature of Talleyrand - L'Homme aux six têtes (The man with six heads), referring to his prominent role in six different regimes

To be the King's paternal blessing,
The man who willingly answers that call,
Highly gifted by God with power and wisdom,
Like a rock in its place stands
And knows no pleasure but his duty,
The people entrusted to him
Turn evil round if he can, who with force
Controls vice and quiet virtue
To knowingly seek with eagle eyes,

The man exercises a higher kind of civic virtue
And his head deserves the oaken wreath.
He sacrifices the pleasure of quiet leisure,
Snatches slumber's strength when opportune
And never stops working, for the well-being
...of thousands — his ceaseless work.

Such a man — who cannot see him now?
Today celebrate his day of honor,
I do not call him, but his name is called
From the Lower Rhine to the Saarland far
And always with blessing he is called.
Who German honesty and steadfast sense,
Justice paired with deep insight,
Restless striving for the welfare of the citizens
With undemanding silent dignity.
HE has already named him.
I name him not.
But bring in the name of everyone,
Congratulations from the heart
And consecrate him the oaken wreath he deserves.

As already mentioned, Sack had also made a special effort to get the Rhine a university again, namely in Bonn. On December 26, 1815, Sack wrote the following letter to Goethe:

1.[88]

---

[88] These letters, already printed once in No. 42 of the *Taube* of October 1907, were at that time a contribution to our family bulletin by cousin Privy Councillor Prof. D. Karl Budde of Marburg a. L., who received permission to print them from the administration of the Goethe and Schiller Archive in Weimar, where the first letter is kept. The director of this archive, Privy Councillor Suphan, gave permission at that time mainly in the hope that perhaps by publishing it in the *Taube*, the owner of Goethe's original reply, which was to be assumed within our family, would come forward to make it available to science for a short time, at least for compari-

Hon. High Well-Born, as I know from my friend the Minister of State Baron von Stein, is engaged in research on art and antiquity on the Rhine and the public awaits the announcement of the results of this research with that longing impatience of which it is moved every time there is talk of a new work by the immortal hero of German literature.[89]

An Hon. Highly Beloved, personally unknown but therefore no less fervent admirer of your high creative spirit – in whatever form the Proteus may appear – I await this announced work with an exquisite longing. An important part of the classical soil, whose art and antiquity, as well as the demands of its inhabitants for the promotion of any subjectively connected spiritual development, has been under my administration for almost two years and has been partly entrusted to it anew for the future. I can bear witness to the fact that during this period of my administration, although now and then under unfavorable circumstances, I never, in what could and must have happened from above, neglected the spiritual for the sake of the earthly but rather always sought the true center of gravity and find support for it in the spiritual. I have also made many efforts to revive the people's sense of patriotic possessions in the field of art and many other higher aspects, which had almost been lost to them during their long years of French rule. However, now that the above-mentioned definitive organization of the local administration is talking about taking hold of the newly awakened and stimu-

---

son with the concept and its imprint in the *Grenzbote*. Whether the desired success has been achieved, I have unfortunately never been able to ascertain. (The author).*

89 Goethe's writing, to which Sack refers at the beginning of his letter, is entitled "Kunstschätze am Rhein, Main und Neckar 1814-1815" ("Art Treasures on the Rhine, Main and Neckar 1814-1815") and was the first of three volumes "Ueber Kunst und Alterthum in den Rhein- und Mayn-Gegenden" ("On Art and Antiquity in the Rhine and Main Regions"), which the old master published in 1816 and 1817. Primarily the two sections "Cologne" and "Bonn" come into consideration among the two letters, furthermore under Goethe's letters the one from August 1, 1815 to his son August about the Rhine journey with Baron von Stein.*

lated spirit for all higher things in art and science through permanent institutions and guiding it in its more distant development, I am called upon by my authority to give an expert opinion on the place and plan of the educational institutes to be founded for this purpose in the Royal Rhine Provinces. Since the work itself has not yet been published, I am entering the path of written communication in order to request from Hon. High Well-Born's kindness a preliminary understanding of how far my main ideas about how the art and science of the Prussian government on the Rhine must now take place, may perhaps hope to coincide with yours.

The Prussian Rhine provinces need, in my opinion, a central point for higher scientific education, a similar one for the old German art, a similar one for the ancient art or art based on the study of the ancient world, and finally a scientific-artistic association which is placed above all these different points and leads them all to the necessary interaction. Wherein, under the direction and participation of the Government and under the name of a general Rhenish scientific deputation, all that is eminently available of illuminating and spiritual power on the Rhine itself or, relative to the conditions and needs of its inhabitants on the banks in the whole of the rest of Germany, shall be gathered together for that purpose and for closer or more distant participation in it.

In addition, the Rhine Provinces need an educational institution for Catholic clergy, separate from the university and a sufficient number of small seminaries for elementary school teachers, suitably designed according to a common plan.

The first of the above-mentioned central points, or the University of the Rhineland, will I believe and for many reasons not to be countenanced here, thrive best in Bonn. Cologne, on the other hand, will have a beautiful vocation through an Academy of Old German Art to be founded there, richly endowed with existing and easily augmented art treasures of this genre as its constant nurturer and carer, as well as through a spiritual seminary to be received in its lap as protector and preserver of the faith of the fathers. Furthermore there should be a Rhenish archive established there as depositary of the most venerable monuments of the patriotic past.

Düsseldorf, with its pleasing forms and cheerful surroundings, with the easy sense of its inhabitants and all the memories of the splendor and love of art of previous rulers still alive there, seems to me suitable for an art school in which art is not, as in Cologne, understood and treated under a certain historical form or category but in its generality from the point of view of the ideal and consequently with the predominant studio of antiquity.

It may still be premature to express an opinion on the seat and further definition of the generally scientific association of German scholars and artists capable of working in the Rhineland or of German scholars and artists who are in some way meritorious of the Rhineland, whose watchfulness and work should hover above the whole of all the Rhineland educational institutes, sometimes stimulating, sometimes organizing, sometimes mediating.

This sketchy presentation of my views about the object in question can only be justified by *sapienti sat'*. My concern to be taking much time and attention from Hon. High Well-Born's precious time can only be justified in order not to sin against the public, which is jealously taking account of every moment. That I am bothering Hon. High Well-Born with this letter at all is certainly an excuse, considering the importance of the subject matter, and assuming a high degree of importance, which would have your judgement for me and for everyone entrusted with the organization of the Rhenish educational institutions, if they would be kind enough to send it to me, on the main aspects of my view which I have just mentioned above.

Please receive in advance my sincere thanks and the assurance of my high esteem.

Aachen, December 26, 1815.
The Privy Council of State and Crown President

the K. Pr. Provinces on the Rhine.

Sack

To

the Grand Duke of Saxony Weimarschen
Privy Councillor, Knight pp.
Mr von Goethe
High Well-Born
in Weimar.

(Only the signature is handwritten and the letter consists of three sheets).

Goethe's answer was:

II.

Hon. High Well-Born

This trustful and, for me, so honorable letter has given me the pleasant feeling that my failure to wait for last autumn's visit to your honorable self is at least partly compensated for. Just as the Minister of State, Excellency von Stein, by recommending the work I am about to undertake, has given me the pleasant feeling that I am adding a new and excellent letter to the many good things I owe to this excellent man.

Since the matter is of great importance and an explanation of it has many difficulties, I will allow myself to express myself aphoristically but before I do so I will give a little information about the creation of the booklet whose edition was unfortunately delayed.

During my two stays on the Main and Rhine in both summers last year, after not having seen my native region for so long I wanted to find out what, after so much misfortune, was to be found there in terms of art, antiquity and science and how it was to be preserved, multiplied, ordered, revived and used.

I inspected the objects, heard the desires, the hopes, the intentions of individuals and whole societies and, since I opened my thoughts towards them, I was asked to write down what was discussed, perhaps to give a public view of the whole and to provide a text for private negotiations. Since, however, I only touched His Royal Majesty's States in flight on an imaginary journey, it is easy to see that this part of the essay will be the leanest and most inadequate even though what is said about other places and regions may be more satisfactory.

Above all, however, I could only proceed from the assumption that I would observe what was available and what, if anything, was to be desired from it. On the other hand, I have excluded the how from my considerations, because this can only be judged by those to whom the execution of the objects is entrusted under the given conditions of time and circumstances.

The Rhine and Main areas, taken in the broadest sense, show, like the rest of Germany, larger and smaller points of hope.

The nature of the states that are situated side by side means that we can never attain the advantages which the Parisians enjoyed wrongly but only for their own benefit but rather for the benefit of the rest of the educated world. All conceivable things which the man of many professions might need for his purposes were found in one place, so that men like Humboldt and Gall, if they did not want to shorten their own lives, might not have been able to shorten their stay.

This body has fallen apart and if the German friend of art and science looks around where he could find any similar advantages, he will have to consider himself a traveller, since he can freely seek and use the greatest treasures of science and art little by little at random.

The main direction of my little essay is therefore to allow each place to have its own and to grant it its merits, while making what is available more widely known, so that it is easier to see how it can be preserved and revived and used by locals and foreigners alike.

But if the foregoing applies mainly to that which really already exists, then a new consideration takes place with respect to that which is to be set up first.

The education of our time is so high that neither the science of art nor those who pursue it can do without it. Since the efforts of Winckelmann and his successors, philology without the concept of art is only single sighted. All more or less educated peoples have had a dual nature around them through the arts that has grown in tradition, national character and climatic influence. For this reason all ancient remains, from statues of gods to broken pieces and bricks, remain respectable and instructive to us.

And so the different branches of science promote each other just as the different branches of art promote each other. The medalist merges with the sculptor, the engraver with the draughtsman. A connoisseur and lover of natural history cannot do without the happily imitating talent of careful artists. Thus it continues through everything until science and art finally call upon technology and craftsmanship to help and also ennoble them.

Whoever thinks of such a whole in a lively way will wish it into a great place where all the limbs directly touch each other. For it is precisely this touch that gives rise to mutual life and a supportive spirit that would otherwise be unthinkable.

In this sense, the desire to see this totality in Cologne need not appear blameworthy to a stranger, even if he dared to express it in a problematic way and even though he was unaware of the special circumstances. I find myself in the same situation and I have kept to this in my publication and let the question hover between Bonn and Cologne.

A new division of the provinces, however, which I have not yet been aware of, seems to make the division of the various institutions more reprehensible. The Hon. High Well-Born has expressed himself clearly about this and I believe that he also understands the reasons for this to some extent. How could anyone who has long since taken provisional action to ensure the best possible progress of a new institution to be set up by them have considered their reasons for doing so?

For the sake of brevity, I would like to paraphrase: In the space between Mars and Jupiter a large planet, possibly surrounded by satellites, has long since been sought and at last four small ones have been found at this point. So now, according to imaginary suggestions, the separate institutions will move around the central sun of the scientific association. Everything united in one place would make it easier for the supervisor to overlook and act upon the reality and vitality of the place, instead of it becoming in the present case an ideal point which has to arm itself with powerful means of attraction and repulsion, if it wants to keep all the orbits around and under itself in regular motion.

I am not saying this in order to argue against the proposed institution but only to say what I am sure has already been taken into account, namely that each of these two cases would require different treatment from the outset.

However, I must express my concern that Germany, as large as it is, will hardly supply so many mobile individuals who are qualified to truly enliven a large public institution on the Rhine, although some could intervene in various subjects and benefit from multiple talents. But to be a distributed institution a much larger staff, which at the same time has more ability, efficiency and good will is required. It is impossible to think of other more serious and sustained efforts on the part of the superiors that will be necessary to maintain the elements that are already separate in themselves and which are now also separated by distance, in a reciprocal and benevolently connected activity.

I have no doubt that it would be possible to afford this strong, energetic, experienced and tested man, with sufficient authority who would constitute himself at the center. I am speaking here only as one who presumes for a moment to speak about how to air his concerns.

As soon as my essay or at least its first issue is printed, I will take the liberty of sending it to you. It will not contain anything concerning the royal provinces that is not already known to the Hon. High Well-Born. There may be some useful notes on how to invite and interest the cities further up in an association though.

To whom, once again, with sincere recognition of the value of such a precious confidence, I ask forgiveness for the thoughts that have been expressed in passing. I received this letter only on the twelfth day therefore I have hastened the present one. If I should receive anything else that I might consider worthy of the communication, I will be obligingly granted permission to add it. Thus with the most perfect respect I have the honor of recommending myself most earnestly to continuing confidence

Hon. High Well-Born
Your most obedient servant
J. W. v. Goethe.

Weimar, January 15, 1816.

The days of the *Rheinischer Merkur* were already numbered when the arch-reactionary Prince Witgenstein received the supreme supervision in late autumn 1815. In his sense of right and duty, to serve only the genuine German patriotic cause, Görres did not even think of moderation, because he would have had to be unfaithful to himself. On January 3, 1816 the King issued a decree prohibiting the further appearance of the *Merkur* in Germany. The Cabinet order to Sack issued in response to this is listed under no. 1 in the appendix of this second section.

Just a few days after settling this matter however, Sack was to write the following letter to his friend Stein about his own indignation. The disgruntlement expressed in the letter that immediately prompted Sack to write to the King, was only too understandable. His pure soul felt that the punitive transfer that had obviously been contrived in

Berlin, was as much a disgrace to his good Rhinelanders as it was to himself. Now it became clear to him that the incomprehensible division of the province, which he alone administered, into two Crown Presidential districts was just the beginning. He wrote to Stein:

"When you wrote to me under the 3rd of December from Frankfurt, you yourself had not yet learned from the conversation with the State Chancellor, which cabals my old enemies, the Hatzfeld-Schuckmann-Witgensteinische clique at the head of the remaining obscurants, played against me and they had already come a long way before the State Chancellor came to Berlin. The reckless, genuinely selfish Westphalian minister B. with his squire or rather his master R., who found himself offended that I had not received them with a French spectacle in the province and accompanying them through it, which is why they did not go to Düsseldorf, were easily drawn into the clique and so the State Chancellor could not stand up to them. In a truly Napoleonic way, it already appeared in the official newspaper on December 30, when I was transferred to Swedish Pomerania and on the 18th I received the cabinet order of the December 10, that Mr v. Ingersleben was transferred to Coblenz as Crown President over the governments of Coblenz, Trier and Aachen, Count Solms-Laubach over the governments of Cologne, Düsseldorf and Cleve and that I was transferred to Cologne. I was transferred to Stettin as Crown President over the government there and Cöslin but without being given the slightest reason. I wondered why I deserved this, considering that I had received such treatment after thirty years of service in which I served the kings and state with the greatest sacrifice in all circumstances — for an administration of two years, in which I can boldly ask anyone whether he would have led it better — where I was appointed to the outpost and probably carried out the most difficult things. I have nevertheless maintained the confidence of the whole people and succeeded in bringing the Prussian State into the spirit of the latter in a way that no one has ever succeeded in doing. The inhabitants of Aachen, for example, have to walk for thirty to fourty hours through a foreign state presidium to get to Coblenz, where they have no transport at all, since the Rhine and Düsseldorf are only ten hours away. And for my honor I could do no other thing than to explain to the King the cabal of obscurants and dodgers against me and now I have declared that if the King did not want to put me back in my post in Düsseldorf and let the operation be run differently, I would have to ask for my leave. You will recall that I explained this to you last year when I told you of the pitifulness of those people, especially the pitiful minister. At the time you dissuaded me and the Chancellor's most concise assurances that he would protect me gave me hope that things would get better. However, when he put the whole organization of the country into the hands of the reckless Mr v. B. and Mr R., who, employed as an auditor for a Warsaw chamber, may have been quite good but not have a clue about general administrative terms, yet giving away presidential positions as well as messenger positions, I saw my political end already coming. The Schuckmann-Witgenstein obscurants found this quite à propos and probably did me the honor of placing me at the head of an opposition party against the King, because — Görres, Arndt and Koppe live in my governorate! — they did not have a go at Hon. Exc.,

but rather decorated on the 18th, for which I would congratulate, if it were not for such poor company, e.g. a
Crelinger and other Jewish comrades! But friend Gneisenau thinks that all those who have rendered the most fruitful services to the state should be persecuted as enemies of
it. I will remain true to my principles in all circumstances:
Tu ne cede malis sed contra audentior ito[90], convinced by the
applause of all the honest and strong, and therefore yours
as well.

On February 19 he continued: "Your friendly letter of the
first of February was as encouraging as it was uplifting.
When one is innocently maltreated and persecuted by bad
or wretched people, the applause of the noble and the
good is the strongest comfort and reason to hold fast to the
principle: *Tu ne cede malis*".

He then tells us that the King had tried to reassure him
about his transfer by an acknowledging cabinet order but
he still considered it to be the work of the Obscurantist
party, which hates the *Rhenish Merkur*......

"For among the pitiful militarists around the King, the
most ridiculous things have been accused of our friends
for some time now—Coblenz Wallenstein's camp, etc.. In
a confidential reply I have now made even closer openings
to the King about these activities of the obscurants. I have
now given him the name of the Lord of Knesebeck as the
one who, in 1809, told me in Berlin "that he and the Märk-
ish nobility would not admit to the execution of the Edict

---

90 Never give in to evil but proceed ever more boldly against it—
from Virgil, Aeneid, 6, 95.

of Liberation of the Peasants and would consider it the greatest misfortune" and that these persons were only trying to put themselves between the people and the throne and to create discord between them. I have presented His present Ministry to Him as one under which no man of duty and honor could serve, made up of cowards and wretches—from a Ministry of Finance in the French Westphalian manner—and I have proved this with evidence.

Despite or perhaps because of this open statement, Sack found himself forced to give up his position in Düsseldorf, because the State Chancellor had set out to prove to him that "obedience" should be returned to the administration. As governor-general of the allies, Sack had had too much free power and with his love of the Rhenish population had at the same time acquired the disfavor of his later Berlin superiors.

When the news of Sack's dismissal from the highest city spread in the spring of 1816, an inhabitant of Aachen, R., who had been bitterly wronged by the French by having his possessions taken from him but who had been restored to his rich possessions by Sack, believed that the long-awaited moment had finally come to show his gratitude to Sack, "Now he is leaving, the associations end here for him so no one can say I am grateful out of self-interest."

He had a box of precious silverware of high value and rare beauty sent to his house by mail from afar "One to whom Hon. Excellency owes all his happiness, asks you to accept the following memento as a token of his unlimited gratitude." Sack reasoned that it was for nothing—he knew that nobody could say in truth that he owed all his happiness to him. Pondering over the past, he thought back to earlier days. Finally he got the idea to call the wealthy and decent R. to him.

Looking at him with his pale blue eyes, pointing at the box, he said, "You had this box sent to me from Liège!"

R., wanting to deny, is confused by the fixed gaze that remained firmly directed at him.

He was obliged to stammeringly confess but he did it so imploringly, so deeply humble and touching, that he disarmed Sack. The latter took him by the hand in silence, led him in front of a mirror and breathed on its glass surface.

"You see dear R., the conscience and reputation of an official is like this mirror. Neither of them should be clouded by the slightest breath. Even the appearance of suspicion is perdition.

I thank you sincerely for your faithfulness and good will. You will have the box picked up from me this very day. If you wish to honor my memory, he softly and benevolently added, So will you, a rich man, use some of its value for charitable purposes."

R., deeply moved and shaken, was only able to draw the right hand offering it to his lips while a few hot masculine tears fell upon it.[91]

---

91 Told in *Die Spinnstube*, a Rhine Westphalian family magazine, after Sack's death, in even more detail.*

"On April 4, 1816 the City of Aachen gave its retiring Crown President a solemn farewell party" was written on the front page of the City of Aachen Newspaper no. 42 of April 6. Here an excerpt from the detailed report which filled it:

A company of 200 people had gathered in the new Ballroom. The first toast to the King's health was given by the celebrated person himself. It came from the heart and went to the heart while the hall was filled with the loud cry of blessing, "Friedrich Wilhelm!"

In solemn speeches and toasts, the Lord Mayor and the Lord Consistory Council expressed the thank you and farewell sentiments of the many, untold people to whom the departing person had shown good will. His officials praised him as a shining example of what is good and right—"lenient towards the person, strict and zealous for the cause, bold for the truth, virtuous, wrathful of lies and falsehood and tireless in promoting the common good of the State and humanity."

"A precious and rich treasure of love and veneration for the person of the King, collected from small beginnings and under difficult circumstances, Sack's successors will already find it amassed in the bosom of the entire Rhine people and, as we have no doubt, will know how to preserve it, indeed, how to increase it. But the first taler is more difficult and more deserving of a large fortune than the second million!"

Both city and country had felt its impact and its fruits had been recognized everywhere as a blessing that rested on his work. "When later reapers are glorified with the rich harvest, then we will remember with deepest gratitude the sower who prepared the soil so excellently and who sifted the seed and separated it from impurity turning it into the blessing of the future. A long farewell poem recited by Mr von Guaita closed the uplifting and atmospheric farewell moments. Countless poetic greetings and poems were even waiting for him when he returned home.

Sack had only been granted two years to work in his home province on the Rhine. His day and his working hours in it had mostly been 14-16. There were 22,506 issues to be dealt with from his arrival in March to the end of 1814, 33,011 in the course of 1815 and 11,220 in the first three months of 1816. This gives a rough idea of his eminent diligence and efficiency. Aachen had been allowed to own him at the zenith of his life at the age of fifty.

He left there on April 11, with tears of emotion in his eyes and an expression of pain on his face. The streets were crowded with people, surrounding his carriage to see him once more and to catch a last glimpse of him. In his book *Darstellung der Provisorischen Verwaltungen am Rhein* ("Representation of the Provisional Administrations on the Rhine"), the District Building Director Neigebaur talks about it thus:

"Even emperors have come and gone in Aachen without such a lively participation of all having taken place as at the departure of Governor General Sack. His last words were, as they had been at his arrival, exhortations to trust in Prussia's just King. So he left in all of them the conviction that he was not only the best official but also the most faithful servant of his King."

On May 1, 1816, an inquiry had arrived at the newspaper monitoring office in Liège, to which the *Merkur* surveillant, probably enlightened by Sack, gave the following answer:

Liège, May 2nd.

Un de nos abonnés de Cologne nous écrit qu'il manque quelque chose à l'éloge de Mr Sack, ancien gouverneur pour la Prusse des provinces du Rhin, inséré dans notre No. 25, c'est la suppression de la particule „de" qui a été placée au devant de son nom, lequel n'en a pas besoin pour être noble c'est à dire illustre.
Non seulement Mr Sack n'est pas noble par la naissance – ce qui est un effet de hazard et non une vertue – mais il a refusé des lettres de noblesse qui depuis longtemps lui avaient été conférées par son Souverain.
Ces distinctions héréditaires dont ceux là peuvent se prévaloir, qui manquent d'un mérite personel, étaient inutiles à cet administrateur intègre, conciliant, déclairé, même libéral / il faut le dire dussant certaines aurioles en être déchirées. Aussi s'en est il tenu à l'estime, à la consideration, à l'attachement de ses administrés,qui sont a ses yeux le plus précieux de tous les titres, comme leurs regrès sont la plus douce récompense.
Il n'y a pas de disgrace possible pour celui qui emporte de tels biens dans sa retraite. Il sera toujours plus puissant que le pouvoir, plus riche que l'opulence l'habitude d'ennoblir les roturiers, qui se distinguent par leur talens ou l'administration des états. Il en résulterait un préjugé fâcheux pour la bourgeoisie, en la faisant pas croire, que celui qui mourt

bourgois n'a rien fait de bien en sa vie.
Mr Sack a sans doute voulu faire obstacle à ce préjugé en
réfusant d'accepter cette faveur de son Prince. Il y a réussi, car
parmi ceux qui le connaissent et l'apprécient il n'en est pas un,
qui n'aime mieux être roturier comme lui, que d'être noble
comme tant d'autres.[92]

Stein had returned to Nassau in April after a winter in
Frankfurt. Here he enjoyed the complete sense of freedom
for the first time as he was away from all struggles and
disputes. The quiet peace of his fields and forests filled his
soul with only one longing—to give his powers even further to the inner strengthening of his fatherland, unbound

---

92 One of our subscribers from Cologne writes that something is
    missing from the praise of Mr Sack, former governor for Prussia of
    the Rhine provinces, inserted in our no. 25, and that is the deletion
    of the particle "von" which should have been placed in front of his
    name that does not require it in order to be noble or illustrious.
    Not only is Mr Sack not noble by birth—which is an effect of
    chance and not a virtue—but he has refused letters of nobility that
    would long since have been conferred upon him by his Sovereign.
    These hereditary distinctions, which those who are entitled to
    them can avail themselves that lack personal merit, were useless to
    this honest, conciliatory, enlightened, even liberal administrator. It
    must be said, however, that some halos were torn from him. So he
    has held on to the esteem, the consideration, the attachment of his
    constituents, who are in his eyes the most precious of all titles, as
    their achievements are his sweetest reward.
    No disgrace is possible for one who takes such riches with him
    into his retirement. It will always be more powerful than might,
    richer than opulence to ennoble the commoners who are distin-
    guished by their talents or the administration of their affairs. It
    would result in such an unfortunate prejudice for the bourgeoisie
    if caused them not to stop believing that he who dies a commoner
    has done nothing good in his life!
    Mr Sack no doubt sought to counter that prejudice by refusing to
    accept the favor of his prince. He succeeded, for among those who
    know and love him, there is not one who would rather be a com-
    moner like him than noble like so many others.

and voluntarily in quiet seclusion. What did he care about superficial honors? What did his personal fame mean to him today?

Before his departure from Vienna at the end of the Congress, the Emperor of Austria had awarded Stein the Grand Cross of the Order of St. Stephen for his services to the common cause during the same. The Emperor Alexander had already presented him with his highest order in Paris in 1814. Another proof of satisfaction was intended for Stein. He was asked what his wishes were. He decided on the Johannisberg Monastery, not far from his property in Nassau, which had been given to Marshal Kellermann of Napoleon and which had now become abandoned. Soon afterwards, in April 1815, Gneisenau had also applied for Johannisberg near Stein and the latter had replied evasively, "Although his wishes did not coincide with his own, he had passed them on to the State Chancellor". In fact, he had, whether out of recklessness or envy, already handed Johannisberg over to Austria on June 12, 1814. Thus the beautiful property on the Rhine came into the hands of Metternich, so ill-disposed towards Prussia, as an Austrian endowment!

Later, Stein succeeded in lengthy negotiations and Vincke, who had returned to Westphalia, now as the appointed head of this province, rendered him helpful services in exchanging his beautiful, lucrative but too distant possession of Birnbaum in Poznan for the former domain, the one-time monastery property "Cappenberg" in Westphalia. The King gave his permission on June 21, 1816 and the provisional transfer took place on August 20, 1816.

Stein had finally turned down the offer to become parliamentary envoy in Frankfurt for Prussia. He had been deliberating for a long time and the final decision had only been made after the presence of the State Chancellor who had come to Frankfurt, where Stein lived in the winter[93], on his return journey from Paris on November 28 to December 1, 1815. The refusal was then made verbally.

---

[93] In his short outline of his life he gives the real reason for his rejection: "I refused the Prussian Legation because of my reluctance to put myself in the relationship of dependence on a man I respected as little as the Chancellor of State. I foresaw, that he would sacrifice me on any occasion or for any reason, and who, out of jealousy or frivolity and in any case with great falsehood, had just completely abandoned a matter entrusted to him by me, which he had taken over with the greatest assurances of willingness, in Vienna and Paris". (Johannisberg?)*

The minister Prince Witgenstein[94] had increasingly succeeded in gaining a strong hold over the King and the influence of his party was now evident in the highest ranks
of the army and the administration. Gneisenau demanded
his dismissal — even where other unjustified reasons influenced governmental measures, public opinion blatantly attributed them to the same source, causing great concern
throughout the country. As early as 1813, a liaison had
formed in Berlin, which at that time wanted to refuse to
withdraw the volunteers called to Breslau for the great uprising. When the King insisted on it, the ministers and
state councillors Schuckmann, von Bülow, Graf v. d. Goltz
and Kircheisen, who felt relegated, joined together to over-
throw the state chancellor. Prince Witgenstein and General
von der Knesebeck had joined the alliance. At that time,

---

94 Stein remarked about Witgenstein in his life records, "Prince W.
possesses all the qualities, without knowledge, inner content and
efficiency, to obtain an advantageous position in life; cold, clever,
calculating, persistent, flexible to the point of sycophancy. The
maxim, *qu'un vrai courtisan doit être sans honneur et sans humeur*
[that a true courtier must be without honor and humor], suited
him. He strove for money and for secret back door influence. He
began his career at the court of Earl Theodor, playing the games of
the Antichambres, then seeking a connection with the Abbess of
Lindau, interested in her natural daughter. Soon afterwards, in
1792, following a decision to elect Franz II's electoral envoys assembled in Ehrenbrettstein and arrested for suspicious connection
with the French envoy in Mainz, he was dismissed. Lord Chamberlain of the deceased Queen Elisabeth, associate of Mdme. Rietz
and accompanying her to Italy, envoy in Kassel, head of a banker's
house, for which he obtained the funds from the Elector under
guarantee of his elder brother, confidant of Count Haugwitz, and
Lord von Hardenberg, to whom he advanced money, entrepreneur
of Plettenberg's bankruptcy, which he disturbed even more, after
the battle of Auerstädt soon in Hamburg soon in Königsberg, in
Hamburg in connection with Bernadotte, he tried to approach me
with the Bonds Venture (with the Elector of Hesse)".*

Stein had pressed Hardenberg for the immediate removal of Goltz and Witgenstein from the vicinity of the King but the chancellor of state did not think he had to fear them or at least he was afraid to touch them. Hardenberg now had to put up with them.

Sack had travelled directly from Aachen via Cologne and Koblenz to Nassau in order to talk to Stein. One of his government councillors in Aachen, Cleve-born Carl Focke, who had been one of his marshals at the homage ceremony in 1815, had applied to accompany Sack to Stettin and waited to see how the die would fall for him. Soon after his arrival in Berlin in April, Sack first had a detailed but highly distressing report given to him by Privy Councillor Knuth via Stein. "Not only does it confirm everything we have discussed but it is even more striking". After he had to admit about the State Chancellor and most of the ministers, whose most pathetic gossip Hardenberg had been listening to, he talked his head off and described the hopeless confusion of the finances. He said that, thank God, there were still enough men but that most of them did not want to come close to the Chancellor anymore, that they saw the unfortunate consequences of the loose economy as the only salvation and therefore all advised him not to step out of the game, "But only when all efforts to effect change fail here, will I go to Stettin. Here, I would have to live a terrible life, whereas there, among the good people of Pomerania, I would perform ordinary work and at least I would not be a witness to this evil here. However, I hope, *Deus dabit his quoque finem*[95] and that we will be able to enjoy a better tomorrow together. Stein replied to

---

95   God will put an end to these also. Virgil, Æneid (29-19 BC), I. 199.

him on May 1 and gave him, among other things, the friendly advice to go to Pomerania regardless of the circumstances and to do his "ordinary work" there. Thus Sack then also went to Stettin.

He had previously demanded public satisfaction from the State Chancellor for the injustice done to him by unfounded hostility, which he had been able to openly confront.

The King then relieved Sack's appointment to Pomerania from the character of a punitive transfer by appointing him as a Royal Privy Councillor with the title of Excellency. (He remained a member of the Council of State as before).

Wife Marianne, however, received the Order of Louise[96], which the King had awarded on August 3, 1814 for her dedication to the cause of women and maidens and of which Princess Wilhelm had been appointed protector, with a dignified and flattering handwritten letter from Princess Wilhelm for her sacrificial services at the head of the Aachen Women's Association.

Stein, reporting this result still from Berlin, on July 5, thanked for his letter from May 1, saying:

---

96 The Order of Louise (German: Luisen-Orden) was founded on August 3, 1814 by Frederick William III of Prussia to honor his late wife, the much beloved Queen Louise (née Luise Auguste Wilhelmine Amalie, Herzogin zu Mecklenburg-Strelitz). This order was chivalric in nature, but was intended strictly for women whose service to Prussia was worthy of such high national recognition. Its dame companion members were limited to 100 in number, and were intended to be drawn from all classes.

"Such a judgement coming from a trusted friend who pays homage to truth alone is the strongest encouragement to remain steadfastly faithful to truth and justice, no matter how dangerous and unpleasant the risks and inconveniences may be, even if it seems to be the lot of the present world. I can only compare the consecration which the valiant Schleiermacher so beautifully proclaimed to us yesterday, at the commemoration of the death of those who fell in the struggle for the holy cause. He said that not only the warrior, but everyone in his position should presume to fight the bad and weak with chivalry to the death, for the good of his brothers, to uphold national honor and prevent disgrace! I thank you very much for the attention with which you have read my administrative report".[97]

Two letters, still dated from Berlin, from August 22 and 26 to his faithful Marshal Focke, deal exclusively with Stettin-related questions. They deal with the questions of moving house and furniture and additional purchases — even wife Marianne's care of the cooks and the stables as well as the supply of hay for the carriage horses are carefully discussed with the young future housemate who is ready to help and has already hurried ahead. Sack was hoping to arrive in Stettin with his wife on August 31. He had mentioned in one of the letters from his brother-in-law Sethe that he had received interesting news about the Rhenish judicial system. While his brother-in-law had taken over the office of Councillor von Reiman, Sack's deputy until

---

97   In December 1815 Sack had sent the King a special administrative report on the excellent attitude of the Rhinelanders and their overall performance and had received thanks from the cabinet for the same, which he announced to them by publication.*

his successor von Ingersleben joined the presidency. His brother-in-law Sethe, President of the Higher Regional Court of Düsseldorf, had been appointed by the King on June 16, 1816 as President of the Immediate Justice Commission, which was to lay the foundations for a new organization of justice, since the governments worked according to Prussian legislation but the courts still rendered judgements according to French standards. Sethe soon called upon the cooperation of all the competent and knowledgeable men of the country—not only the officials of the judicial profession—according to genuine Stein principles. They had to wait two years for the ministerial decision, which when it arrived was in stark contradiction to Stein's liberal views! However, as Sethe had advocated, many of the French laws that had proved to be more effective remained in force or were incorporated into the German organization. In July 1816, Gneisenau handed over the command of the Prussian troops on the Rhine to General v. Haake, his successor and like Sack, went to Stein in Nassau before he retreated to his Silesian estate Erdmannsdorf. It seemed that his word, which he had written at the time of Sack's transfer was to prove true, that "all those who have rendered the most fruitful services to the state are now persecuted as enemies of the state". In 1818 the King, who then recalled him, appointed Gneisenau governor of Berlin and later in 1825 field marshal general. He remained in friendly correspondence with both Sack and Stein.

Some excerpts from private letters and the letters to Focke from this time of Sack's turn of fate are included in the appendix.

Sack, Crown President of Pomerania

The First Ten Years of his Work there from Summer 1816-1826

The Sack Couple
Left: Dr. Joh. August Sack, High State Privy Councillor and Crown
President of Pomerania
1764-1831
Right: Marianne Gertrude Johanna Sack née von Reiman 1776-1851

Thus the dream of his life that he would spend the rest of his years in his home province on the beautiful Rhine, working and acting as he had done so energetically and joyfully in the last two years, was over and it was again a matter of banishing one's own feelings into the background as in the time of the servitude of the fatherland and to let fulfilment of duty be his sole guide.

He knew exactly what difficult task had been assigned to him. He knew the desolate conditions that awaited him in Pomerania as he had had to administer most of the province when it was still under French occupation. During the French passage to Russia it had been bitterly devastated and robbed of almost all means of self-help. The children's verse:

"Cockchafer fly...
Your father is at war
Your mother is in Pomerania
Pomerania is burned to the ground
Cockchafer fly!"

had become all too hard a truth.

Very well, so be it! In the saddest province that Prussia once again could call its own, he wanted to regard himself as the chosen one who they entrusted with its re-construction — yes! he would show the gentlemen of this base influence on the King which blessing, with God's help, would allow itself to be created out of the Pomeranian desert. *Ne cede malis sed contra audentior ito.*

As early as 1805, when he and Stein had travelled to Pomerania together to visit the large new salt works and the port in Swinemünde, they had seriously considered plans to expand it. At that time they had been forced to shorten the journey because of the imminent danger of war and then the sad events of the war had left all great plans for improvement unfulfilled. Even when he later had to co-administer Pomerania from 1808 to 1810, business in the Kurmark with Berlin during the French occupation had been too extensive for him to have extended his duties as head of the presidency more intensively to the neighboring province. No doubt he had personally installed the new government in Stargard in 1809, had negotiated with the estates about the raising of contributions and it had always been a pleasant memory to him that the Pomeranian estates had shown a much more pleasant sense of sacrifice than the Kurmark estates. How pitiful Berlin now seemed to him!

When the ministerial posts were filled two years before, it had already been thwarted that he, the citizens' pride who himself had fought so hard against the constant preference accorded to nobility instead of proof of ability, should be taken into account in the filling of posts in Berlin. Alas, since the backlash had regained control, had it not just always gone downhill in the victorious kingdoms? To have to be in Berlin today would only be torture for him! Yet if in his fifty-second year he had decided to withdraw completely, as his friend Stein had preferred to do, he would not only have lacked the estates but also the years. After all, Stein was seven years older than he was and was not a well man, while he himself experienced and proved in Aachen that he had surpassed all his subordinates in his ability to perform, albeit somewhat at the expense of his health. Since Marianne too preferred to move to Stettin rather than to stay in Berlin, the decision was clear, even though it was one that had been forced upon him. Stein himself had advised him not to give way yet but to calmly and forcefully emphasize the reforms everywhere as before.

And his faithful Rhenish Government Councillor Focke joyfully went along with him and would be a great help to his mood.

When he looked back on the years he had spent in Berlin since he had first been appointed from his home in the Lower Rhine region to the East as a member of the General Directorate and Privy Fiscal Council, he had to admit that he had not lacked variety in his positions, offices and places of residence in the fifteen years of the new century. His extraordinary ability to find his way in ever new matters and to familiarize himself thoroughly with them had always called him to solve difficult tasks. From 1802-04, as the right hand of the Minister v. d. Schulenburg, he had already peacefully managed the classification of the Westphalian imperial cities and church areas together with Stein and had later to witness these areas, to which he had lent his hand and his heart together with the left and right Rhenish homeland, being torn away from Prussia. No wonder that he, as a passionate patriot was already hoping for a just retribution after this robbery and that he himself, in his responsible position as civil governor of Berlin during the French period of 1807-09, had always nurtured and favored the desire for a new uprising of Prussia and the liberation of his old and new homeland from the French yoke. The fact that he was one of those who secretly prepared such an uprising, that he was in any case not the man to tolerate the encroachments by the enemy that had been proffered to him as head of the Tilsit Peace Commission, had been the reason why he had been temporarily relieved of this office at the request of the enemy and had been appointed by his King to the cabinet in Königsberg. There he was able to work with Stein again on the elaboration of the necessary reforms until he had to return to Berlin in November 1808 as Crown President to administer the areas of Kurmark, Neumark and Pomerania that had been evacuated by the French. It was only natural for him to put all his energy into the practical implementation of the reforms after he had been involved in them in word and deed from the very beginning. But soon his provincial activities had to cease because after Stein's banishment, it seemed to him to be necessary to support the Chancellor of State Hardenberg who Stein himself had once recommended to take his place. When Hardenberg gave him the Department of Domains, Forests and Taxes in 1810 (the French again forbade him to hold a higher office) until the Department of the General Police in the Ministry of the Interior was entrusted to him in November, he had at least always been treated equally, even if the positions of the Crown President created by Stein had meanwhile been abolished by Hardenberg. Only when in the year 1812 the French friend Prince Hatzfeld denounced him in Paris as a follower of Stein, he had to exchange the police with the more apolitical Department of Trade and Commerce. He had to come to terms with all of this and then with all the passion of his hot-blooded Rhenish temperament, together with Gneisenau and Scharnhorst, he organized the re-armament and had belonged with them to the extraordinary commission that in as early as 1811 had longed for a union with Austria. When the uprising finally broke out in 1813 and Gneisenau handed over the large memorandum on national defense that he and Scharnhorst had prepared to Hardenberg, Hardenberg was able to write to Eichhorn at the same time, "Councillor Sack has been informed of our proposal. He is fully aware of the principles it expresses." At that time, he was the civil governor of the country between the Elbe and the Oder where he had to watch over the security of the country and especially that of the capital, set up the army and the militia and help to procure the means of war. Until then, after the liberation, the call to the homeland had reached him at the suggestion of his faithful friend Stein. The central government over all the German lands, whose princes had been on Napoleon's side, had been transferred to him and at the same time also over the left Rhine areas that had already been occupied for twenty years by the Corsican usurper. He had fulfilled the highest wish of his life and had been given the most beautiful task by being allowed to devote his entire working power to his home province for two years. Hardenberg had now disappointed him very much despite some good qualities upon which he had first placed so much hope. Stein had already been right in saying that he was moving further and further away from him when he realized that the State Chancellor did not have the backbone to intervene in the necessary measures of renewal in Prussia but rather preferred to return to the old, comfortable ways increasingly weakening his friend's far-sighted reforms. Only the few months that he had last continued as Crown President in Stein's unchanged sense had been enough to make him a victim of the conflict which had also caused his friend in Nassau to renounce all Prussian service and not even to take up the position of Prussian Parliamentary Delegate under Hardenberg. Nevertheless, the more this became clear to him — the more he would not give up the struggle to strengthen the foundations of the state which he had once worked out together with Stein — on the contrary, he felt a double duty in himself to assert them even more firmly and tenaciously against the shallow ministry and the Chancellor of State, who had been won and found too weak.

On July 11 he already took the administrative threads into his hands in Stettin and was visibly pleased and touched when his higher and middle officials surprised him with a welcoming poetic eulogy. Thus he had already unconsciously created a warmer feeling of goodwill for himself through his earlier activities. When on August 28, 1816 he had to confess to his friend Stein how much different and more favorable it would have looked in Pomerania than it does now, the powerful factor of compassion for this poor province and his old motto, "Always moving forward for the better" came to the fore with a renewed desire to help and support, victorious over all the disappointments he had experienced.

It soon became apparent that his predecessor had only favored estate management and had neglected all the other issues. The main task now was to make the Stein reform clear from the bottom up as a blessing especially for the economy of the peasants who had a lot in common with the stubborn Westphalians familiar in the ponderous spirit of the population, resisting everything new. Frederick the Great had already insisted with several strict decrees in 1719 and 1739 that no lord of the manor should enslave the peasants or evict them from their farms without good reason. In the year 1763 the great King had then decreed "Every landowner was obliged to pay a penalty of one thousand taler for every peasant's site that had become desolate and had not been restored from 1756 onwards, five hundred taler for every half peasant's and cossack's site and two hundred taler for every gardener's or cottager's site. However, despite the most severe means of coercion, the regent's charitable intentions were not carried out and it was astonishing that even by 1807 so little had been changed. Thus appeared the edict of October 27, 1807, in which it was already indicated that the nation was to be given a purposefully established representation, both in the provinces and for the whole. This was supplemented in 1810 as follows: "We wish to grant and secure the property of those of our subjects who have not yet enjoyed any ownership of their possessions." Finally, the cultural edict of September 14, 1811 was issued for the same purpose. So it was not the fault of the holders of government, i.e. the Prussian monarchs, that the majority of the estate owners were still unrestricted owners of the farms. The laws had remained without implementation for decades. That was the ponderous Pomerania! Particularly complicated rural, urban and political conditions had to be overcome because until 1815 the whole of Western Pomerania had been under Swedish rule for one and a half centuries and King Gustav the Fourth had never been able to gauge his plans according to his powers and the means at his disposal. With his clearly expressed hatred for Napoleon, he had loudly expressed the belief that he would not dare to attack his troops and his preconception had even gone so far that, in spite of the French advance in the winter of 1807, he himself, after the already concluded peace at Tilsit, cancelled his armistice concluded in the summer of 1807 — despite the resistance of his generals! "He could not and would not believe that the French should dare to march over his border". In the evening of the same day forty thousand French stood before and around Stralsund! When in 1810, after the peace treaty of Paris between Sweden and France, Vorpommern was returned to Sweden, Gustav's successor Carl XIII had called

some of the most capable men of the nobility and bourgeoisie to Stockholm to draft a new constitution for the
province:

1. that the national constitution, as introduced by
   King Gustav IV, was maintained

2. that a Royal Swedish Government be re-estab-
   lished, according to which the King of Sweden
   could only be directly invoked, and

3. the judicial constitution remained the same as that
   of 1806, only the introduction of the Swedish Code
   of Law and the liturgy was to be omitted.

In the old Prussian part things had gone badly during the
French period as well. A great recklessness had taken hold
of the authorities, even the War and Domain Chamber of
Stettin hastened to place itself at the disposal of the French
ready for service. The District Administrator of Naugard
travelled to Stettin to pay homage to Napoleon and left his
district and its affliction to the aged Mr Friedrich August
von Bismarck of Kniephof (Konarzewo)[98]. Thus, poor
Pomerania had become the province that suffered most in

---

98 The Kniephof estate was originally a knight's seat and fief of the
    Dewitz family, which later, together with Jarchlin and Külz,
    passed into the possession of the Bismarck family by purchase in
    1725. The buyer was Colonel August Friedrich von Bismarck-
    Schönhausen (presumably an ancestor of the person referred to
    here who could not be traced). Around 1780, Kniephof had a
    manor house and four households.
    From 1816 onwards, the future Chancellor of the Reich Otto von
    Bismarck experienced the first years of his childhood in Kniephof.

1811/12. Its damage alone had been calculated at over twenty-five million.

And how did the bargain work out! Already in 1805, when Napoleon occupied the English Hanover[99], England took revenge by taking away all Prussian ships without further ado, with 600 becoming its booty. The Pomeranian shipping industry had thus fallen into decline and when Napoleon's Continental Blockade followed in 1806, it suffered the ultimate blow. Only through the smuggling trade did the maritime towns of Colberg, Rügenwalde and the towns of Köslin, Naugard, Massow and Stargard, which led from there into the country, eke out a living. Napoleon himself actually found it advantageous to take part in the flourishing of the smuggling trade by imposing a fifty percent continental tax on it, instead of fighting it. Of course, smuggling only caused an intolerable increase in the cost of all necessities of life. The need had become so great that the very wealthy General von Rüchel, who owned the entire dominion of Amalienberg, which still included the villages of Raden, Güstemin and Friedrichsgnade and a total of 6,350 acres, had this property gambled away in a state-approved class lottery! With such a state of the province however, Sack's proven versatility was necessary to bring the barren state of the region back onto a more or less regular course. A small farmer had coined the saying about Sack, "*Hei set vele Pötte an't Füer, von de vele nicht tom Koken*

---

99 From 1714 to 1837 Hanover was by personal union the family seat of the Hanoverian Kings of the United Kingdom of Great Britain and Ireland, under their title of the dukes of Brunswick-Lüneburg (later described as the Elector of Hanover).

kommen"[100]. But how could the small farmer judge, if this caring provincial father did not leave any means untried and did not spare any difficulty in order to make the sad part of the country entrusted to him equal to the rest. It was certainly not his fault that not everyone was happy. When he heard that someone had a matter to put forward but was afraid to raise it before the highest officials, he shouted encouragingly to the man, "Is it about Pomerania? I'm always ready to talk about Pomerania!"

He travelled the province incessantly so that he could only give his orders after he had seen things for himself. What a depressing landscape was offered to him here yet what a favorable environment to carry out Stein's reforms without any restrictions! Sack set to work with zeal. In 1817, he set up a general commission in Stargard, which, under his personal supervision, first surveyed the entire farmland, then merged and distributed it. The lords and peasants then dealt with the matter in such a way that half of the land they had worked up to that point, which had not been liberated until then, became free property, the other half reverting to the lord of the manor. The beneficial effects increased from year to year and the rural population was so stimulated that the yield of the half of the land they had been granted was greater than that which had previously been obtained by the unfree whole. Heath lands that had never seen a plough were cultivated, quarries and moors were drained by dams and ditches and turned into usable land.

---

100 Low German dialect – roughly: He set many pots on the fire, from which very few will come to the boil.

By 1822, 1160 Pomeranian villages with ten thousand farmers had already applied for this regulation and in 745 villages it had already been implemented. In the process, 6,004 farmers had already received 633,189 acres as their own property, which amounted to a fortune of six million taler, while they themselves replaced their previous manual and harness services with nine million taler. In three decades the wasteland decreased by fifty percent. Not only the farmers, but also the lords gained advantages. Their possessions became more rounded and manageable, as the conflicts ceased. What used to require thirty-two farm horses, now ten farm horses were needed. From 1817-21 the population, in the districts of Stettin and Köslin alone, increased by 70,063 souls.

He found the school system in Pomerania frighteningly neglected, as he had already experienced in the Rhine Province. While in farther Pomerania it was the Wends[101] and the Kaschubs[102] who knew how to elude themselves

---

101 Wends is a historical name for Slavs living near Germanic settlement areas. It does not refer to a homogeneous people but to various peoples, tribes or groups depending on where and when it was used. In the modern day, Wendish communities exist in Lusatia, Texas, and Australia.

In German-speaking Europe during the Middle Ages, the term "Wends" was interpreted as synonymous with "Slavs" and sporadically used in literature to refer to West Slavs and South Slavs living within the Holy Roman Empire.

102 The Kashubians, also known as Cassubians or Kashubs, are a Lechitic (West Slavic) ethnic group native to the historical region of Eastern Pomerania called Pomerelia, in modern north-central Poland. Their settlement area is referred to as Kashubia. They speak the Kashubian language, which is classified either as a separate language closely related to Polish, or as a Polish dialect. Analogously to their linguistic classification, the Kashubs are considered either an ethnic or a linguistic community.

and their children from any cultural constraints, in Western Pomerania it was not easy to fight against the over-bred Swedish particularism and the caste spirit, the pampered and the Western Pomeranian concepts of nobility. There was no obligation to attend school beyond the River Peene, there were only schools at the whim and arbitrariness of the lord of the manor as a secondary occupation held by shepherds, tailors and women for an annual salary of two to three talers. However, he found much understanding with the clergy and teachers of Old Pomerania because of his own accommodating disposition. In 1816 he founded the Bible Society of Stettin, whose presidency he assumed. By decree of August 21, 1818, the school supervision of the rural schools was transferred to the respective pastor of the parish, as he had already done successfully in the districts on the left bank of the Rhine. Meanwhile he succeeded in introducing compulsory schooling in Western Pomerania nine years later in 1825 by cabinet order.

He helped the disreputable gymnastics to a new appreciation—at his instigation and the Marienstift Board of Trustees sent a teacher to Jahn in Berlin to train as a gymnast and on October 18, 1817, the first public gymnasium, to which the city had contributed the funds, was opened in Stettin. He even applied to the ministry for the name Neuturney for a new suburb of Stettin, "because it borders on Old Turney and reaches up to the new gymnasium, which

---

The Kashubs are closely related to the Poles. The Kashubs are grouped with the Slovincians as Pomeranians. Similarly, the Slovincian (now extinct) and Kashubian languages are grouped as Pomeranian languages, with Slovincian (also known as Łeba Kashubian) either a distinct language closely related to Kashubian or a Kashubian dialect.

is such a necessary requirement for national education under the new military system of general conscription.

A fine testimony to Sack's selflessness in the tremendous workload he took upon himself is provided by his answer to his Government Councillor Focke, which he was to lose after only one year of working together as Sack struggled with the ministry to achieve his many goals, (see Appendix V, 3). Without reprimanding or criticizing his wish for an immediate transfer back to his home country, which was expressed to him in writing via Berlin, instead of verbally at home, he even offered to support his wish.

Yet Focke himself seems to have changed his mind, for he did not remain alone in the service of his high superior but in 1819 the 36-year-old councillor became the fiancé of Sack's 20-year-old niece Agnes Sack from Liegnitz, who had been invited to Stettin by the Lady President to make extended visits. Only a few days after this union of hearts, which was sanctioned by the parents of the bride in Liegnitz, the father of the bride died suddenly and cloudy shadows fell immediately in the sunny rose season of Stettin. Probably the widowed mother, Madam Privy Councillor Focke, who lived in Berlin and was soon herself deeply shaken by the death of her second son Reinhold in October, had met her charming daughter-in-law in late summer, with radiant eyes matching the deep warmth of Agnes' heart along with her business acumen. However, both mothers were unable to attend the couple's wedding, which the generous Uncle August and his splendid wife Marianne gave in their home in Stettin. Focke's sister, who had been married to the local government councillor of

Mittelstädt since 1818 and a second brother of Focke, Fritz, were however present. Because of the love of his heart, Carl Focke's desire to return home that had long since calmed down, was completely overcome and he only became more and more attached to his now uncle August.

However, this family event has put us one year ahead of the chronological sequence.

In 1818, Sack was able to tackle the plan he had already drawn up in 1805, first together with Stein and which he considered absolutely necessary. This was the deepening of the Swine River at its mouth. It remains his greatest merit to have brought about this expansion of the port of Swinemünde (Świnoujście) and the resulting revival of trade, which at that time was totally in a state of collapse. The improvement of the waterway through Swine, which had already been started by Frederick the Great and had since been neglected and dilapidated, was now purposefully tackled by his tireless efforts. After all, the need for a secure entrance to the port of Swinemünde had also been established at the time in full agreement with Stein. On May 17, 1818 the first sinkhole was let into the sea in Sack's presence and after 5 years the large pier in Swinemünde was completed. The fairway at the mouth of the Swine had been deepened by 16-18 feet, compared to the Oder which was only 11!

Interested in the great enterprise with which Sack set to work so energetically, the King himself came to Stettin on his return journey from Russia in autumn 1818 and had Sack discuss his plans on the spot. The monarch must have been impressed by the way the unjustly transferred Crown President was able to put his slogan "*Tu ne cede malis sed contra audentior ito*" into practice in the noblest sense. Sack also took care of overseas interests:

In 1823, a nautical elementary school was established in Stettin on the Lastadie[103] and a navigation school in Stralsund. In April 1826 the first Oder steamship, the "Kronprinzess (Crown Princess) Elisabeth", was launched, and the merchant navy counted 411 ships.

Nevertheless, these are the results and we are now continuing to accompany Sack in the rebuilding work. Fishing and the fish trade, which used to be so flourishing in the past, are the areas to which he devoted his attention and support. The salting and smoking of fish, already practiced in Pomerania centuries ago, was soon put back into operation at his suggestion and brought new income to the coastal towns and villages.

He issued a new fishing decree for the Oder, the lagoon and the three estuaries of the Oder and founded the two colonies Hammelstadt and Karlshagen for the herring fishermen. The village of Osternothafen, where smaller vehicles found winter shelter and emergency help, developed from the settlement of the workers employed in mole construction. However, Swinemünde had now suffered a loss due to the construction of the harbor, as numerous workers and lightermen had moved away from there. Sack thought about compensation and persuaded the King to

---

103 Lastadie was a quarter of central Königsberg, Germany. Its territory is now part of Kaliningrad, Russia.

give money from state funds for the construction of a large bathing establishment and a community center. Under Sack's guidance, a warm bath house and surrounding facilities were built, so that the foundation of Swinemünde as a seaside bathing place took place in the same years.

Through the establishment of even more bathing establishments at suitable beach locations, the seaside resorts Misdroy, Rügenwalder-Münde, Putbus, Sassnitz and Heringsdorf were also founded by him over the years and brought to ever greater development.

He founded the first non-profit savings banks and thus at the same time the Citizens' Emergency Institute for the Stettin craftsmen in need. This was a main foundation for improving the situation of the workers and later also led the Stettin merchants to form a Merchants' Corporation in 1821. Previously it had been organized as a guild but by the Royal Statute of 1821 it was able to develop into a free corporation and elect its own leaders. This institution then had to be endowed with new goals and its interests had to be raised and expanded. Sack worked tirelessly to drive the ponderous Pomeranians who had become unenthusiastic after their tough experiences. He introduced them to new possibilities and opportunities, which can be clearly seen in the records of his administrative period. He prompted them to write countless reports and memoranda to the ministry. Once he had awakened their spirits to fresh aspirations, they even realized later in Berlin that the Oder trade, which had formerly been the more important, could no longer be allowed to lag behind the Elbe trade and was disadvantaged.

He was able to report to his friend Gneisenau on October 12, 1819 that at his request the King had granted him permission for the very costly extension of the severely damaged St. Mary's Cathedral Church in Kolberg (which had been hit by 20 bombs on July 2, 1807 while Gneisenau was defending it) as well as a church and house fund for the church in Magdeburg-Neustadt, which had been destroyed by Napoleon in 1812. A new organ was inaugurated in the St. Mary's Cathedral on June 24, 1827 in the presence of the Crown Prince, financed by the surplus of the collection and an additional payment from the King. At the same time Sack had been able to report to Gneisenau in 1819, "that today I have recommended the retired Lieutenant Nettelbeck, who was recommended to me by Hon. Excellency, to the Royal Government of Köslin for consideration as soon as possible."

Sack's ethically robust nature meant that he was able to create or strengthen charity wherever he lived, regardless of denomination. In 1820, he had the old Count's castle at Naugard, which had been an inadequate *Spinnhaus*[104] and penitentiary since 1720, redesigned and founded a penal reformatory there, to whose beneficial goals he then gave his special protection.

---

104 From the 16th century onwards, the term *Spinnhaus* was used to describe prisons, which were generally used to house women who were impoverished, begging or accused of prostitution. The name refers to the spinning activity that the imprisoned women had to perform. The work imposed was intended to be disciplinary, as the underlying purpose of the institutions was to rehabilitate rather than punish. Spinning houses are thus regarded as the beginning of the modern penal system.

While in the first years the Crown President had devoted himself almost exclusively to the most urgent material necessities, he could gradually turn his attention to beautification and spiritualization, which were so dear to his heart. He was the first person in the Stettin citizenry to suggest the idea of creating a recreation park. His influence immediately enabled the military authorities to determine and allow the project to be carried out. As early as 1819 he founded a landscaping association, which commissioned the construction and later the extension of facilities on the Glacis[105] through trees and paths, flower-rich ornaments and playgrounds, the likes of which Stettin had never known until the walls had been removed and the ground space made available for them. The war had brought the foundation of an "Economy Society"[106] to a quick end, Sack knew how to revive the foundation of a similar association in Demin.

Just as his friend Stein in his leisure time devoted himself to the promotion of history and called the *Monumenta Germaniae*[107] into life, so Sack, in addition to his innumerable

---

105 A glacis in military engineering is an artificial slope as part of a medieval castle or in early modern fortresses. They may be constructed of earth as a temporary structure or of stone in more permanent structure.

106 "ökonomische Gesellschaft". Evidence can be found for this in the *Amtsblatt der Regierung in Stettin: 1817* in a notice signed by Sack. The first General Meeting had apparently been held on February 12, 1817. The Economic Society was a scholarly society that was devoted to questions of economics and traditionally, in particular, to agriculture.

107 The *Monumenta Germaniae Historica (MGH)* is a comprehensive series of carefully edited and published primary sources, both chronicle and archival, for the study of Northwestern and Central European history from the end of the Roman Empire to 1500. Despite

tasks, also found the time, in the midst of his restless activity, to support literary undertakings and to help bring them into being.

The Pommeranian Provincial Gazettes for Town and Country, published by Superintendent Haken zu Treptow a. d. Rega, were to help in this respect. Sack himself introduced them as a patriotic enterprise to the inhabitants of the province with a longer announcement on January 1, 1820. In it he stated "that after thirty-five years of experience in the most varied of posts and after the close observation he has given to this Province and its inhabitants, he entered into closer relations with them for the second time three years ago and such a country and such a people are worthy of every instrument for their culture", calling the enterprise itself a true national need. Even Vincke's friend, Crown President of Münster and several other Cleve

---

the name, the series covers important sources for the history of many countries besides Germany, since the Society for the Publication of Sources on Germanic Affairs of the Middle Ages has included documents from many other areas subjected to the influence of Germanic tribes or rulers (Britain, Czech lands, Poland, Austria, France, Low Countries, Italy, Spain, etc.). The editor from 1826 until 1874 was Georg Heinrich Pertz (1795–1876); in 1875 he was succeeded by Georg Waitz (1813-1886).

The MGH was founded in Hanover as a private text publication society by the Prussian reformer Heinrich Friedrich Karl Freiherr vom Stein in 1819.

The project, a major effort of historical scholarship, continues in the 21st century. In 2004 the MGH, with the support of the Deutsche Forschungsgemeinschaft, made all of its publications in print for more than five years available online, in photo-digital reproduction, via a link on the MGH homepage. These things cause us to reflect on what sustainable influence the characters in this book founded for us today.

friends there are on the list of the 972 subscribers who immediately supported the new newspaper.

The first volume of this rich publication, which was supported by scholars and writers with detailed essays and poems on both the history of Pomerania and the present day, was already able to give a detailed account of another visit by His Majesty the King, which he extended to a full fortnight, from June 1 to 15, this time to take note of the military and civil achievements of the province. As early as May, the Crown Prince, as Royal Governor of Stettin, had been there for a few days to inspect the garrison preparing to take part in the great manoeuvers. At that time he had had breakfast with the Crown President Sack and then made a water trip with him to the charmingly situated Frauendorf. He was accompanied by his father and 9,400 troops had already been drawn to the capital for ten days to participate in the great military show, while others were accommodated in neighboring garrisons. The princes Wilhelm and Karl joined the monarch as well. The show of troops took place on the very first two days after the arrival of the highest rulers. These were exhausting days for the Crown President, who was constantly on the move with the King from then on following this great military spectacle. One usually dined around on the estates of the nobility and Sack had then also in the evening, whenever there were no balls in the larger cities, to be always ready for discussions about what had been seen and for new sightseeing in the morning. On such an occasion, this time a trip along the coast, a rest was made in a fishing village, where Sack had taken precautions that some herrings were presented to the King. Having witnessed the catching, salting and packing of the fish on several occasions, the high lord then ate the fish with visible pleasure, drinking at the same time to the continued prosperity of this important foodstuff. The place was named Heringsdorf ("Herring Village") after the King's visit and from then on it developed into a popular seaside resort. Wherever the King got to know the province, adorned with decorations in the cities and in the countryside from bridges and ships, cheerful people greeted him and cheered him as their beloved ruler, while Sack himself, with inner satisfaction at what he had achieved in such a short time, was allowed to bathe in his glory.

The royal satisfaction expressed itself in a special letter of thanks:

To the

High Privy Councillor and President Sack.

"During My presence in the local province I have found unchanged the attitudes by which the Pomeranians belong to the Fatherland and which they have worked so hard for the same. I may also expect the same devotion from the inhabitants of New Pomerania and through them their indissoluble consolidation with the Prussian States all the more confidently, the closer it is to My heart to establish their happiness and prosperity as firmly as possible. The conviction that the authorities in this are in conformity with My patriarchal intention gives Me a sure guarantee of this success and I therefore return satisfied with the endeavors which I have perceived everywhere in this respect and in which I have not overlooked your active influence".

Stettin, June 12, 1820

Friedrich Wilhelm.

A letter has survived from the fall of the same year 1820, which Sack sent in response to an inquiry by the Consistory Councilor Monicke of Stralsund. Even from this semi-official letter, one can hear an echo of Sack's complete reconciliation with his present place of work, after he had gained distance from the circumstances of the Rhine province during the four years he had been away. Therefore, it seems valuable to include the letter here:

To Consistory Councillor Monicke in Stralsund.[108]

Hon. Highly Reverend

I would like to thank you sincerely for the message I received in yesterday's post about your request to be transferred to Coblenz and for the confidence you have shown in me.

Since Mr R. Director Heuer was still here this year and is going back there tomorrow, I informed him of this. We have discussed it and through him I will share my opinion with you briefly, discussing the details with you orally.

The proposal of Mr Stm. Frhr. v. Altenstein Exc. is honorable and gratifying and you have done well not to reject it immediately but to ask for some time to consider it. It also merits such consideration, especially at the present moment when there is still talk of abolishing the government there which appears to me to be probable. In this case it would be possible to consider whether you would like to remain in your religious office there or be transferred here to the government and to the Consistory without pastoral care but without loss of your previous service remuneration, which seems to me to be a good idea. In the other case, you are aware of the existing circumstances that are not those awaiting you in the new professions.

---

108 In the possession of the German Reich Railway Councilor Dr. jur. Ed. Sack of Marienburg in West Prussia. A consistory is the assembly of cardinals in the Roman Catholic Church, a church court or an ecclesiastical authority in the Protestant churches.*

Dr. Joh. August Sack from an oil painting 1824

I cannot describe them as appealing to you as I know them to
be here and in Stralsund. Where there is much light and
therefore also much shadow together, as is indisputably the
case on the Rhine, there is also much conflict between the
former and darkness. Without being intolerant of anything, I
have always found myself more free and cheerful in a Protestant country than in a Catholic one, where even a Görres has
not been able to free himself from the Ultramontanist[109]
shackles, as his last writing says, and where one has to fight
daily against incidents of superstition and stupidity, which
we know only from lectures in the Protestant countries.

---

109 Ultramontanism is a clerical political conception within the
Catholic Church that places strong emphasis on the prerogatives
and powers (infallibility) of the Pope.

Friedrich Ambros Graf Veterani (1650-1695)

Director Heuer will say even more about this and if I take into account your family and other individual circumstances mentioned by you, I cannot advise you to accept the offer. However, I am far from, in any way, least of all from intervening in the fate of a man so esteemed by me. If you do decide to do so, I wish you and your dear ones in it God's blessing. If you decide against it for those reasons, your minister cannot rebuke you, nor interpret it badly and I will gladly participate in this process.

So may God direct your and His heart to that which gives you the best happiness and satisfaction! I ask you to count me among those who will always be most sincere in sharing this hope.

With these sentiments and with my most sincere recommendation to your wife, I always remain with the highest esteem

Hon. Highly Reverend

most obedient
Dr. und Freund
Sack.

On the King's birthday, August 3, 1821, the province
hosted the secular celebration of the unification of Pomerania. One hundred years previously, in August 1721, Frederick Wilhelm the First had already received the homage
of the estates, citizens and peasants when the area between
the Oder and Peene, which had been under Swedish
sovereignty, fell back to Prussia as its original owner. Sack
gave the ceremonial speech at the secular celebration and
with the King's consent a silver commemorative coin was
minted for the occasion, which was opened with a church
service throughout the country at the monarch's request.
For not only in Stettin but in every place in the province
Sack had ensured that this festival was celebrated in a patriotic manner. For as and where he could, the Crown President favored all the historical days of commemoration to
reinforce the spirit of unity in the province.

He also had another Yearbook of the Province of Pomerania published in 1821 by his secretary in the Upper Presidium of Salfeld, the XVIth, 406 pages long, providing it with
a foreword to give constant encouragement and guidance
for the new uplift of the Province and to petition for it. The
lithographic title hinted at the unification of all three administrative districts with the Prussian House that was
completed in 1815. The Prussian eagle above two inter-
twined hands with the date 1815, the new iron cross and
the old Pomeranian griffin, formed the outer decoration.
(The symbol of Pomeranian freedom which the Pomerani-

ans often had to defend is the griffin, i.e. a flying lion with a hawk's head under its griffin pennant).

The King took part in this large-scale and organized patriotic commemoration — the description of which in the Pomeranian provincial papers alone takes up 78 narrowly printed pages and which was used in almost all larger towns to unveil monuments, found charitable institutions, feed the poor, establish church foundations, school records, collections, illuminations, the founding of associations, processions, parades, shooting matches etc. through three awards of religious orders and the amnesty of a country soldier sentenced to life imprisonment in Naugard. The City of Stettin presented its Crown President Sack with a letter of honorary citizenship. The University of Halle, where Sack began his legal studies almost forty years before, awarded him a doctorate in law, the Pommeranian Region presented him with 3 vases.

The silver and copper commemorative coin minted for the celebration shows the three heads of the Great Elector, Frederick Wilhelm I and Frederick Wilhelm III, and on the reverse the province of Pomerania (female figure), presenting its scepter to the ruler of Prussia (male figure in the coronation regalia). *Patria Patribus — Fida Felix.*

The Royal Mark Economic Society of Potsdam, which had just published a draft for a collection of materials for the chorography of Brandenburg in print in 1821, set Sack as an example to be imitated and called upon the men of spirit, knowledge and patriotism in Pomerania to also compile a work comprising three sections: natural history,

history and locality description. He advised to first publish the relevant essays in the provincial gazettes that he had co-founded and to encourage other interested parties to collaborate. In any case, he succeeded in bringing to light some valuable works of the more talented scholars and silent researchers and in awakening in the readers a desire for education and love of their homeland.

> "On Sunday and Monday 30th IX and 1st X of the same year Stettin was unexpectedly surprised by another visit of His Majesty the King and the whole royal family. On Sunday evening the two princesses and Prince Albert of Schwedt arrived and on Monday evening the King with the other princes. On Monday morning, Sack gave the former a breakfast in Zülchow (suburb) at Thielebein's house. On both evenings, the royalty were at the theatre, leaving again at noon on Tuesday.
>
> (Excerpt from a letter Carl Focke wrote to his mother.)

On June 15, 1824, the same day that Sack founded the Society for History and Antiquities by presenting its statute to it, he had also organized a seven hundred year commemoration of the conversion of Pomerania to Christianity by Bishop Otto of Bamberg with much love and effort. In all churches and schools the day was celebrated as a high feast and in Pyritz the foundation stone for the Otto Seminary and Otto Fountain[110] was laid under four ancient lime trees.

The Pomeranian Provincial Gazettes had already successfully stimulated the sense for the provincial past and the urge to explore had developed more and more, so that Pomerania was already on the honorable way to contribute its part to Steins *Monumenta Germaniae*. If something touched Sack with nostalgic pain in all his delightful creations, it was the fact that the friend himself shunned the long journey and could not decide to visit him in Sceczin.

Stein now limited his excursions mostly only to his change of residence from Nassau to Cappenberg. Probably he had once again had to decide to follow the request of the Emperor of Russia and on October 30, 1818, he had occasionally followed Alexander's call to the Aachen Congress for a talk. It had been extremely painful for him to repeatedly hear the harshest judgments from the foreign business men. "Prussia," it was said, "does not count, nobody respects it, it has no government. The Chancellor is completely worn-out and is a vain self-serving man who would rather let the state and the monarchy perish. It has

---

110 "In front of the town of Pyritz there is a spring which bears the name of the holy well after Bishop Otto of Bamberg, a wise and holy man who converted the idolatrous Pomerania to Christianity. Since 1824 it has been worthily renewed by the grace of the pious King Frederick William III. It is now enclosed in hewn granite, and comfortable steps lead down to it. A large granite cross rises above it, with a matching pious inscription. Not far from it, near the road from Pyritz to Arnswalde there is a building resembling an abbey, built as a seminary for country school teachers, and bearing the name Ottostift (Otto Foundation)." Taken and translated from https://de.wikisource.org/wiki/Der_heilige_Brunnen_bei_Pyritz

no finances and incompetence and squandering are exhausting it." According to Stein's own judgement, Prussia, wavering between Russia and Austria, was dragging behind both of them in the Aachen negotiations. However, in all this, Stein's love for his own King — despite what he himself had had to overcome — was not denied for a moment. When he came out of a confidential conference of the King and the two Emperors in Aachen, he turned to go to Legation Councillor Eichhorn with the words, "You know how much I think of the Emperor of Russia but Frederick Wilhelm is the first and best of all, he is completely true and faithful and honest. At the banquet he then said to Gentz that he himself was tired of politics and was going to withdraw completely from it. He only wanted to help promote the sources of German history on his own. In 1820, from July to May 1821, his work on this subject had taken him through Switzerland to Rome and Italy, where he met Niebuhr who was in Rome to examine the Vatican manuscripts and documents. At that time, the Vatican Library contained in separate collections the manuscripts of the Palatine Library (Palatina), the manuscripts of Queen Christina of Sweden and the Ottobonian and Urbino manuscripts, which had been seized from Heidelberg by the French. On his return to Nassau, the King had presented Stein with a gift of a thousand talers for the work — the Prince of Thurn und Taxis had assured him 100 ducats each for ten years. The House of Anhalt did the same and the City of Frankfurt promised a one-time donation, so that Stein could immediately pay his larger obligations to the illustrator Merian and continue his scientific work with new confidence.

The restoration of the Castle of the Teutonic Order, the Marienburg a. d. Nogat (Malbork Castle)[111], which had been suggested by the Crown Prince (later Friedrich Wilhelm IV), was carried out in 1823. The Crown President of the Province of West Prussia, von Schön, offered everything to ensure a dignified execution of the building through contributions from the knightly families whose ancestors had belonged to the Order. Stein also received an invitation and, together with his sister Marianne, made a contribution of 400 talers, which he wanted to see used for the construction of the two granite pillars in the hall in front of the great aisle. He justified this with the fact that he had two brothers in the order, of which the younger one defended the Veterani Cave[112] — a fortified place at the Danube — for three weeks against the Turks and handed it

---

111 The Castle of the Teutonic Order in Malbork (Polish: Zamek w Malborku; German: Ordensburg Marienburg) is a 13th-century Teutonic castle and fortress located near the town of Malbork, Poland. It is the largest castle in the world measured by land area and a UNESCO World Heritage Site.

112 In 1691 Friedrich Ambros Graf Veterani (1650-1695) succeeded in conquering the fortress of Lippa, his main focus was now entirely on the defence of Transylvania, especially the prevention of Turkish activities on the Danube. Thus, in 1692, he had the cave on the bank of the Danube, until then known as "Piskabara", explored by the imperial captain d'Arnau, occupied and fortified by 300 men. At the end of March, began the attack of a Turkish army on the fortified cave. First attacks by Turkish tchaiken — ships with a crew of up to 300 men and 3 cannons — were initially repulsed but after a 45-day siege from repeatedly attacking land forces, the imperial contingent finally had to surrender to the superior force. Due to these battles the cave was named Veterani Cave. In the course of the Russian-Austrian Turkish War (1787-1792) the Veterani Cave was again defended by imperial troops against the Turks. Again the commander, Major Stein, had to bow to the Turkish superiority and capitulated after tough defense on August 31, 1788. The imperial troops were granted free withdrawal.

over only after he had no ounce of bread or ammunition
left. He wished to see his coat of arms on the cross of the
Order and his name underneath, with the name of the
armed act, which still lives in the annals of Austrian history, attached to one of the pillars. This was done according to Stein's wish and the coat of arms of Ludwig von
Stein, placed on the German cross, with the mention of the
act of arms, still lives on at the Marienburg.

The first volume of the *Monumenta* was printed in 1825.
There was no financial contribution from Berlin. However,
all the important historians had supported the success of
the great enterprise with promises and achievements. Dr.
Pertz[113], who later became Stein's outstanding biographer,
had placed himself entirely at his disposal, he directed the
printing and made the necessary journeys with stays of

Today the cave is flooded by a Danube power station at the Iron
Gate and therefore not accessible.

113 Georg Heinrich Pertz (28 March 1795 – 7 October 1876) was a German historian and used as the basis for some of the information in
this book.

Born in Hanover, from 1813 to 1818 he studied at the University of
Göttingen, chiefly under A. H. L. Heeren. His graduation thesis,
published in 1819, on the history of the Merovingian Mayors of the
Palace, attracted the attention of the Prussian reformer Baron
Stein, by whom he was engaged in 1820 to edit the Carolingian
chroniclers for the newly founded Historical Society of Germany.
In search of materials for this purpose, Pertz made a prolonged
tour through Germany and Italy, and on his return in 1823 Stein
entrusted him with the principal charge of the publication of the
series Monumenta Germaniae Historica, texts of all the more important historical writers on German affairs down to the year 1500,
as well as of laws, imperial and regal archives, and other valuable
documents, such as letters, falling within this period. Pertz made
frequent research visits to the leading libraries and public record
offices of Europe.

several months in Rome, Paris and London, all at his own expense.

The foundation of the Pomeranian Historical Society already gave Sack the satisfaction and joy of continuing to prove his loyalty and dedication to his old friends in Nassau and Cappenberg.

Sack also still found time to conduct a confidential correspondence with his old friends Stein, Gneisenau and Vincke about everything that moved his patriotic heart. However, it is always Stein who, right off the cuff, expresses his experiences and feelings. From this correspondence it is clear how Sack became increasingly independent of the Chancellor of State who died in 1822 and whose great weaknesses he had fully recognized in 1816. Since then, Sack had gone his own way, the straight path which his humanity and conscience alone dictated to him, seeking and finding his only satisfaction in the consciousness of fulfilling his duty.

As early as in 1817, a bank account of the Berliner Bank had been established and in 1824 the Association of Pomeranian landowners, supported by the Crown President, founded the *Ritterschaftliche Privatbank* on shares.

From the very beginning of his work in Pomerania, as a great gardener and fruit grower himself, Sack had founded a fruit tree nursery in Stargard for this purpose in 1818 and had also tirelessly spoken out in favor of increased sheep breeding in the countryside. By introducing better varieties of sheep and helping flock owners to make the yield more profitable, he crowned this effort in 1825 with the establishment of the Stettin Wool Market, initially held on Lastadie, later with its growing importance (from 1831 onwards) on Paradeplatz. In the past, Pomeranian wool had to be brought to Landsberg on the Warta River but now the market in Stettin was supplied by 430 wool producers with 10,000 hundredweight of wool right at the beginning and buyers from home and abroad came in large numbers. The inns, such as the *Hotel de Prusse*, where the landed gentry had their lodgings, were extremely satisfied with the new lively traffic.

The editor of the provincial gazettes, Superintendent Haken, after all these various successes, felt moved in 1824 to publicly acknowledge in a rally that what was expressed in the Royal Cultural Edict of September 14, 1811, had already come true:

"It is most gratifying to Our (the King's) sentiments that We have finally come to the point where We can set all parts of Our faithful nation in a free state and open up the prospects of happiness and prosperity to even the lowest classes. We implore the blessing of Providence for our good people and for the efforts which we shall all make together to improve the state of the whole and of the individual as far as possible. Yes, and one may add to this that the daily more than visible fact proves to be true what Mr Sack said on the occasion of the announcement of the *Pomeranian Provincial Gazettes* on January 1, 1820, "...and the assurance shall then be fulfilled, given to our most gracious King and to the highest state authorities on several occasions, that a second and third Pomerania in culture and population is to be created in Pomerania.

The new second Pomerania was already there! Full of industrious life and joyful striving, serious work and accomplishment prevailed everywhere. The construction of the first Chaussee in Berlin had been pushed through by Sack and dragged on longer than Sack had wished, for the young *Provinzialbank* that financed it was not yet working satisfactorily. But where there is a will there is a way and a beginning had been made with the internal traffic connections that were still completely missing in the province.

Sack's nature as a leader could look back on truly eminent successes after his ten years in 1826. He was now sixty-two years old and was still inspired by zest for action and devotion to duty. Schön up in Prussia, Vincke in Westphalia and Merckel[114] down in Silesia were the only ones successful like he was! The latter had only returned to his post of Crown President in 1825 after five years of resignation and since then the four-leafed lucky clover of the friendly and

---

114 Friedrich Theodor Merckel, from 1828 von Merckel, the first Crown President of Silesia, also a man of high administrative duties. which he was able to perform in the wars of liberation in Silesia and through which he gained special favor with the King. At the request of Gneisenau, then military governor in Silesia, Merckel was appointed civil governor on June 8, 1813. On his retirement in May 1845, Friedrich Wilhelm IV awarded him the Order of the Black Eagle, he died on 10 April 1846. He came even closer to Sack's family through the marriage of his daughter to Guido Sack (1179 [9/22]), landowner of Steinsdorf, (a nephew of Dr. Joh. Aug. Sack), whose youngest sister Minona Sack was still in her first marriage to the assessor Gustav v. Merckel, in her second marriage to the Crown Government Councillor Felix von Merckel, both younger sons of the Crown President.*

equally energetic supporters of their provinces had been at work again. In addition, Gneisenau, who was close to all of them and Stein, administered the capital now in Berlin as their governor, and Stein, the unremitting one, devoted himself with exemplary zeal as Landmarschall to his Westphalian provincial assemblies and was soon reinstated to them as State Councillor in Berlin. How splendid and delightful everything had turned out above expectations — yes, it was a joy to be able to continue working!

Sack, Crown President of Pomerania

The Last Five Years of his Work 1826-1831

At the end of April 1826 the King had appointed Stein as a member of the Council of State and on May 3 Stein accepted "this proof of considerate benevolence" as he expressed himself in his letter of thanks.

Upon the news of his arrival, Sack and Schön hurried to Berlin to give a warm welcome to the now returned employee in the State Council. Princess Louise von Radziwill had also rushed from Poznan to welcome the old friend. In a later letter Stein spoke out with respect to her and about the reunion with the old friends but also about the uplifting and reassuring change that had taken place in Berlin and the progress that had been noticed everywhere.

In the Ministry of Finance, the insignificant and recently helpless Minister von Klewiz was followed by von Motz. Motz, a Hessian by birth, had already been introduced to Stein when he studied with his fellow student von Vincke in Marburg and Stein met with his brother in Kassel and Giessen in 1792 to protect his property in Nassau. Sack had also met Motz earlier in 1801 in Berlin when he was appointed to the General Directorate. There, in addition to all the departments of the Westphalian and Lower Saxony provinces, their mining and forestry, justice, commerce and excise matters that he had to deal with, he was also a member of the Finance and Law Commission but also of the Higher Examination Commission. Motz had to take his state examination before him as an assessor. The bourgeois family of Witzenhausen, Motz, had become "von Motz" (nobility) through his grandmother, a daughter of the Hessian Chancellor Göddaeus, whose ambition as a widowed Privy Councillor had been to have her children, including the father of Motz, the lawyer and procurator Justin Motz who lived in Kassel, awarded the imperial nobility by the Vienna Hofburg[115]. Justin Motz who was promoted to Chief Appellate Court President under the French King Jerome died soon after Jerome's escape in 1813. His son Friedrich had not been a diligent pupil at the Carolinum College—when he moved to the State University of Marburg in 1792 and joined Vincke's eleven months older son there. It was probably the cheerful, carefree nature that attracted the older, serious Vincke, who at the time lived with the Pietist Jungstilling, to move to him. It was characteristic of Motz even then that when Vincke later moved to Erlangen, he told him of his affection for Marianne N. and he worked against his serious intention to marry her and tried to talk him out of it, because his Marianne was of bourgeois origin. While Motz describes the seven Marburg semesters as the happiest time of his life, his father was highly dissatisfied with his son's use of time, especially when Vincke encouraged him to enter Prussian service. Despite all his encouragement, Motz did not have the diligence of his student friend. He did not hurry to take the

---

115 The name translates as "Castle of the Court", which denotes its origins when initially constructed during the Middle Ages. Initially planned in the 13th century as the seat of the Dukes of Austria, the palace expanded over the centuries, as they became increasingly powerful. From 1438 to 1583, and again from 1612 to 1806, it was the seat of the Habsburg kings and emperors of the Holy Roman Empire, and thereafter until 1918 the seat of the Emperors of Austria.

assessor's examination together with him but preferred to be called upon for all pleasures as director of the ball. In the course of his cheerful life he soon fell in love with a lady who was of course a noblewoman. He was introduced by the Chamber Assessor von Arnstedt to his brother-in-law, the District Administrator of the district von Hagen, and soon passionate flames of love were burning in him for his much celebrated little daughter Albertine. The public engagement took place after Motz had passed his bar exam in 1798. His father-in-law, known as the "great Hagen", granted him residency in the ancestral estate of his first wife, Nienburg, on December 22, 1799, when he led his bride to the altar, since he himself, through his second marriage, remained the owner of the valuable two estates of Eilenstedt and Vollborn. Thus the young junior lawyer from a very recent Austrian aristocracy entered one of the oldest Hessian noble families and as a lucky man was also ensured materially by the fact that the bride brought him the income from Vollborn not far from Nordhausen in Eichsfeld as an inheritance from her mother, Hagen's second wife, into the marriage. Gradually, the young husband thought about taking his assessor's examination and when he registered for it in Berlin, the bourgeois Privy Councillor of Finance Sack was one of his examiners. His school report was not exactly favorable, since the sunny boy of happiness had been making his way in life without the benefit of the burden of knowledge. Only two of his papers had found favor with Sack, the third, the legal one, was declared insufficient. At the oral examination his companion, the Markish chamber student von Rappard, did much better. Finally, after some hesitation, the grade "fair" for Motz was changed to "good".

Motz, who had now been given the position of District Administrator by his father-in-law at the age of 26, had become the father of a daughter before his exams, followed by his first son one year later. He now tried to establish useful contacts with the noble families in his neighborhood and strove to administer the previously leased Vollborn estate himself and become District Administrator in Eichsfeld. Again, in this he was soon to succeed. His father-in-law took over his old position in the Halberstadt district again. When Napoleon took possession of the whole of Eichsfeld after the Battle of Jena in 1806, Motz hurriedly agreed to have the new French government proclaimed by messengers on horseback on the same day and after the Tilsit Peace he soon decided that his Prussian career was over. His father had already been in the service of Jerome and so in 1808 he accepted the post of a royal French tax director in Heiligenstadt, which he held for five years. However, when he first heard news of the victorious Battle of the Nations near Leipzig in 1813 from gypsies, he suddenly decided to become a Prussian District Administrator again. Soon he was able to get a recommendation from his patron von Krusemark to the State Council of Klewiz, whose government had been transferred to Halberstadt, where Motz knew well enough to hand over to an advisor. On December 9, Motz took the oath for the King of Prussia once again and on the 18th of the same month he was appointed director of a new finance commission in the Halberstadt district. From 1815-16 he was appointed governor of Fulda, which was to be incorporated into Prussia as Hessian territory from then on. On October 14, 1815, Motz met the monarch personally in Fulda, where the King of Prussia spent a night in the post house and not in the castle while passing through. Since he knew the King's weakness for the military, he immediately presented the ruler with the schedules for the troops' forthcoming transit marches. He also made a bold move to emphasize his own efforts to defeat Hanau and Fulda at the same time as Prussia and through his skillful eloquence he later knew how to win over Stein and Hardenberg for this plan. The Fulda settlement was to bring him, without Hanau, many disappointments, until he finally managed to achieve a certain amount of success. This monstrous settlement matter could only be concluded in 1845 but Motz had earned his first merit for the Prussian cause. From 1816-21 he was Vice-President of the District of Erfurt, where he often had to negotiate with Humboldt, whose property Burgörner was located in his area. When the district president of Magdeburg died suddenly, Motz stood in for him and while retaining Erfurt, he also became provisional Crown President of the Province of Saxony. As such, he was seen as the man to save the day in the financial calamity that had risen to its highest level in Prussia under Klewiz in 1824. After a long back and forth, calling for memorandums and proposals how to remedy the deficit, Motz, by the favour of the heir to the throne, won more and more of the favor of the still timid King until he appointed Motz as Minister of Finance on January 9, 1825. The appointment decree was not signed until June 11, and the term of office was to begin on July 1.

From the above brief account of Friedrich von Motz's curriculum vitae, one can gauge the feelings with which Sack in Stettin viewed this occupation of the highest financial position in the state, on which he always remained dependent with his far-sighted and far-reaching plans. Henceforth a man eleven years younger than himself was to occupy this position, a man whose educational background he had become thoroughly acquainted with, a man who, unlike himself, had not devoted the greater part of the best years of his life to a hard test for the fatherland and who had always fought the battle as one of the most loyal and best Prussian citizens and liberation helpers but instead, one who had risen on the wings of favor and skill in seizing the opportunity of the moment. Such a man was now appointed to the highest financial post in Berlin, which, after the flagrant handling of his predecessor, was in urgent need of a strong, purposeful remedy. How great this need was, he himself had experienced, for he wrote to Stein in confidence from Berlin as early as the summer of 1817, "Against the immaculate Finance Minister, fate has given me the greatest satisfaction in that I have been appointed here with von Schön to investigate his financial affairs", this is also mentioned in the letters to Focke (see Appendix V, 3).

Very soon the personal attitude of Motz towards Sack when he described a measure taken by the Crown President in Stettin in favor of the Stettin trade, whereby from 1825 the goods via Sundinia were granted a tax reduction of 2½ per cent and the receipt of such goods through the Elbe and Havel was charged with crane money of four silver pennies per hundredweight, to be mistaken, "The advantage of some Stettin trading houses has been bought at too high a price".

Motz, the former chief president of Saxony and district administrator of the Halberstadt district, could not tolerate that the Elbe trade, which he had consolidated by the Elbe Act, suffered losses in favor of the Oder trade, although the State of Prussia and its Minister of Finance could not care less where his customs revenue came from. Even against von Schön in the province of Prussia, who at first was hostile to Motz's customs policy, he soon dealt equally heavy blows as against the Pomeranian Crown President. Later however, the new Minister of Finance achieved great external successes with his customs and excise policy, although nobody knew better than he did to whom he actually owed them.

It came as a great credit to Motz that it was largely the fruit of the effectiveness of his General Tax Director Maassen, whose name deserves a place among the most glorious in German history (but neither his contemporaries nor posterity has given him sufficient recognition). The fame that was due to him was carried off by another. Maassen, the meritorious creator of the Customs Act of 1818 and later successor of Motz in the ministry and who was responsible for concluding the contract that finally brought the German Customs Union into existence, was not a glowing and dazzling personality. Born in Cleve in 1769, the son of a tax receiver, he was more of a scholarly nature. Quiet, modest, cheerful, benevolent, a little stiff with subaltern manners, he distinguished himself in practical business life by his comprehensive knowledge, great clarity of thought and prudence, thoughtfulness, firmness and perseverance, in the Council of State and also later in the ministry as a capable speaker. He and his knowledge however, concentrated on finance alone, while Motz's character, free and bold and animated by verve, also reached over very eagerly to other ministries, so that one soon got the opinion from him that he was even striving to become Prussian Prime Minister.

Maassen, who was six years his senior, was soon able to cope very well with Motz. At times the thoughtful Director General would fall into the bold minister's hands and the latter would laughingly call out with a subtle double meaning, characterizing the position of his employee, "Everything only with moderation!" More serious and true is another well-vouched for exclamation from Motz, "Maassen, I can't live without you!"

In order to ward off the harsh criticism of the Sund customs duty, which had been introduced to boost Stettin's trade, the Stettin merchants submitted a 36-page memorandum through the Provincial Assembly, in which they applied for quite different preferences for their trade in order to bring it back to the level of former times. "The decline of their trade was due to the Elbe Shipping Act of 1821", which Motz at the time had strongly supported.

For Motz, these views and wishes were above all fun. He refuted them in detail and called upon the Stettinians, among others, to prove that they had the capital at their disposal to replace the millions which Hamburg, with the Elbe port and trade, was now crediting to all Prussian industry and world trade. If they had given their case more thought, the angry minister concluded after a long discussion, they would undoubtedly have been decent enough to support a project which was designed in the ruthless interest of the merchants of a single city, incompatible with the existing legislation and the welfare of other provinces and which denied any public spirit! And President Sack lets such things just go through!

Even Cotta's newspaper *Das Inland*, which cautiously worked for Motz's trade policy, gave a detailed refutation of the Stettin paper in three issues. It is possible, says Hermann von Petersdorff in his Motz biography from which these excerpts are taken, that the article was prompted by the circle around the Prussian Minister of Finance.

Stein, who came to Berlin in 1829 to personally support important standing requests for cadastre[116], additional

---

116 A cadastre (also spelled cadaster) is a comprehensive land recording of the real estate or real property's metes-and-bounds of a country.

In most countries, legal systems have developed around the original administrative systems and use the cadastre to define the dimensions and location of land parcels described in legal documentation. A land parcel or cadastral parcel is defined as "a continuous area, or more appropriately volume, that is identified by a unique set of homogeneous property rights".

In 1808 Napoleon ordered a general parcel survey for the areas on the left bank of the Rhine in order to establish a land tax cadastre. The Kingdom of Prussia followed this procedure in 1819 with an instruction regulating this. Around 1822 to 1835, the entire western provinces were surveyed according to the boundary markings made by the landowners and systematically recorded in the original cadastral register of the Rhineland. In the eastern provinces, which were dominated by the nobility, nationwide surveying and recording could only be enforced from May 21, 1861 onwards by taxes and law renewal, which had been made in the first Westphalian state parliament to which he was appointed in 1826, (of which cadastre remained unchanged as well as the additional taxes still being raised by von Motz).

About the journey Stein wrote "it was unsuccessful in regard to all financial matters. Several applications concerning the business of other ministries were considered. The fact that applications relating to the tax system failed in the case of v. Motz can be explained by his personality. He is strong, active, thrifty, chooses his businessmen well — his cash registry system is of good merit, also his participation in the trade associations with the neighboring states of Germany — on the other hand he lacks general scientific education. His former situation was one of a small Hessian Junker family, from which follows narrowness and subalternity of views and a rigid adherence to the preconceived opinion — *Il ne doute de rien*[117]". On Motz's death he even ruled that he lacked education in constitutional and state-economics and a delicate sense of justice. (From Pertz: *Stein's Leben*.)

Pomerania seemed to become a particular cross to bear for Motz and with the province's fervent advocate, Crown President Sack, further controversy arose. Motz had managed to get the King to grant one million taler for road construction in 1826. The *Ritterschaftsbank* looked at Motz with skepticism but since it had once been founded and existed, Motz wanted to use it. In 1827 another 1,200,000 taler were added to the approved sum. The bank was now

---

means of a law that decreed this.
117 He doesn't doubt a thing.

to take over the road construction. Great plans were worked out. Varnhagen and his circle were very disappointed and attributed these measures to the fact that Motz "wanted to get rid of the manor landowners as uncomfortable nuisances by this impractical means". The beginning of the affair was delayed however. Immediately, von Bülow-Cummerow, the director of the *Ritterschaftsbank*, was ready with accusations against Sack. Since Motz was disgruntled against him altogether, he expressed his astonishment at the slow promotion of the matter. Soon however, the party of farmers led by Bülow-Cummerow spoiled its own cause by making repeated demands that were too high. However, the councillors in the ministry became quite irate when the Pomeranian landowners' deputies demanded twice as much money to pay off their private debts to them (probably for the transfer of land to the road construction) as the state was able to use to pay off its own debts. In his battles for the *Ritterschaftsbank*, which was used for the construction of the road and against which one of the aristocratic opponents, von Bülow, the Crown Prince, as governor of Stettin, even attempted to take over (Sack had carried out his first road construction projects with the Pomeranian Provincial Bank), Motz was forced to write in 1828, "This is the third year that the road construction project is being written about but no stone has yet been moved to actually lay out the planned roads". He doubted the seriousness of the government while the province in the meantime had to suffer. Since Sack finally came out in favor of the bank, the King also decided in its favor on 22 March. However, the aristocratic landowners, who believed that the Finance Minister who had became very popular with them, was

Marienburg a. d. Nogat (Malbork Castle)

the main supporter of their welfare, soon made a new demand of one million talers for the purpose of improvement, which the Minister felt compelled to reject on April 30, 1830. From then on, however, the construction of the road continued and in 1830, 30 miles of it already passed through the country.

One sore point in which Sack was hampered by the Finance Minister's lack of concessions, who pointed out the poor state of his finances, was the settling of colonists. He had requested them for the as yet uncultivated barren stretches of his province and was eager to have this carried out.

He was now often hampered by Motz not only in matters of material support for his proposals but also in other respects. Even in the spiritual field, to which Sack had always devoted his special care in church and school matters, the minister believed he had to intervene. The sectarianism of the "revivalists"[118], which was asserted in his province but which was particularly at home in the circles of the landed aristocracy and which only flourished after Sack's death, was repugnant to Sack's soul. He, the thoroughly pious, believing Christian, had been educated and gone through life guided by his Reformed parents as well as by his uncle in Berlin, in the humble, simple confession of the salvation teachings of the Gospels and had never learned anything from the vain separation of the

---

118 Revivalist movements are currents in Christianity that usually owe their existence to a wave of "revival" and that with regard to content particularly emphasize the conversion of the individual, the (individual and community) experience of faith as well as the practical Christian way of life ("life in community with God" and "following Jesus"). Common Christian or confessional dogmas take a back seat to an "original" understanding of a gospel taken directly from the Bible. Revival movements assume that living Christianity begins with man's response to the "call of the gospel" to conversion and spiritual renewal.

Revival in the sense of the revival movement means an incisive subjective experience of sudden seizure by God, which can lead to a radical turnaround in life and complete surrender to God. Revival is especially mentioned when the phenomenon of this experience does not only occur singularly, but when a group of persons or a whole region is affected. Today comparable collective events are usually rather called "spiritual awakening".

In German-speaking Europe Lutheran Johann Georg Hamann (1730-88) was a leading light in the new wave of evangelicalism, the "Erweckung", which spread across the land, cross-fertilizing with British movements.

One can observe two fundamentally opposing theologies here. The revivalist point of view which meant conversion and joining the 'chosen ones' through spiritual rebirth and Sack's view of reliance on the actual teachings of Jesus and living accordingly – a dispute which continues to this day.

rightly believing elect, only from Christ's following simple and docile disciples of old. He was exceedingly tolerant, for he had experienced in the difficult years of the invasion that before the ultimate goal of the rebirth of the fatherland, every selfish, self-emphasizing thought had to give way in favor of the success of the great common cause. He continued unwaveringly to put into practice the beautiful word "that the loss of power must be replaced by the gain of virtue."

However, a diverging assessment between Motz and Sack in matters of religious belief soon became apparent through the agenda question that Sack advocated. In the famous petition of the twelve Berlin clergymen of October 17, 1825 against the introduction of the Agenda[119], on

---

119 King Frederick Wilhelm III intended to establish a liturgical union between Lutherans and the Reformed with the agenda he had developed. The King's aim was to establish a unified Protestant regional church in the state, which had been considerably territorially enlarged after the Congress of Vienna in 1815. To this end, he drafted an agenda that was to be valid in all Protestant churches in Prussia and was to be used literally. In fact, it was intended to go beyond the mere administrative union, a common church leadership for the Lutheran and Reformed Churches. The monarch, who was very interested in the church, benefited from the fact that, as a result of Pietism and Enlightenment, congregations and pastors in Prussia were often hardly aware whether they were Lutheran or Reformed. In many cases the attitude to life was generally Protestant, not specifically Lutheran or Reformed. The King therefore unspokenly presupposed the existence of a doctrinal consensus (and thus a consensus union) between the two denominations. However, the existence of the dogmatic prerequisites was disputed between the Protestant Lutheran Church and the Reformed Church.
The Agenda, which was drafted by the King himself and published in print, was based on the Brandenburg Church Constitution of 1540. The dominance of liturgical elements with the sermon

which Schleiermacher was at the head of the signatories, it was made clear that many preachers would have accepted the Agenda (i.e. a fixed guideline for the leader of the service, which prescribes the choice of Sunday Epistle, the text of the sermon, prayers, etc.) in a second survey only because of the threat of possible consequences. Bishop Ne-

---

at the very end provoked the protest of the Reformed clergy of Berlin Cathedral as early as 1821.

With his attempt to establish this work as the obligatory Protestant service book, Frederick Wilhelm III touched on a controversial point of the Church Constitution: Who in the Protestant Church is entitled to the *ius liturgicum* (right to issue orders of worship)? Some church congregations in Prussia, especially the synods in the Rhine Province and in the County of Mark, believed that this right was not due to the sovereign himself but to the synods and local congregations. The King, on the other hand, insisted on his sovereign regiment of churches. A number of parishes opposed the King's request in 1822. In the same year, the King made the so-called *Unionsrevers* obligatory for ordinations. In 1824 two thirds of the parish priests agreed. Friedrich Schleiermacher, under the pseudonym *Pacificus Sincerus*, criticized the King's request in his paper *Über das liturgische Recht evangelischer Landesfürsten* (On the Liturgical Law of Protestant Princes), which the King attempted to refute in 1827 with the anonymous paper *Luther in Beziehung auf die Preussische Kirchenagende* (Luther in Relation to the Prussian Church Agenda). Schleiermacher again reacted anonymously with the paper *Gespräch zweier selbst überlegender evangelischer Christen über die Schrift: Luther in Bezug auf die Preussische Agende"* ("Luther in Relation to the Prussian Church Agenda").

From 1827 onwards, the dispute was defused by compromises reached separately for the Prussian church provinces: the so-called Berlin Agenda was formally accepted but an appendix with liturgical characteristics and traditions of the respective province could be printed and used. The Cultural Union in Prussia had thus effectively failed. In 1834, King Frederick Wilhelm III also declared that there was no causal connection between the acceptance of the union and the adoption of the Agenda. Accession to the Union was voluntary and did not mean the abolition of the confessional denominations that had been valid up to that point.

ander, a close friend of Motz, felt moved to write a refutation, for which he wanted to collect as many signatures of
clergymen as possible in protest against this outrageous
suspicion. However, on the advice of the new finance minister the refutation was omitted, among other things "because otherwise the Twelve would probably respond with
Schleiermacher's deft pen."

There was a second violent clash with Minister Altenstein.
Altenstein, in order to please his lord and King, who was
very much concerned with getting the agenda through,
fought against Schleiermacher[120], the greatest Protestant
clergyman, as a "malicious clergyman", who was to be
made "harmless" by legal means. In November 1827,
Motz, although he had also voted for the agenda, lodged
an energetic objection to it at the Ministry of State in 1827.

As a result of the agenda dispute, Lutheran confessionalism in
Prussia grew stronger. Some convinced Lutherans did not join the
Union. In Silesia, especially in Breslau, there was the strongest rejection. Through petitions to the King, Lutherans there asked for
the preservation of Lutheran worship, the independence of the
church on the basis of a Lutheran constitution and the independence of the Lutheran church in teaching and life. The initiator
was Johann Gottfried Scheibel, professor of theology and pastor at
the Evangelical Lutheran Elisabeth Church in Breslau. But the
King did not tolerate such open opposition. Scheibel was suspended and expelled from the country. As a result, independent
Lutheran congregations outside the Union formed in Silesia as
well as in other parts of the country. Some of them were persecuted, expelled, expropriated and imprisoned as dissidents, and
prevented from further using the church buildings, sometimes
with the help of the military. Numerous Lutherans emigrated to
Australia and the USA between 1834 and 1839. They founded the
Evangelical Lutheran Missouri Synod in the USA (2.4 million
members, as of 2010). The persecution of the since then so-called
Old Lutherans ended in 1840 under King Frederick Wilhelm IV.

Altenstein, who knew the majority of the ministers to be on his side, was furious about Motz and, in a report to the King, placed him in the appropriate light. Motz, however, knew how to present the hopelessness of criminal proceedings to the King in a very plausible way, "then the twelve preachers would look innocent and only the authority of the government would be damaged". The King must have been convinced of the correctness of this representation, for in any case Schleiermacher was never summoned before the criminal judge. (By the way, Schleiermacher was a close friend of † Bishop Sack and his son, the then court preacher Friedr. Sack (33/7) in Berlin, and belonged to the closest circle of the Sacks, Spalding, Eylert and others.)

---

120 Friedrich Daniel Ernst Schleiermacher (1768-1834) was a German theologian, philosopher, and biblical scholar known for his attempt to reconcile the criticisms of the Enlightenment with traditional Protestant Christianity. He also became influential in the evolution of higher criticism, and his work forms part of the foundation of the modern field of hermeneutics. Because of his profound effect on subsequent Christian thought, he is often called the "Father of Modern Liberal Theology" and is considered an early leader in liberal Christianity. The neo-orthodoxy movement of the twentieth century, typically (though not without challenge) seen to be spearheaded by Karl Barth, was in many ways an attempt to challenge his influence.

Friedrich Christian Adolf von Motz (1775-1830)

These two final results preceded the battle for the ideas of
tolerance that Motz had to fight with Altenstein, in which
Sack was also involved this time. It was now the Government Councillor von Mittelstädt of Stettin, who was married to the sister of Sack's nephew, Government Councillor
Focke, who is known from the history of Bismarck's youth.
Mittelstädt was a Pietist and was connected with the re-

vivalists of Pomerania, the Thaden-Trieglaff[121], Senfft-Pil-sach[122], Puttkamer and others, in whose circle Otto v. Bismarck later found loyal friends, his liberation from religious doubts and his partner Johanna[123]. Mittelstädt was an excellent civil servant, a spiritually and morally high standing person but certainly not free from spiritual

---

121 Adolf von Thadden-Trieglaff (also Triglaw) (1796-1882) was a Prussian landowner, conservative politician and the center of the Pietist-Protestant revivalist movement in Pomerania. He was the father of Marie von Thadden-Trieglaff, who had a great influence on Bismarck.

122 Ernst Karl Wilhelm Adolf Freiherr Senfft von Pilsach (1795-1882) and became Crown President of the Prussian province of Pomerania.

   Senfft was one of the promoters and active preachers of the East Elbe revivalist movement, such as the *Belovian* movement. After 1848 he became co-founder and leading member of the Central Committee for Inner Mission and founder of a "boys' rescue house". Nevertheless, Senfft increased his property holdings in part in a ruthless manner, probably without becoming aware of the resulting social hardship of the former tenants. After his brother-in-law Adolf von Thadden-Trieglaff, he was the most influential representative of the pietist-protestant revivalist movement in Pomerania. Adolf's daughter Marie von Thadden-Trieglaff had initially also been able to win over Bismarck for the aims of the movement. His later *Kulturkampf* against the Catholic Church, however, alienated the Reich Chancellor from the Pietists and led to a sharp confrontation with Senfft in letters.

123 Johanna Friederike Charlotte Dorothea Eleonore, Princess of Bismarck, Duchess of Lauenburg (1824-1894) who was a Prussian noblewoman and the wife of the 1st Chancellor of Germany, Otto von Bismarck. This has information about her has been included here because it throws light on the pietist connection in the Prussian heirarchy.

   She was born at Viartlum manor near Rummelsburg in the Prussian Province of Pomerania (present-day Wiatrołom, Poland), the daughter of Heinrich von Puttkamer (1789–1871) and his wife Luitgarde Agnese von Glasenapp (1799–1863). Her ancestors of the Puttkamer noble family, first mentioned in the 13th century, be-

arrogance. He worked on church and school matters in the Stettin government and his promotion to departmental director was imminent. Since Sack was very satisfied with his person but had no sympathy for his exaggerated religious orientation, it seemed inappropriate to him to entrust Mittelstädt with the management of Stettin's ecclesiastical affairs and he therefore suggested his transfer in February 1829. The Minister of Culture, Altenstein, fully agreed with Sack and submitted a request for transfer to the Minister of Finance. Accordingly, on July 13, 1829, Mittelstädt's transfer to Bromberg was ordered. His brother-in-law, his former predecessor in Stettin, had also been a Pietist and when Mittelstädt learned of the reasons for his transfer, he could justifiably assert that he was at least as qualified as the latter and that a transfer on these grounds constituted a restriction of the Protestant freedom of religion. He lodged a complaint with the King by means of an injunction. Sack and Altenstein, when the King demanded a report, thought it more advisable to leave Mittelstädt, who seemed to be interested in Stettin, there. This conjured up a storm with Motz and Schuckmann. In December 1829 they protested to the Ministry of State that such a back and forth would damage the authority of the state and they now considered Mittelstädt's employment in a province where separatism was rampant impossible. Altenstein cited as his counter-argument that in Poseidon the same post had even been given to a pronounced atheist who, contrary to his and even the Crown Prince's fears, had proved himself well suited to the leadership of the Department of Church and School Affairs. Why should a pi-

---

longed to the Uradel dynasties of Farther Pomerania and were known for their devoted pietism.

ous man like Mittelstädt, who is also vouched for by the chief president, not take over this position? The Bishop of Pomerania, Ritschl, had also declared the appointment of Mittelstädt as a Crown Government Councillor to be harmless. But Motz thought that a retreat on this point would now be regarded as a victory of the separatists "of this unbelievably coherent party". He even now himself spoke out against Mittelstädt's transfer to Poznan, since during his travels it could have been noticed that also in that province the separatist and conventionist movement was quite flourishing and that it would require a stricter supervision of the government not to see it proliferating there as in Pomerania. On January 13, 1830 there was now a meeting of the Ministry of State. The crown prince, Duke Karl of Mecklenburg, the ministers Schuckmann, Lottum, Danckelmann and Motz were present. Altenstein, Bernstörff and the war minister von Hake were missing. It was decided to recommend to the King to let the transfer order stand.

The conflict of opinions about the report to be submitted to the King was now the source of a heated debate. Only recently, a very ungracious cabinet minister to the Ministry of State had spoken out against "the one-sided reports of the ministers, which more often ignore the underlying factual circumstances and the discussions that have already taken place". On March 13, Motz, the Minister of Finance, angrily put his foot down in response to what he considered to be the usual long-winded remarks of his fellow ministers, "I cannot sign the present report. I consider this mysticism and this conventionism to be pernicious for the state and pernicious for the Protestant Church. It is dangerous to want to talk about such an important subject only occasionally and one-sidedly. I consider these mystics to be Protestant Jesuits. I consider their teaching to be totally contrary to the genuine Protestant spirit. I know from observation and experience that this mystical activity has the most detrimental influence on family circumstances and on domestic life. I am convinced that the unlawful proliferation of this mysticism leads directly to the transition into the Roman Church. I cannot concede that the views of the Minister of State Baron von Altenstein are alone competent in this matter. The views of each of the other Ministers are equally competent in this respect, for it is not theological knowledge that counts but the observance and evaluation of existing laws, a knowledge of human nature and a rational view.

The War Minister von Hake also vigorously voted on March 23 for the pursuit of these "excesses down to the roots". Bernstorff, on the other hand, said he would have sided with Altenstein but at this stage abstained from voting. Schuckmann and Lottum voted for Motz. Five weeks later, the Minister of Culture declared that he, for his part, could no longer sign the report. There was another meeting of the State Ministry on May 19, the day before Motz left for Thuringia. Now the Crown Prince, Duke Karl, and again Altenstein, Bernstorff and Hake were missing. The four ministers present, Schuckmann, Lottum, Dunkelmann and Motz, decided, omitting Altenstein's broad statements, to apply again for Mittelstädt's transfer to Bromberg (Bydgoszcz). Motz believed he could leave calmly but before the report went to the King, Motz had his first nervous fit shortly after his return home, in Berlin on June 9. He died of a nervous breakdown on the evening of June 30th and in the midst of his plans and deliberations he was overcome by merciless death. On June 10 he had answered a letter from the Stettin merchants Goldammer and Schleich, in which they asked him for permission to name a newly built, beautiful, large ship capable of transporting 160 loads, after him and to decorate it with his bust. He gladly granted the requested permission. Soon this ship was to be the only vessel on earth and on the water bearing the name "Friedrich von Motz". On June 12, a liver attack had forced him to lie down while at dinner. The illness was of a very nervous nature, until death struck the 54-year-old at the end of the month, quite unexpectedly and painlessly.

At last Motz had stood there quite isolated in his position. The constant disagreements with the Minister of Culture von Altenstein and the way the Minister of Finance expressed himself led to an unusually deep resentment on the part of Altenstein. Motz was also otherwise inclined to sharp attacks against employees in higher positions. Friedrich v. Raumer, although he did not deny his services to the customs union, later criticized Motz for lacking science and for seeing only hindrance in law and rule. Motz had Friedrich Bucholtz[124] write fierce articles against high

---

124 Paul Ferdinand Friedrich Buchholz (1768-1843) was a German writer. He represented bourgeois, early liberal and Saint-Simonistic positions and is considered a pioneer of sociological and positivist thinking in Germany.
Since 1810 he supported Hardenberg's reform policy in his writing. In 1815 Buchholz founded his own journal, which he initially published and edited under the title *Journal für Deutschland, historisch-politischen Inhalts*. From 1820 to 1835, he continued it under the title *Neue Monatsschrift für Deutschland, historisch-politischen In-*

school education and in contrast spread his ideas on
school policy and his great hopes for the vocational
schools. Among other things, Motz was aggressive in his
manner also against England and Count Bülow as Minister of Trade, who, thanks to Huskin's short administration,
had been able to complete the navigational acts that gave
Prussia a better trade-political position especially towards
England. Motz was almost intent on arousing Russia's jealousy against England. As his son Ernst told in this context,
the wish for a closer and neighborly connection with
North America was in the back of his mind. Already in
January 1830, deeply hurt to the core after two ungracious
cabinet orders, Motz had seriously thought of his farewell
"tired of this unworthy treatment" which dragged on until
March. He had been pacified again by a gracious cabinet
order of April 29 but this incident had diminished his willingness to work. For he had had to experience that the
King, who had already given him many proofs of his good
will, including monetary gifts when the finances improved, and in whose special favor he thought he was
standing, expressed his dissatisfaction with his achievements so far in a cabinet order of January 30, in which he

---

halts.

In his writings on social theory, Buchholz proved to be one of the
first representatives of sociological thought in Germany. He also
adopted the positivism of Auguste Comte as well as the teachings
of Henri de Saint-Simon and the Saint-Simonists to a large extent
and made them known in Germany by translating forty treatises
by Comte, Saint-Simon and his students into German and publishing them in his journal.

In his writings, Buchholz represented anti-Jewish resentments, although his polemics on this subject were often economically moti-
vated. Accordingly, Buchholz also turned against the emancipation
of the Jews.

emphasized that Motz's management had not fulfilled the demands which the Immediate Commission for the financial administration, which was at present attached to Minister Klewiz, had made but was rather still far from the goal. Furthermore, by expressing concerns about the security of the financial situation, he instructed Motz to comment on individual items in his administration and to correct them if necessary. Since then Motz had only ever worked on his justification in memoranda and reports, which obviously had completely worn away his nerves.

On July 17 *Maassen*, Motz' successor, received an Immediate Report from Altenstein for signature in which the appointment of Mittelstädt to the Crown Government Council in Stettin was approved. Maassen refused to sign the report, saying that it was a matter of conscience for him to act in Motz' interest and that he himself agreed with his views. The Crown Prince also sent the report back without a signature. Schuckmann, Lottum and Danckelmann did an about face, indicating now that they did not want to incur the odium of initiating religious persecution.

Thus a cabinet order of August 25 decreed the appointment of Mittelstädt to the Stettin Crown Government Council.[125]

---

125 Ernst von Mittelstädt, born on August 4, 1785, died on January 11, 1870, was probably a friend of the above-mentioned circle of Pietists but himself did not belong to the group of extremists, "the Revivalists". He and his wife Marie, née Focke, were far too worldly and tolerant. Mittelstädt was also later fully recognized in government circles and died as the Consistorial President. Incidentally, Sack was later followed by Fr. Senfft von Pilsach, (1852-1866), from the circle of the "Revivalists", as the Crown President of Pomerania.*

For Sack a more peaceful time began again where he could develop his many ventures and also put his own house in order.

Already on June 28, 1828[126] he and his wife Marianne had replaced their bridal testament, which they had made before their marriage, for the second time with a new one, which they gave to the court in Oberwiek near Stettin for safekeeping. (See Appendix VIIa).

The year 1830 saw the three hundred year memorial festival of the Augsburg Confession, which Sack celebrated in Stettin and in the province with church and popular celebrations everywhere. This summer he used his holiday to see his friend Stein again in Cappenberg and to visit the grave of his father, who was buried 20 years before in the nearby cathedral in front of the Neuthor, in the local churchyard, called *Unser lieben Frauen-Ueberwasser* (Church of our Lady Beyond the Water). An upright sandstone epitaph in Empire style with the inscription marked the lonely place of rest:

Carl August Sack
born November 13, 1721
Judicial Councillor with the Government
of Cleve
Widower of Gertrude Margaretha Notemann;
died April 9, 1810.

From there they went on to the Rhineland where Marianne's brother still served as district president in Aachen. Then they continued to Cleve to the mother's grave. In

---

126 Sack died on exactly the same day some three years later.*

Düsseldorf the art collections were visited — his brother-in-law Sethe and his sister Philippine (whom he was to lose in a few months' time) had long since moved to Berlin, where the former was president of the Prussian Court of Cassation. His brother Ernst was married to Sethe's sister, since 1820 he had already been the financial councillor and provincial tax director of Magdeburg. Under von Inger-sleben's administration everything on the Rhine had changed considerably and had become stranger to him than he would have thought.

When he returned home, he enjoyed the abundance of fruit in the autumn in his beautiful garden out in Ober-wiek. The fruit grew on the trees he had planted himself, because he was a fruit grower with a special liking for the sunny summer in the north. It was a particularly beautiful property that Sack had acquired there by purchase. In addition to the large, stylish residential building, there were, apart from the coachman's house, stables and sheds, an orangery and greenhouses as well as a splendid, extensive park with fruit and vegetables. Here with his own produce he always enjoyed his recreation after the workload of his job. He was especially happy when he could secretly place a well grown fruit onto the plate of his Marianne.

His profound sensibility had found full domestic happiness at her side. Although she did not give him children, he shared with her the joy of those of her late sister Jacobi and the rich child blessings of his own siblings in Berlin and far away. Some letters that have survived in Jacobi's family bear witness to the intimacy of his family relations (see Appendix VI). Two of them date from 1820, when

Sack went to Teplitz to bathe because of his physical ailments. Later, after living in his rural estate with more outdoor exercise, he seems to have had less regular need for this. Later he often visited his friend von Bülow on his estate Rieth near Ueckermünde, where Sack and his wife Marianne also met Carl and Agnes Focke. The loving disposition of the affectionate spouse and caring uncle of the family speaks from the letters of 1828.

In the spring of 1831 on April 18, Sack suffered a severe stroke quite unexpectedly and the doctors gave up hope right away. His will to live and his creative urge seemed once again to be victorious in the fight against death. He felt compelled to hand over the Regional Presidency of his Stettin district, which he had been co-administering since 1816, to his first Crown Presidential Councillor and Vice-President, von Bonin[127] but did not find it easy to become friends with his views and actions. Sack was animated by

---

127 Wilhelm Friedrich Fürchtegott von Bonin (1786-1852) was Crown president of the Prussian Province of Pomerania.

Bonin was a government assessor in Stettin before he took part in the wars of liberation between 1813 and 1814. In 1816 he was dismissed from the Prussian army as cavalry captain and became a member of the government council in Koblenz. In the same year he became the vice-president of the administrative district of Stettin in Pomeranian Stettin, where he held office until 1832. From 1824 he was a member of the newly formed Provincial Assembly of the Province of Pomerania.

From 1832 to 1834, von Bonin was president of the administrative district of Köslin in Köslin in Pomerania and in the same office from 1834 to 1835 he moved to the administrative district of Merseburg in the provincial Saxon city of Merseburg.

From 1835 until his death in 1852, von Bonin was Crown President of the Province of Pomerania and at the same time President of the administrative district of Stettin. In 1843 he was appointed High Privy Councillor with the title of Excellency.

a strict sense of justice and had no respect for the person he was dealing with. He always confronted unwarranted presumption, selfishness and conceit with dismissive sharpness. Despite many a bad experience, he constantly took care of the big landowners, because he did not extend his aversion to arrogant individuals to the whole class. He emphasized time and again that it was desirable and necessary that the old, good Pomeranians of noble families should remain in possession of the estates due to them. Bismarck recounts from his youth that he also remembered the Crown President Sack as a guest of his parents at Kniephof. (Bismarck, *Bücher der Rose*).

It was astonishing and admirable how on April 23, five days after that first breakdown, he once again summoned his faithful Chief Presidential Councillor Frauendienst to present the records. On May 7, in an injunction, in which he advocated the retention of the landowners of Zimmermannshorst in the possession of their farms, he wrote the beautiful words which give a deep insight into his being, "Among the most rewarding and fortunate events of my life I count the happiness of often being the executor of Honorable Royal Majesty's grants of mercy and of the benefactions bestowed upon the Prussian State and especially upon the Pomerania which I love. Honorable Royal Majesty has given me numerous opportunities since my now forty-five years of service as Crown President and I hope, if God gives me life and health, to have many more opportunities to rejoice in that happiness, since Honorable Royal Majesty never tires of beneficence and I still find myself strong enough to be the executor of Honorable

Royal Majesty's commands and benefactions". (From the local calendar 1925 for Ueckermünde district.)

As the warmer season approached, the fierce enemy cholera had already announced itself from the east and soon it had been introduced into the province of Prussia, already spreading epidemically in the neighboring ports. In Riga 2743 persons had fallen ill, 996 of them had recovered, 1332 had died, in Gdansk 87 military personnel, 272 civilians, together 359, 43 of them had recovered, 254 had died. Sack was deeply concerned about his province and spared no means and no decree to prevent further infestation by land or sea and to have all sanitary precautions taken. Eleven days before his end he had a lengthy publication written for the *Königl. Preussische Stettiner Zeitung* ("Royal Prussian Stettin Newspaper"), for preventive care of the population. Although he had delegated part of the management to Vice-President von Bonin, who published the article on July 1, he declared himself ready to negotiate at any moment on important issues. He wrote impatiently with regard to the danger of cholera and the forthcoming wool market in Stettin, "These urgent business matters demand my presence in the city but I must still live here in my garden on doctor's orders".

The bad weather did not allow the intended bathing trip either, "but I do not want to be idle".

Three days later he suffered another nervous breakdown. One had often seen him, who in recent years had worn remarkably fast to old age, wandering lonely in early spring to the place in his garden that he had chosen as his resting place. Could he have secretly felt the invisible companion at his side, reminding him of the near end of his daily work? With the increasing summer heat, the number of minor strokes had also increased until finally, after bravely resisting, his strength broke completely. With that the quiet, worldly mind, as in the days of childhood, came back to his soul, which took leave of everything that was earthly, full of divine peace. "Now the way to happiness is open to me", the daughter Gertrud heard him say to his sister Sethe, who died in the autumn of 1830, the day before the morning of his death. In the night of June 28 he gently slumbered into eternity. In October he would have reached the age of 67. His dear Focke pressed his eyes closed.

On the front page of the *Kgl. Preussische Stettiner Zeitung* ("Royal Prussian Stettin Newspaper") of July 1, 1831, no. 52, the government announced his death with the following words:

"This morning at half past two the Royal Privy Councillor and Crown President of the Province of Pomerania, Knight of the Order of the Red Eagle First Class with Oak Leaves and the Iron Cross, His Excellency Dr. Johann August Sack, aged 67, passed away gently as a result of a nervous stroke. The State, which the immortalized man served with unshakable loyalty, perseverance and rare distinction for almost half a century under the government of three monarchs, even in the most difficult circumstances, loses one of its most trusted servants. The Province of Pomerania, which he served as its head for fifteen years, loses one of its memorable benefactors, to whom it was devoted with intimate and general affection. At the same time, we lose a strong and benevolent leader and a faithful and fatherly friend.

What the deceased did in his long and eventful life, what his strong and religious sense, his untiring activity and his rich and benevolent mind did for the state and especially for the best of the province of Pomerania and its inhabitants that was entrusted to him, secures him a grateful and honorable memory among our descendants and a place in the ranks of our most excellent statesmen.

The Government.

This announcement took up the left half of the title page, on the right was the following obituary:

"Due to the death in the night from 27th to 28th of the same year of the Royal Privy Councillor and President of Pomerania Dr. Sack, Knight of the Red Eagle Order of First Class and of the Iron Cross, the fatherland, science, church and school has suffered a loss, which the members of the undersigned consistories and school colleagues feel all the more deeply and painfully, the more they have had the opportunity to see in the deceased the faithful, bourgeois German man, to venerate the joyful and zealous promoter of scientific culture, the protector of the churches and schools, the courageous and witty representative of everything that could contribute to the advancement of the noble, good and beautiful, in the Pomeranian land entrusted to his care by the King's Majesty that has become so dear to him in a series of 15 years. "The Lord had made his life a blessing for many", that this word of the Holy Scripture applied in the fullest sense to our friend, patron and leader, who is now asleep, will be recognized by all those to whom he was so willingly close through counsel and action. Therefore, his memory remains as a blessing, not only in our Province but also in the whole of our German Fatherland. For from the banks of the Rhine to the shores of the Baltic Sea, the memory of the noble man will live on, who was active for King and Fatherland until his last breath with devoted sacrifice.

Stettin, June 29, 1831.
Royal Consistory and School Council
of Pomerania.

Among the advertisements in the same newspaper issue of July 1, 1831, the death of her husband was placed at the top of the list:

At half past two this morning, following a nervous stroke in his 67th year of life and in the 33rd year of our happy marriage, the gentle passing away of my beloved husband, the Royal Privy Councillor and Crown President of Pomerania, Dr. Johann August Sack, I hereby announce with a grief-stricken heart to our mutual relatives and the numerous friends and acquaintances of the immortalized man.

Stettin, June 28, 1831.

Marianne Sack, née von Reiman.

The supplement to No. 52 of the *Preussische Stettiner Zeitung* ("Prussian Stettin Newspaper") introduced an essay continued in the supplements to No. 53 of July 4 and No. 54 of July 8 entitled: **Memories from the Life of His Excellency Johann August Sack (all titles listed) under the motto:**

Hail to Him, O Messenger of Peace
the one with the green olive branch in his right hand,
to our storm-tossed earth eternal love proclaimed!
Though in sorrow and pain we draw near
His grave, but praying: "Lord let him rest
in peace. Amen!" Noble, rest
for softly you have finished and we shall follow!

The author of the short summary of his life, written with great veneration, was E. Bernhardt of Stettin, a government and school councillor who had come closer and become dear to Sack in recent years. The meaningful and pious dedication concludes with a fiery appeal to youth in the sentences:

"And now I turn to you, young men of my fatherland, with the words of a great German (Johannes von Müller), a voice from the tomb from which we come and on which I have laid down a flower in silent melancholy. Fulfill the place God has given you for in it nothing seems too high for you to reach and nothing so low that you may neglect it. In this way kings are made great and in this way the man of the Spirit acquires eternal laurels. In this way the father of the house raises his family above poverty and lowliness... With every stroke, with every elevation, with every reversal of the wheel on the mystical chariot of the government of the world, the command of wisdom, moderation and order (and of the fear of God, the beginning of wisdom and its crown) re-sounds. He who ignores it is judged. People of the earth and dust, princes of the earth and dust, how terribly this is done is revealed in history. (Ah, also the history of our days!)".

Written on July 1, 1831.

In the main issue of the *Königl. Preussische Stettiner Zeitung* ("Royal Prussian Stettin Newspaper") of July 4, 1831, there was also the following supplication by an unknown author:

At the tomb of our most distinguished leader

We stand at your grave, dignified old man, deeply grieved, humbly bearing the resolution of the divine will which called you from your busy career and we pay you the most heartfelt thanks for your restless activity and your always lively sense of all that is good, recalling in memory the numerous proofs of your strong work and your affectionate devotion to everyone who approached you.

Who, like you, encouraged you to faithful devotion to king and fatherland when your mouth spoke with enthusiasm about the celebrated names? Who knew, like you, with the dignified firmness that must clothe a civil servant of your rank, how to establish such trust in the authorities as you did, who did not spurn it but regarded it rather as a duty to always collect the judgment of expert men before you proceeded to the execution of every object of technical reference? Who has ever possessed the art, as you did, in the way of the modest participation granted to the citizen, of voting for your orders with love? Therefore, my dear fellow citizens, let us use as a shining example his sublime example of restless activity, strict legality, ardent love for the throne and fatherland and true religiosity, offering to our adored King the most heartfelt and sincere thanks that he has given him, especially him, to our Province. We respectfully beseech our beloved Sovereign that he may be content to appoint as successor to our good Father Sack a man who is, as he was, a man of the people and who will bring to fruition the seeds which he has sown with loving care in our hearts and throughout Pomerania.

The same No. 53 of July 4 brought the following acknowledgement under three stars:

*   *   *

The great sympathy expressed yesterday in the many people accompanying me on the last course of the earthly remains of my dear husband, who had fallen asleep in repeated loving remembrance of all those who remained behind, was particularly comforting to me. With a touched heart I therefore express my deepest gratitude to all those who in this way showed me their sympathy for my great and irreplaceable loss and humbly submit to the Almighty

God, his wise and inscrutable counsel that he may mercifully preserve them from a similar fate for a long time to come.

Stettin, July 2, 1831.

Marianne Sack née Reiman.

This newspaper No. 53 published the following report in its front page about the funeral celebration, in which the participants were estimated at 600 people:

Stettin, July 1, 1831.

This afternoon between 3 and 4 o'clock the solemn funeral of the remains of Excellency the Crown President Dr. Sack took place in his garden in Oberwieck near Stettin (formerly Velthusian).

The ringing of all the bells in the city at noon already indicated the impending funeral service. When the hour of the funeral came, the procession also set off under the ringing of all the bells on its way to that place. The choir of the local town musicians, who played the song „Jesus meine Zuversicht" (Jesus my Hope), was followed by the coffin, on the lid of which the medals of the deceased lay upon a black velvet cushion. The four corners of the shroud were carried by four governmental officers. The coffin was surrounded by the servants of the deceased and then, led by two clergymen, the head of the Government Councillor Focke was the next mourner present. These were joined by the entire Protestant and Catholic clergy and behind them all the royal civil servants and military officers, some in groups and some in deputations. Deputies of the estates and the countryside, the magistrate, the town councillors, the merchants, the riflemen's guild, the high school and a large number of local citizens, without any further particular order or observation of a hierarchy as if by chance and free choice of those present, none of whom were invited to the funeral, had brought them together.

Arriving at the tomb, the Consistory Councillor Dr. Richter delivered the eulogy, in which the long, active work of the immortalized man, his unshakable love and loyalty for king and fatherland, his faithful love for his husband, was recited after the seminarists had sung the first three verses of the above-mentioned song. His benevolently comprehensive mind and above all his strong, simple and religious understanding were emphasized and the remains of the deceased were honored in such a way that his earthly and with God's help blessed work acquired a well-founded entitlement. (For the funeral oration see Annex VIII)

There was a deep silence in the countless assembly.

Everyone felt the great loss with pain and countless tears following the man who had fallen asleep into the silent tomb.

Peace to his ashes!

Among Meinhold's[128] poems the following is found as a funerary inscription dedicated to him:

Here lies August Sack in the Lord God.
A man who was great without ribbon or star,
A man who a father would never become
Left many thousands of orphans on earth,
A man who was noble, without being,
By his virtue, by his heart alone.
Go home wanderer and do your best,
That you also die as such a nobleman!

Sack's resting place was located in the middle of a large rotunda, at first surrounded at a distance by seven young oak trees, then by a lawn, which was bordered by a wide garden path, also in a circular form, followed by higher bosquets with flowering ornamen-

---

128 Wilhelm Meinhold, as a young poet dealing with the history of Pomerania appreciated and encouraged by Jean Paul, rector and preacher of Koserow on the Island of Usedom.*

tal shrubs, through which two small connecting paths led from the large park to the consecrated place, to which a room of 8 square rods (one rod is 4 square metres) was dedicated.

The city requested and a decree of the King published in the *Kölnische Zeitung* ("Cologne Newspaper") in 1831 approved that the garden arrondissement with the grave of the outstanding civil servant should carry the name *Sackensruh* ("Sack's Rest").

In the same issue of the *Preussiche Stettiner Zeitung*, which had first announced Sack's death, it was published from Berlin on June 27 that the King had deigned to appoint the Government Councillor Focke to Stettin as Crown Government Councillor and Director of the Department for Domains, Forests and Direct Taxation at the Government Council of Liegnitz.

Marianne received the news that Baron Karl von und zum Stein had been recalled to his heavenly home in Cappenberg on June 29, 1831, the very same day. In this way the friends united on their way to the hereafter. On June 30, in Münster in Westphalia, the Crown President von Vincke wrote in his diary, "Letter from Krüger, who brought me the loss of the honest Crown President Sack, also a dear friend, fellow traveller and ministerial colleague of von Stein.

Marianne received the following handwritten letter from His Majesty the King in the first half of July, among the countless expressions of condolence from all parts of the country:

Even before receiving your honored letter, I had become aware of the great loss that you, the King and the country had suffered through the death of your husband. How much I esteemed and honored the deceased and with what true friendship I was attached to him is known to everyone, including you. Your great kindness led you to tell me yourself of the sad event, thus giving me the desired opportunity to express to you the sentiments which inspired me towards the deceased and which now make me feel his loss all the more painfully. My condolences are all the more vivid, however, and my sympathy is all the more heartfelt for your just pain, my esteemed one. Receive the expression of it with the kindness of which you have given me so much evidence and may you continue to do so.

To your most devoted servant

Frederick Wilhelm.

Potsdam, July 7, 1831.

Marianne wrote to the brother-in-law Jacobi, Privy Councillor at the State Chamber of Auditors in Potsdam:

Stettin, July 23, 1831.

Dear brother!

For your loving letter I thank you most sincerely. Also your dear wife for your participation in my great loss. Even though I had long been prepared for the fact that my dear husband would not be with us for long, I was deeply saddened by the certainty of his death. I saw how gradually his strength was diminishing, becoming very thin and how, in the first seizure that occurred on the 18th of April, his memory was severely affected, for his brain and spinal cord were very weakened by the stroke. There have been four relapses. However, my good man had recovered nicely here in the garden, walking around a lot. Eight days before he went to sleep a nervous stroke occurred. He himself believed that it was a nervous fever because he felt so weakened but this was not the case. Unfortunately, my good man was paralyzed, especially on the left side and the sick man had to take every little help he could and fantasized a lot. Only the last two days, when he could not get out of bed, his thoughts were clear. He must have felt very weak and so he said goodbye to all of us in the most loving way — oh it was terrible for me to be so brave. My dear husband laid his hand on my head, blessed me, thanked me for all my love and care. As often as I came to his bed he recognized me, extended his hand to me in a friendly way and gave me a kiss. His last words were greetings to all my loved ones. He died with the greatest peace and all his utterances were full of love. Forgive me dear brother, if I make your sorrow revive, I know how much you loved your brother. But I thought it would be nice to hear about some of the dear departed one's last days.

Fourteen days before my husband's illness I asked him if I should not answer the last letter he received but my dear husband wanted to write himself. However, he did not answer private letters and up to ten days before his end he had not yet handed over the business, although he had been on vacation here for fourteen days. All our entreaties and suggestions did not help. The only thing that annoyed my husband was when I asked him not to work. Otherwise he was ill, which actually lasted for ten weeks and he was always friendly and calm, never excited and indescribably patient, never complained and had a lot of courage until two days before his death. Finally, all that was necessary was to ask heaven to take him in, for his condition was very distressing.

I intend to stay here in Stettin. The garden is now twice as valuable to me where my beloved had chosen his own quiet spot two years ago. The place is very beautiful and he expressed his wish to Gertrude Sethe that I should one day be placed with him and that is also my wish. I have been by his side for so many years and for the last eight days I have not been permitted to leave him for a moment and have found peace of mind in the fact that I could always be with him. In the first days of September I am thinking of bringing Gertrude back to Berlin. My brother-in-law Sethe has been kind enough to offer to help me with my financial matters. Whether I will still have the pleasure to see you this autumn my dear brother, I cannot yet determine.

The participation in my husband's death has been very great here. People speak of him with great love and respect. Today a great funeral music of Mozart was performed in the Jacobi Church. At his funeral, where certainly six hundred people were gathered here in the garden, the mourning and participation was very great and now many people walk to my husband's grave every day. The city will call the area around the garden *Sackensruhe*. A deputation that came to me eight days ago asked for this. May I ask your wife and children to send their warmest regards. Gertrude is recommended. Farewell,

M. Sack.

The great general mourning that had spread throughout the province was expressed on July 25, 1831 in a moving commemoration ceremony in the Jacobi Church in Stettin, where Mozart's Requiem was performed in honor of the deceased.

The leaders of the Merchants' Corporation, founded by Sack in 1821, had already issued an appeal for the erection of a memorial on July 8, 1831. The location chosen was a hilly elevation in the part of the grounds in front of the Anklam Gate, which extended as far as the Unterwiek. The King's permission was required because of the fortress fund to which that part still belonged. It was granted on August 11, 1831. In the last five years of his life, Sack had achieved a great deal for this first green belt around the town, the so-called plantation had flourished wonderfully. "Simple and unpretentious as the deceased himself had been, a monument in cast iron was to rise in the shade of those trees (oaks) he loved so much." The Privy Construction Director Schinkel in Berlin was approached and two drafts were made, one of which was then executed. A cast-iron pyramid in the shape of a cabinet was then erected corresponding exactly to the four points of the compass, after a barge from the iron foundry of Woderb & Egells had transferred it from Berlin to Stettin with a weight of 21½ hundredweight. In the open sections of the upper half, one Genius each, with laurel wreaths in their hands, was depicted hovering. The inscriptions were placed underneath on the east and west sides. The front, facing the city, bears the words in translation:

Monument of Gratitude and Veneration
from the Merchant Community in Stettin
1831

On the back, facing the River Oder, it says:

The Royal Real Privy Councillor Crown President of Pomerania.
Knight of the Great Red Eagle Order and the Iron Cross
Dr. Joh. August Sack
Born in Cleve on October 7, 1764
Died in Stettin on June 28, 1831

The memorial was ready to be erected at the end of August 1832. However, since the latticework cast in Gleiwitz only arrived after another six months, the unveiling could first take place on March 31, 1832, "early in the morning in the silence". The modesty of the gift harmonized best with a silent procedure, according to the records. Eight oaks were planted around the fence, four of which have grown into mighty trunks with overshadowing crowns.

The monument had to be freshened up once in 1871 and on the day of the hundredth birthday of the person it celebrates. On October 7, 1864, a wreath of artificial flowers was placed on it by an unknown hand. The same donation adorned in again on June 15, 1874, the 50th anniversary of the Otto festival, which Sack first called to attention in his Pomerania, on which Archbishop Otto of Bamberg had successfully spread the message of Christian salvation 700 years ago in the still pagan coastal region.

The laying of the keystone for the large fortification of the deepened harbor took place on the pier in Swinemünde (Swinoujscie) on August 3, 1831. Mr Busch, director of the port, emphasized in his speech:

> Now that the work has been accomplished, it is fitting that we should remember with melancholy gratitude the spirit of a statesman who, with his rare energy, gave the first impulse for this work. He first showed his monarch the advantages and presented the necessity of the construction, a task which he then promoted with his youthful fiery zeal, which remained undiminished even in old age.
>
> What the Crown President Sack worked and created in Pomerania the annals of the province will not conceal. Here above all we hear his glory in the murmur of every wave that breaks at this mighty bulwark. We cannot give

him a jubilant cheer, but in the tears we weep over his grave, a silent libation is brought to his memory.

General Feldmarshall August Count Neidhardt von Gneisenau died in Poznan during the night of August 23-24, where he had been travelling from his castle Erdmannsdorf near Warmbrunn, as he had been given the supreme command of the four eastern army corps against the Polish uprising approaching the Prussian border. He had been killed by the rampant cholera epidemic at the age of 71. All three friends were born in October, Sack on the 7th, Stein on the 26th, Gneisenau on the 27th. They were all members of the Council of State and were all recalled to their eternal homeland in the same year.

The *Kölnische Zeitung* (Cologne Newspaper) reported on October 20, 1832, that a new work of art had been created from the medal coin of the Royal General Wardein[129], the medal in memory of the highly deserving Royal Privy Councillor etc. etc. Joh. Aug. Sack. The commemorative coin shows the portrait of the completed work together with an inscription on the main side. On the reverse the province of Pomerania in female form is decorated with the mural crown, which has just completed the inscription of the name Sack on a monument and is about to decorate it with an oak

---

129 This would have been Gottfried Bernhard Loos (1773-1843) who was a German *Wardein* and entrepreneur. The duties of a *Wardein* included supervising the *Münzmeister* (minting master) and the stock of precious metals used in minting. He was also responsible for the quality of the alloys and the accuracy of weights and measures.

wreath. The explanatory caption reads: *Tantae Virtutis Tantique Meriti Immemor Pomerania*[130].

In the district of Rügenwalde (today Darlowo) the memory of Crown President Sack lives on in the village of Sackshöhe (today Zakrzewo), which was founded on September 28, 1828, 5 kilometers east of Rügenwalde and named after him. In 1859 the three settlements at Ober-, Mittel- and Untersackshöhe became an independent municipality. In 1863 and 1895 the school was extended — since 1925 there is a new school building — in the same year the population was 263 persons.

Grave in the old Grabov Cemetery in Stettin

In Cleve, Sack's birthplace, a new street was named Sackstrasse in his honor. The burial place, which was once consecrated to the *Sackensruh*, was to remain there for only 14 years. On the grounds outside in Ober-

---

130 Regardless of merit and power mindful of Pommerania.

wieck, where the Sack property and park was located, the old passenger station of Stettin has been standing for almost nine decades. On April 23, 1841, the entire Sack property, including all residential buildings, orangeries, stables, etc., had to be purchased by the Berlin-Stettin Railway Company which in turn assumed the obligation to "leave the burial place of Blessed Crown President Sack in its present condition for eternity". This contract of sale concluded before the royal district court was, however, invalidated only a few years later by the fact that the Berlin-Stettin Railway had to cede this part of the garden with Sack's resting place to the tax authorities and could no longer keep the obligation to care for *Sackensruh*. As a result, the body and gravestone were moved to the municipal burial ground in front of the King's Gate in 1845 and Mrs Sack's representative took over the maintenance of the memorial, which was newly planted with a young oak tree. On July 7, 1848, Privy Bourwieg signed an agreement on behalf of his mandatary, according to which the tax authorities retrospectively reimbursed the total costs of the translocation and also paid the city a redemption capital for the future maintenance of the gravesite, which was followed by a redemption payment on July 24, 1848. On October 24, 1848, the City Council and the City Assembly of Stettin committed themselves forever to maintain the tomb, vault, latticework, tombstone, mound and tree section in the best condition as taken over on October 23, and to hand over the key to the widowed Lady President at any time.

Vice-President von Bonin was not immediately appointed as Sack's successor; from 1832 to 1836, the Royal Privy Councillor von Schönberg was the first to administer the business of the Crown President. In 1836, the Royal Privy Councillor von Bonin was then appointed as Crown President of Pomerania and remained so until 1852.

Marianne, who had initially remained resident in Stettin, moved to Berlin at the end of the 1830's, probably when her brother, the former Government President von Reiman, was appointed to the capital as Royal Crown Privy Councillor.

Since according to the mutual will made by the spouses in 1828 the surviving partner, i.e. since 1831 Marianne, was the sole owner of the entire property, she drew up a new will in Berlin on February 14, 1841, which she still provided with a codicil on December 1, 1846. When it was drawn up, she withdrew an earlier will made on November 20 and deposited it with the Court of Appeal.

Marianne lived in Berlin, Unter den Linden 56, with a society lady, Miss Emma von Römig, to whom she granted a life pension in her last will and testament.

Marianne Sack followed her husband in death on November 9, 1851 and was buried at his side, according to her wishes, in the old Grabow cemetery in Stettin, in the same crypt that had contained his earthly remains since 1845. From her last will, which was published in its 28 paragraphs and many subsequent provisions on December 27, 1851, and supplemented by an extensive inventory, it is remarkable that the Crown President owned a fine collection of commemorative coins, about fifty pieces, in gold, silver, bronze and iron, all of which had been minted on historical occasions. As the only gift donation, which he, the conscientious official (see section 2 of this commemorative publication) probably could not refuse this one and only time, three porcelain vases from the King were found in his estate! The Berlin Manufactory awarded him the Pomeranian General Landscape as a gift of honor on the occasion of the unification festival in 1821, while the city authorities of Stettin honored him with their letter of honorary citizenship. Marianne determined that the vases should be distributed (by lot) under the Privy Fiscal Councillor Ernst Sack of Egeln and the Chief President of the Higher Regional Court Max. Sack of Ratibor and the Assessor of the Higher Regional Court Guido Sack of Breslau. In family portraits the will mentions the will of the Crown President himself, ("to be kept by the Privy Fiscal Councillor Ernst Sack, as well as all documents, letters and decorations"), the painting of her father-in-law, Judicial Councillor Carl August Sack (inherited by the mineralogist August Sack of Halle[131]), the painting of Sack's mother-in-law, née Gertrude Nottemann (inherited Crown President Sethe of

---

131 This August Sack, a godson of the Crown President, later also called Stein-Sack, then had the other Sack ancestral portraits of Georg Sack and his wife painted, which always continue in the male Sack line in branch XXVIII at his behest (today located with Justice Councillor Detlof-Sack, Mühlhausen) and are supplemented there as far as possible. These are not, as was assumed, from the Crown President.*

Berlin). Her own oil painting and that of her immortalized niece, the Majoress von Zalukowsky, Mrs Marianne bequeathed to her nephew, the then Higher Regional Court Assessor, later Supreme Court Councillor August Jacobi.[132]

When these few testamentary dispositions are presented from among the multitude of the same, we are once again greeted by a breath of fresh air from the twenty years of private memories that the companion, who had the privilege of being Joh. August Sack's wife for thirty-two years, shared after his departure. It is clear from all her instructions that she cultivated communication with his relatives as with her own, with the same family love and that she guarded his memory in a respectful and reverential way in her fidelity to him.

---

132 The portrait of the Lady President in this document was taken by the kindness of Miss Lucie Jacobi (1333 [12/2125]) from the oil painting of Marianne by means of photography.*

Monument of Gratitude and Veneration
from the Merchant Community in Stettin
1831

Conclusion

Thus, the writer concludes the compilation of the manifold details that were presented to her while investigating the traces of the outstanding Sack ancestor's works and achievements. How many more have been erased and faded or withheld from her? Yet it is now incontrovertibly certain that despite all the fates of the post-(first world) war period, which have once again battered down the trade and transformation of Pomerania's landowners, the memory of Dr. Joh. August Sack lives on in indelible gratitude.

The celebrations at Sack's gravesite, such as at the memorial to the Merchants' Association, on the occasion of the hundredth anniversary of his death on June 28, 1931, bear eloquent witness to this. In addition to the memorial speeches and meaningful wreath donations with dedication ribbons, first of all by the representative of the Sack Family Foundation, among them especially the members from his home province in the Rhineland. Furthermore, the current President of Pomerania, the State Governor on behalf of the Provincial Administration, the Mayor as representative of the city of Stettin and the Chairman of the Society for Pomeranian History and Antiquity, all again emphasized the great merits of the immortalized person at his newly restored burial mound. It was the current president of the Chamber of Commerce and Industry who commemorated Sacks' immortal importance for Pomerania's trade concluding his speech with a quotation from the poem by Dr. O. Altenburg on Sack, with which the then head of the Merchant's Association had ended his speech at the inauguration of the monument in 1833.

The wording of the poem was as follows:

He who sees his life's purpose
in fulfilment of his duties,
with undying loyalty
for Fatherland and King,
even dying, still his duty done
finds sweet solace in death,
whose praise shall not be stilled,
who blessed the whole of Prussia.
So do not shun admirer's hand,
to add leaves to the wreath
sworn to state and King with thanks.

With the words: "Whoever recognizes the highest aim of his life only in the fulfilment of his duty blesses the whole of Prussia", the present speaker laid down the same golden yellow evergreen wreath on the steps of the monument, as it had already been dedicated there in the commemorative years 1833, 1864 and 1874 to the spirit of this unforgettable man.

Arolsen, in October 1931.

Gertha von Dieckmann,

née Sack.

Appendix 2

Prior to Sack's Transfer from the Rhine to Pomerania

I. Cabinet Order of Friedrich Wilhelm III to Crown President Sack

The editor of the *Rheinischer Merkur* in Coblenz has, quite unlawfully and in spite of the warnings issued to him, not been able to renounce arousing the discontent of the people against the government by unbridled rebukes and obvious appeals to the people and at the very moment when a general peace obliges every well-meaning citizen, even where not all expectations are satisfied, to secure the good of the same for everyone and to promote trust and harmony. He has attacked the conditions of this peace publicly and in a manner which, rather than working for that purpose, is likely to arouse, spread and nurture concern and disquiet, hatred and discord.

I will therefore no longer permit the continuation of the chosen journal and order you to immediately prohibit it. My ministry is working on a law on the freedom of the press, which will issue regulations for the subsequent period which will be in accordance with public opinion and the best interests of the State. But until then, you must keep the newspapers and daily journals in particular under control.

You have not been following my orders in this. I hereby inform you of my serious displeasure and I want you to reprimand the Censor for his total neglect of duty on my behalf.

Berlin, January 3, 1816. Friedrich Wilhelm.

II. To the Editor of the *Rheinischer Merkur*

School Director Görres

His Majesty the King has, by means of the Most High Cabinet Order of Berlin on January 3, 1816, decreed that the publication of the *Rheinischer Merkur* should be forbidden because it is completely unlawful for them to deliver and spread articles which stir up and nourish the discontent and discord of the people and disturb their minds by unbridled rebukes and obvious incitements. The Privy Councillor of State and Crown President Sack has inclined to instruct me to comply most punctually with this sovereign prohibition under the 9th of this month.

I therefore disclose to you this sovereign intention to be complied with in the most unconditional way possible. I call upon you, from this day onward, not to publish a single page of your journal. To this end, the appropriate injunctions will be issued to the censor, the printer, and, because today's journal has not been published, the necessary instructions will be given to Mr Mähler, the police inspector.

You shall immediately acknowledge receipt of this Regulation.

Coblenz, January 12, 1816

The Commissioner of the Government General
Sack
(Ernst Sack, brother of the Crown President.)

III. A Final Word

By the Royal cabinet order of January 3, the further publication of the *Rheinischer Merkur* is prohibited in the Prussian states. The copies in stock were immediately sealed and the printer was arrested, so that since the publication ceased on the tenth of this month, the honored subscribers of the same, who had paid in advance for the new volume, would have the amount returned to them by the various post offices, having previously agreed to a reasonable deduction just for the dispatch of the five published sheets. Those who, for the sake of completeness, prefer to receive the first half of the 1814 volume of their prenumeration will therefore make their declaration at the post offices and return it within four weeks.

Koblenz, January 18, 1816.

Extracted from the collection *Der deutsche Staatsgedanke* ("The German State Philosophy"). Joseph Görres, *Rheinischer Merkur* by Arno Duch, Drei Masken-Verlag, Munich 1921.

IV. Excerpts from Private Letters, Referring to Sack's Transfer from the Rhine to Pomerania

The mother of his young Marshal Focke writes to her son Carl, Berlin July 19, 1816:

"The *Berliner Zeitung* contains a very enthusiastic article about your boss."

Sister Marie Focke to her brother Carl, Berlin July 25, 1816:

"The relationship with Sack is undoubtedly very pleasant for you. So you are now literally invited everywhere with him as his attache." (Sack was already present in Stettin for days.)

The mother to son Carl F., Berlin July 28, 1816:

"Just back from a visit I paid to Mrs Privy Councillor Sack. Her Excellency has told me various things about your joys and sorrows there, especially about the wet session on the island, where you and your husband chose to sleep on the sofa. She is receiving letters all the time and is expecting him, who will need a whey cure here under Dr. Boehm's supervision, any time now".

Carl initially lived "in the country house" above the boss, as long as Sack's wife had not yet moved in and ate at his place, at least for lunch. Sack was also kind enough to invite the eleventh grade high school pupil Wilhelm Focke, when he visited his brother in Stettin from July 24 to August 7, to join him daily for fourteen days.

The mother to Carl F., Berlin August 21, 1816:

Carl had a recommendation from Berlin to a wealthy Stettin merchant family Lutz (apparently in the north-western suburb of Züllchow), where there was also other stimulating contact. Mrs Lutz wrote to Berlin that Carl had "made a visit there with Mr Sack".

Sister Marie Focke to brother Carl, Berlin August 29, 1816:

"The Sack couple came yesterday to say goodbye. I always like him very much when I see him with his expression of honesty and openness. I am glad that he has remained your boss (N.B. Before the Stettin employment, Carl's relatives had hoped very much that he would get a good job on the Rhine and they could then move in with him). On August 30th, Sack travels to Stettin with his wife."

In this and the following year, 1817, Focke received letters of congratulation and, in part, envy from his former friends who had been with him in Aachen. The conditions at the six new Rhine governments were mostly quite unsatisfactory. It is understandable that those who were worse off mourned their former governor. But the voices of devotion from those individuals who were doing quite well, for example from Koppe in Minden, are equally loud.

Chief Justice of the Higher Regional Court Neigebauer, Cleve April 11, 1818 to Carl (he had also been with him in Aachen):

Since then, the Rhine has become a tidal stream for many people. But "I have enjoyed myself quite a bit. I was in Aachen last week, where everything still depends on him. In Coblenz too and the royal family in Neuwied loves him as their benefactor[133] Tell him that when I ate there, everyone talked about him in glorious terms. In Cologne I was quite refreshed by Bruckner, who is also a very good *Sackian*."

V. Three Letters from Sack to Government Councillor Carl Focke in Stettin During the Years 1818 and 1817

Berlin, August 22, 1816

To Government Councillor Carl Focke Stettin:

---

133 From June 1815 onwards, the Nassau acquisitions had brought Sack into frequent contact with several mediated princes and rulers of the nobility, such as Wied and Neuwied, Wied-Runkel, Solms-Lych and Solms-Braunfels. Since he approached these houses with openness and trust, he could expect the same and not a single unpleasant discussion had taken place. He took the Royal Prussian Edict of June 21, 1815 as a guideline and proceeded mildly but purposefully, while the lords of the house were reasonable enough to recognize his treatment of the matter as a thoroughly just and considerate one.

That the nobility of the Rhineland were fundamentally opposed to Sack is quite wrong. However, there were always individuals who remained averse to Stein's reforms and saw Sack as the representative thereof as a "grumpy pigheaded fellow". Nor was it surprising that they knew how to castigate him as a "ruffian" in reactionary Rhenish Witgenstein, given the whole political wartime shift in the ownership of the Rhine Confederation princes and their followers. The fact that Hardenberg had listened to these machinations, about such a proven, outstanding, and royal-loyal organizer and administrator, remains characteristic of that chancellor of state at all times.

Hon. Well-born, I thank you most sincerely for the letters and messages sent to me, the best of which is that nothing significant happened there.

It is certainly the same case here. After a two-day incognito stay in Glienicke, the State Chancellor went through to Doberan to take a bath there for four weeks and then spend a fifth with his son in Holstein. Since the Minister of Finance is away and von Schuckmann is preparing, as they say, to leave for the Rhine, there is a dead silence in all business dealings here and I have not tried to wake them up.

Since Thursday evening, when I arrived here happily, I have been taking *Taraxaci Extract*[134] and *Egerwasser*[135] under the guidance of Dr. Böhm, packing my things and books, and yesterday we moved out of our house and moved in with our brother-in-law Jacobi, where we will stay for the rest of the days. The boat, which was rented solely for our belongings, will leave here on the 28th and we ourselves on the 30th to be there on the 31st when everything runs smoothly.

According to this plan of mine, I now ask

---

134 Dandelion Root with Herb. A herbal medicine for the treatment of loss of appetite, urinary tract and genital disorders and gastrointestinal disorders.
135 At least since the first quarter of the 17th century *Egerwasser* was also shipped in clay bottles. It was the first mail-order healing water in Bohemia.

1. To ask Mr Sanne whether Mrs Commercial Councillor Oegler can let us move into her Grabow apartment on the 31st, as I have no doubt she will.

2. Whether she wants to leave us her furniture, like you also promised me. Then...

3. It is only a matter of bringing out the beds, which we could easily get because in any case we would arrive in my quarters in the city and would then be informed by you through Mr Sanne.

4. Hear what the situation is like in Oegler's apartment and what we have to take care of, which includes whether Mrs Oegler wants to leave me her stock of hay, oats and straw, which I would also ask Mr Sanne to do.

5. To tell Mr Griebel that he should have the hall or some other rooms in the new house completely made ready, so that when the ship with our things arrives there in the first eight days of the new month, they can be taken there at once, so that they will not soon be transported a second time, which is so important and valuable for the furniture.

6. If everything is correct in item 1, then you do not need to bother about moving out, although I have seen in the Tuesday newspaper that your brother (Reinhold Focke) has now been appointed to Frankfurt and you will probably move into his apartment anyway. Only if the item 1 would not apply, you

would have to make room for a small family who would then live upstairs.

Please give my recommendation to Director Mühlendorff when you see him and tell him that Mr von Rohr wrote to me and asked me to extend his vacation but I replied that he should rejoin the colleagues as soon as possible because his presence is really necessary for the first department of the government. Otherwise I would not know what to say to him for now but I intend to write to him with the next mail.

7. If Mr O. L. v. Schulenburg should have something to write to me about the Prenzlau horses, please send me his letter as soon as possible, otherwise I will keep the Dewitz horses, which used to be well-behaved.

8. Mr v. Schulenbürg also asked the cook hired by his wife to tell her that she would be coming to our quarters on March 31, so that my wife could consult with her about the kitchen. Otherwise I wouldn't know where to order anything. However, I thank her in advance for her kind offer to provide me with the above. To Mr von Hiller, Mr Böhlendorf and all those who remember me, a most sincere recommendation. All is well in your house. Your brother Wilhelm was with me. Your mother wants to visit me first. Here the weather is one degree worse than there, wind, rain and thunderstorms alternate. There is nothing from the Rhine but lamen-

tations, including one from Merrem, which I just don't have at hand. My wife recommends herself with myself to your friendly remembrance

Humbly, Sack.

Berlin, August 25, 1816.

To Councillor Carl Focke, Stettin.

I have received Hon. Well-born's courteous letter dated 22nd of this month, while you will already have received my reply to the first letter. The broken seal does not mean anything, rather it is a pity that you did not read the letter. It was from Mr Sethe and contained some news from the local Justice Commission that would have been interesting to you. On the whole, Sethe is very satisfied with things. He himself is in better shape and will now be in Aachen to strengthen his foot.

I thank you for the other news and the effort you have put into my orders. I have now received a reply from Mr Sanne, according to which Mrs Oegler is very kindly leaving us her house in Grabow with the furniture. I am therefore thinking along the lines of my plan, which I helped you with the other day, to move out there with my family straight away and if Mr Sanne simply would like to get our beds and kitchen utensils there, then I would ask him, with my grateful recommendation for the effort he has put in, to let him know that the bedsteads and beds, all of which were in the country house for me and which Mrs Schulze will order to be brought to Qegler's house, some of which are in my apartment and some of which are up-stairs.

The kitchen utensils are out on their way but if they had the kindness to let our cook, ordered by Mrs von Schulen-burg, know that she might acquire a quantity of earthen-ware, which of course is not coming along and is certainly available on the local market, it would be very beneficial to our stay in the country.

You don't need to be worried about your apartment, be-cause you will not be disturbed upstairs and I will keep the lower one for me as a work office.

I would ask you to tell Mr v. d. Schulenbürg that, because of the horses, I can only make up my mind when I get there, since I have not yet received a reply from Mr von Dewitz to my letter sent before my departure, and since I have taken his horses with me, I will have to wait all the more, since I have taken his horses with me — so if the Jew cannot wait until then, I would ask him to forget the horses.

Mr Abegg from Emden, who replied very kindly but not cordially, informed me that he had sent herring from his own catch to me with a ship "Vrouve Kartje", Captain Ebeling, and that Mr Sethe had the Düsseldorf furnishings addressed to me by H. Melcher from Amsterdam. Should I receive any of these things in my absence, please have them received but hand them over to Mr Griebel immedi-ately, as he can take up mainly these things, wine etc. into one of the new rooms and into the unused cellar.

I would like to tell Mr Friedrich that I received his letter from Swinemünde (Swinoujscie) yesterday, that I am very satisfied with it and that I will soon thank him orally for the good execution of his orders.

I saw your mother and had her letter delivered immediately. The one left by Mr Merrem will be delivered here. The poor man will be embarrassed like many on the Rhine. Old Mr Heuberger complained about it loud and clear. The State Chancellor intends to go with Mr von Schuckmann, which will be good.

The weather here is so bad that one believes to be in November. I drink water sometimes but it doesn't agree with me. I hope it will be better there. On Saturday we think to arrive there and send the ship with our things beforehand. It does not seem to be necessary to make any further arrangements than to meet the people indicated.

My wife reciprocates your compliments and I remain respectfully yours

Hon. High Well-Born most humble servant

Sack.

Berlin, July 11, 1817.

Hon. Well-born, I may have received both letters of May 11 and June 22 on time but suspended the answer because I hoped to give you reasonably satisfactory results orally or in writing but the items in question have not yet been ready for this.

So now, to begin with the spiritual things. Only in the last few days have I received the report on the General Superintendents' offices, which you co-signed, and I took it up with Mr Nicolovius Rath. If one could receive from the outside a highly worthy man κατ εξοχήν[136], I would be willing to hear your private opinion but what is missing completely and so much is that one has been looking in vain for years for some such postings. I know the Reverend Spiess you are referring to by all his qualities and visited him last year in Frankfurt a. M., also suggesting him for the local Court Preacher position. However, he is of Reformed religion and in Pomerania we would have to have a Lutheran General Superintendent. Yet there is no one in our province who has more claim and quality to this than Mr Engelken[137]. I therefore signed the letter with the reservation that if he and Mr Schmidt could not properly pay the compensation into the consistories, which depends on the forthcoming instructions for the Consistory and the governments, which have now been promised as soon as possible, I would have to apply for a third funded

---

136 par excellence

137 Friedrich Ludwig Engelken (1749 -1826) was a Protestant theologian, pedagogue and general superintendent of Pomerania with the title of bishop.
  In the agenda dispute after the Union (1817) of the Lutheran and Reformed Churches to the Protestant Church in Prussia, Engelken took a clear stand for the Union. For his merits in general and for the introduction of the Union and the Agenda in particular, he was appointed Superintendent General of the Church Province of Pomerania on January 30, 1826. He was awarded the title of Bishop on February 5, 1826.

Consistorial Councillor with own salary. In addition, I consider the preacher Wolfs in Poznan to be the best whom I have met here and whom Mr Natorp has recommended so highly to me, the friend and relative of Lütger, who was born there and who would so gladly come to us.

The appointment of Mr Bernhard as School Councilor is also waiting for the intended instructions, because only then will it be determined which of the educational matters should actually remain with the consistory. I hope that they will not be separated from the whole province but the Minister of the Interior is of a completely opposite opinion and that is why one just gets nowhere in these matters.

Mr Kahle has completely spoiled the Stargard educational matters with his lecture and we now have to restore them the hard way, similar to what happened with the Interest-Meliorations thing, which the State Chancellor finally decided in favor of the government against the Minister of the Interior and about which the latter is very angry. He allowed me, under oath, which I could only view in general terms because I had not seen the order and despite the fact that I had ordered the communication from there, that I would do everything reasonably decent but change a lot more when I got there. So if something has not already happened, please wait until I get there before starting.

I have held on to the things suggested by Mr Bernhard in order to consult with him and the other gentlemen, especially since he has been absent until recently. Please tell him that, with my best recommendations and that he should not leave there next week.

Unfortunately, I do not yet know when I will be able to leave here. The other Crown Presidents were able to leave at the beginning of this week after the conclusion of the Council of State but both Mr von Schön and I are here at the express written request of the State Chancellor to assist at the conferences investigating the state budget. These were to be held every day since then and on this I had based my plan to leave here next Sunday, stay there for 8 days and then begin my spa vacation. However, since the conferences have not been held until today, I doubt that the plan will come to fruition. Please tell Mr von Rohr there that I will write to him as soon as I know something concrete.

I had also put off your own important matter until we had a chance to talk face-to-face. The first thing I want to do is to report the preliminary results to you. Although I cannot wish any change in my situation from the present point of view and although I would not like to see you leave, it is completely contrary to my way of thinking to put some kind of obstacle in your life plans, especially since they are so far-reaching. That is why I have informed Mr Solms here of your wish as legal adviser to be transferred to one of the Rhenish governments, namely to Cologne, and since there was talk of reconsideration of such men, he has included you among them. Before he left, he only told me that the matter had not yet been signed but that there was a chance for you to come to Aachen. For my part I believe that for this reason, as with all the appointments on the Rhine, the decision will only be made after the arrival of the State Chancellor and Minister of the Interior but I will leave it to you to decide whether you wish to write to him

and openly repeat to you the assurance that as much as I would like to remain in the same business relationship with you as before, I am far from destroying your life's plans but am prepared to promote them in everything you wish for their welfare.

By the way, I didn't tell anybody else about your project, not even your mother, with whom I visited in Steglitz on Sunday a fortnight ago when I had the opportunity to do so.

When it is known, there would be no shortage of enthusiasts who would apply for the current position, especially friend Neigebaur, who is here on a holiday trip to Silesia. He expressed his most ardent wish to rejoin the state administration, being very dissatisfied with the justice system on the Rhine in all respects and giving a very sad description of the business in our fatherland.

I have not yet been able to find the Jäkler document which you wish to have but I will arrange for it to be sent to you. I believe, however, that the Prince's constitutional notices will soon be assembled and sifted differently and therefore the wishes expressed in this regard to Mr Eichmann and Mr Andrer can be left at that.

A petition was filed with the Ministry of Finance against the decision of the fourth General Administration has no effect in itself as far as your position goes. If you want to do something, write to the State Chancellor and ask him that he may, when he is there on the Rhine, examine the equity of your petition and decide there.

Due to the uncertainty whether we will already be there by next Monday, my wife asks whether you would like to call our cook or have her tell her that she should use the present time of the good young beans and so that they don't get too hard soon, to bottle a considerable amount of them. There is no shortage of the bottles in our house in the cook's custody and if she does not quite understand the way of preserving them she should go to Mrs Colonel Lehmann, who last year preserved 35 bottles, which have kept well until the end.

This morning Refr. E...... was here with me to go to Carlsbad and told me that Frederick had wanted to leave for the island of Usedom. If he is still there, tell him that he should be back there by the middle of next week, because I have a lot to discuss with him and cannot stay there for long. I have many things to initiate there, both in consideration of the taxation system and other things. Therefore I have also decided to send Mr Böhlendorf back and during my absence many things will occur which I will carry out in Sept. and Oct. So I hope that my absence will not be prejudicial.

Just now my wife said, she had spoken to her eldest sister and her mother had not been well since the first of the month when we were happily together in Steglitz but she would not be going there now but perhaps to Frankfurt. My wife recommends herself to your memory and I remain your most devoted servant

Sack.

Margin notes:

On the first page of the letter:

You probably already know that Mrs Merrem has given birth to a son and Mrs von Düring a daughter for the second time — otherwise the news. So you must also make sure that you catch up, so as not to be left behind too much.

S.

On the 3rd page: I will probably not be able to leave before Thursday because then the Lord Chancellor of State will also leave, but I wrote on Monday.

VI. Three Letters from Sack to his Brother-in-law, the Privy Crown Fiscal Councillor Jacobi of Potsdam in 1820 and 1828

Magdeburg, September 2, 1820

My most esteemed brother,

It is one of the pleasant events of our trip that all things worked out as planned and so it was a great pleasure for us to find your letter of 22nd when we arrived on the evening of the 30th and to see that you completed your trip so well and happily with all your lovely company. My wife was very happy to receive the letters of Elisha and Julchen and I was delighted to receive yours and that of the brother von Reiman. We had anticipated coming here for only one day and so surprised our dear ones here. The following two days we were in constant company with them. The two brothers and I are making a promised visit to Mr Nathusius in Hundisburg and my wife is staying here to rest. Tomorrow, Sunday, we will continue our journey to Genthin to be with you in Potsdam on Monday evening. It is our heartfelt wish to meet all of you, who are so close to our hearts and so dear to us, well and healthy and my wife in particular has a fervent yearning for this. She is not writing much today because I am travelling and have to send the letter to the post office before she gets up, so she does not answer Elise and Julie but welcomes them warmly and we are reserving everything and anything for conversation. We will, however, have to keep in mind the amount of news and stories to be communicated to each other, because I have planned to take two months off from the beginning and this time will end on September 12th. Consequently and according to the plan drafted above, I would stay there only on Tuesday, Wednesday and Thursday, except for Monday evening, but in the evening of the last day I would go to Berlin to stay there on the 8th, 9th and 10th and return to Stettin on the 11th and 12th.

We are pleased that you want to hospitably receive us in your apartment. We only hope that it will not bother you, dear sister and Elisha, and we are satisfied with every comfort. If the horses and carriages can stay with you at all, Codelius, who also keeps horses, may be kind enough to let me pay for the necessary feed, otherwise Frederick will probably talk about it with the nearest innkeeper for the time being.

I was all the more pleased to receive a letter from von Reiman's brother, as he told me that he had given you the upper hand in all matters of calculation and that we can now take the important decisions on everything there to regulate scientific and personal matters.

My wife, who benefited from the trip to the seaside resort more than I did, extends a friendly greeting to you and all our dear friends and I remain your most faithful servant and brother with the familiar sentiments,

Sack.

Stettin, October 15, 1820.

My most esteemed gentleman brother!

We ought to have written to you long ago and thanked you and our dear Sister most sincerely — as we do now — for the many friendly kindnesses shown to us during our stay in Potsdam and Berlin but in the early days of our stay here, distractions caused by the presence of the Crown Prince were to blame for our omission and afterwards we awaited the answers to the letters we received from you and your brother-in-law Eichmann, so that we could write. This is what we are doing today and I, in particular, am answering the warm letter of May 28 of this year. It is very pleasant that Reiman's brother, because he was prompted by you to move on, is now continuing his business down there, so that we will soon hope to straighten everything out. I will check the items sent to me with the others as soon as I can get to work on private matters, given the amount of detailed and daily increasing official work. Cousin Forell from Mühlheim an der Ruhr has also written to me and I now want to regulate my private affairs with him. The main content of his letter, however, consists of lamentations about the present sluggish relationship in the Provincial Treasury Offices and he is right in this respect, as the Minister von Klewitz generally always concedes to me, that the Provincial Treasury will soon be just as disrupted as that of the State. Too many cooks spoil the broth. He wanted to sort it out in September and I have now officially requisitioned the items from him most urgently. Yet if, as Cousin Trout writes, he has been commandeered by the 14th and 15th from General v. R. to rejoin the Corps of Engineers after his tenure, then he has done wrong, for he would have climbed very high and could have had a brilliant career and since Herr v. R. is on the Rhine, he should still try to do so.

I have nothing against your and Reiman's brother-in-law's plan to suspend the distribution for one year and I will also advise the Sack Family co-heirs, although the new brother-in-law v. Kottwitz is in a hurry to make progress with the sales process. The idea from R. P. Coh. I have therefore also sent off by mail.

My wife and Julie write about the other family matters in the enclosures. I only add that my wife's spa experience has been consistently excellent but I have not yet felt any benefit from it. Which is why, after the Crown Prince has left us, I continue to drink the water from the six jars of spring water I brought with me on the advice of Dr. Heyn. This seems to relieve my suffering and improve my sleep, so that I think everything will go well this winter. Before the winter comes I have several more journeys in mind. Especially because Minister v. Schuckmann has come here and wants to visit the large Magdeburg penitentiary with me and to talk to Mr Glt. Müller of Swinemünde in Pomerania as soon as Minister v. Bülow is back. He seems to play a right role as Minister of Trade on the Rhine. I certainly wish my friend Julius Urtheil to know about this and will soon write to him myself. If you see him before then, please tell him so, with our best recommendations to him and his dear wife.

I sincerely thank you for your and everybody's kind wishes for my birthday. We have celebrated happily in the circle of our friends and would have liked to celebrate with you among us. So we had to make do with a toast to your good health. The day on the calendar was marked *Espero* [expectation], and so we were comforted by the hope of seeing you again next spring in good spirits. I will write to August especially, since he is doing so well. In the next year I would advise him to spend time in a good institution, where physical and mental education can be combined and where he can be given sufficient occupation to keep him lively. The various political movements which are now taking decisions on the Troppau (Opava)[138] project seem to have a great influence on the paper and money markets, as they do everywhere, and we shall find out more only when more precise decisions are known. According to my arrangements there, Mr Fr. invested r 3,000 in our new bonds and r 10,000 in West Prussian mortgage bonds on my behalf. I wanted to leave it at that for the time being, until we see how things go in *politicis*.

The paper on the Chancellor of State caused a sensation with the declaration of the same. It was ascribed to Mr Sch. but I immediately took Mr Neigebauer for the author, whose style and one-sided view could not be mistaken. His note from Cologne only reported the dispatch of the barrel of *Laubheimer 1819*, which Mr Merrem had selected for me and stated that after a happy arrival and some rest I would like such poison. From this I conclude that it could soon be drafted into smaller barrels, as it contains 7½ *Ohm*[139], according to the comments I have gathered from

---

138 From 20 October to 20 December 1820 the rulers of Austria, Prussia and Russia met in Troppau for the so-called Troppau Congress of Princes, which was held on the occasion of the civil uprising in Naples. Tropau today is in the Czech Republic and has been renamed Opava.

139 One *Stückfass* was the standard barrel of wine. It was about 1000-1200 liters, depending on the region. 1 *Stückfass* = 7½-8 *Ohm* depending on the region. Smaller barrels would improve the *Barique* flavor of the wine after storage.

you. About whether both are correct, I would ask for your assurances sometime, in order not to proceed incorrectly when it arrives. I also ask you to tell me how the Moselle wines you ordered turned out, which Mr Dietert wanted to send directly to you and just to take it out of his wine depot or directly with the local friends Roloff and v. Heyne.

In the newspapers there I saw an announcement of the fifth Department of the Minister of War, according to which for the Major 145 r 20 gr per cent are to be had on deposits. Don't you want to inquire about it and make this increase for the poor woman v. H., who is certainly the sole heiress of it and who would be entitled to such an increase? E. Jacob greets you. Your other friends are doing well. Mr v. Rohr has become a little thin because of all the pleasures he thinks he has to give his daughters during the day and to himself playing games in the evening. He is now reflecting on the position of Chief President in Liegnitz, which has come about due to the death of P. Klinkhöfer. This is more for the sake of honor than for the sake of advantage, because otherwise he does not think he will again be able to skip over those who are preferred to him. What vanity! My wife wrote about Focke's child and the fact that I baptized her the day before yesterday. Otherwise all the young women in the government of Aether have given birth to boys. Mrs Hamman, Solzer, Focke, Kollike and Feltheim. Now put Mrs von Mittelstädt in front of them and let us wish them the best. Poor W.(overgrown) daughter of Mrs B, unfortunately gave birth to a dead child and is still in great danger of dying herself. I have told my wife and Linchen that I will pay the expenses necessary for the latter, the former has 10 r for this month and does not need anything yet. I will collect everything in due course from the Weimar interest. Since the trip of old Ribbentrop, which was announced in the newspapers, the military have been predicting considerable armament on the Rhine but it will mainly consist of picking up his daughter and remarrying with his former wife v. Emden. To all our relatives and friends the warmest greetings, especially to dear sister, Elise and August — always and without reproach, your brother-in-law and friend,

Sack.

Stettin, December 20, 1828.

My wife had just finished wrapping some small Christmas greetings, also intended for your dear Lucie, when the District Administrator v. Gerlach visited us, who is traveling there to visit his father-in-law and his sister. He wants to pick up his wife and children, who have been with the former for six weeks and offered to take anything along. However, since his arrival in Potsdam will probably not happen before the festival, we only asked for a greeting to be addressed to all of you and instead sent the box directly by mail.

Inside there is a dress for dear little Lucie for Christmas, one belt, one work box with accessories and a small house or church also mountain and valley. My wife wishes me only that these little presents may bring joy to her dear daughter and apologizes for not writing because of her sickness. Her gout is quite active and her face is always swollen. Her nervous system is very affected and she, like me, has to take it easy on herself. We want to wish her and you a better winter than autumn, which makes writing difficult for her. However, since there was still a little place left in the box and she wanted to give a little Christmas present to August, she enclosed a parcel for him with the request, since you will also send him something for Christmas or some other occasional, to send it at the same time.

It was dear to me to hear that finally in the Cohausen(?)[140] matter the power of attorney went to their authorities and will now probably let brother-in-law v. Reiman or Julius hear something of the success when they have recovered from the horrors of the earthquake[141].

---

140 This probably refers to Salentin Heinrich Ignaz Florin von Cohausen (1782-1864) who was a Prussian district administrator of the Saarburg district from 1818 to 1847. Although Cohausen was always concerned about the welfare of the district during his time in Saarbrücken, he lacked a sound knowledge of the relevant legal situation and the desire to make this the guiding principle of his work. Rather, he often acted hastily and passionately. For the superior government in Trier, this resulted in a weakening of the district administrator's authority over the mayors' offices. These did not obey the orders of the district administrator, but complained about them to the government.

141 On 3 December 1828 at half past six in the evening, the border region between Belgium and Germany was stricken by a moderate earthquake. Among the testimonies, we also retrieved a questionnaire sent by the Prussian government to local authorities with the purpose of quickly obtaining information on the earthquake effects in the western part of the kingdom of Prussia. This inquiry is the oldest of its kind that has been discovered to date in this part of Europe, suggesting a rare concern by a national authority about the seismic hazard, and prefiguring the seismic inquiries that scientific institutions use today. (https://www.researchgate.net/publication/283495497_The_3_December_1828_moderate_earthquake_at_the_border_between_Belgium_and_Germany).

Merrem himself did not send a report to Berlin after he had got to know the terrain there. Only the good Linchen had had a hard time to get closer to her loved ones, which could be excused but not advised, even if Mr Merrem could assert his claims.

Mr Bödecker is doing well with the road construction. He is allowed 2 r. for running planks, for him as well as the contractors when they are finished with his work. Next week the costs of the insurance company shares will be paid and I will collect them for you when the receipt is here. Dividends are now being paid again, just like in spring, and Rumschöttel still finds them profitable, even though this autumn has brought a lot of taxes and losses.

Otherwise I have nothing to report at this time. If you want to inform me of something that you want to make sure will reach me, please do so through Mr v. Gerlach, who will pass through Stettin on his return journey. My wife sends me her warmest greetings. She, the dear sister and Julchen and I would like to ask you to pass on our greetings to the friends there: Mr Ritschl, Eylert, Colonel v. S., Pred. Damm and Mr Brun, when you have the opportunity.
Always with the familiar sentiments,
Your most devoted brother and Fr.
Sack.
To the King!. Crown Privy Fiscal Councillor
Mr Jacobi
in Potsdam.

4 pounds 8 loth[142] postage free, hereby a little box drawn in wax canvas H. Z. J.

---

142 Old German measure of weight: 1 loth (or lot) was approximately 14 grammes.

Note about the Family Letters

With the few letters that have been preserved from Sack's private life, it seemed appropriate to have those kindly provided to me printed above. Those from the Focke family have been contributed by Dr. Carl Focke (1109 [9/111]) of Düsseldorf, those to the Privy Fiscal Councillor Jacobi of Potsdam by the sisters Frau von Wietersheim (1327 [12/2122]) and Fräulein Lucie Jacobi (1333 [12/2125]) of Berlin. The following testament from the year 1828 is thanks to Mrs Excellency Glt. Voigt, née Sack (1180 [9/221]), who also has preserved the later one written by Sack's widow in 1841, as well as the complete inventory of the estate.

The author would like to express her warmest thanks again to all those who were helpful and enriched her compilation by loaning them to her.

VII Dr Johann August and Mrs Marianne Sack's Last Will and Testament when Married

a. Testament as a married couple

In order to remove all uncertainty about our estate after our eventual death, we, both husband and wife, I, the Royal Privy Councillor and Crown President of Pomerania, Dr. Johann August Sack and I, the Royal Lady Privy Councillor and Crown President of Pomerania, née Marianne Gertruda Johanna von Reiman, in good physical and mental health and after careful consideration, have considered it expedient to make the following last will and testamentary disposition, in which we hereby annul and destroy the will deposited with the Royal Chamber Court of Justice in Berlin on June 5, 1813, according to the Recognition Certificate of Berlin.

§ 1.

Foremost it retains everywhere what was in the one from us of January 3, 1799. Hereby we enclose a copy of this, since the main copy is attached to the previous will and testament, according to which our assets brought into the marriage and acquired during the marriage, whether by inheritance, gift, savings or other assets, are to be common and the principles of general conjugal co-ownership prescribed in the Prussian General Land Law are to be applied in general. In the same way, if our marriage should still be blessed with children, the intended marriage foundation remains in force.

§ 2.

However, in the event that one of us dies without having any children from our marriage, we commit:

a) that no sealing or any kind of inventory of the entire common property should take place, but that the surviving spouse should remain in undisturbed possession of the estate, which is why we made the necessary remark on the envelope of this last will and testament and let it be noted in the Recognition Certificate;

b) that the surviving spouse is entitled to inherit all the property which will be available on the date of the death of the deceased, regardless of what it is, both movable property and real estate and assets, and to act and administer it at will and without any restriction, in particular to sell it, to dispose of it among the living, and that neither he nor his heirs after his death shall be obliged to render any account thereof. We exclude the provision of the General Land Law Th. 1 Tit. 12 p. 469, according to which in the case of *fideicommissarial* substitutions, the heir is not authorized to make gifts out of mere generosity, and we also grant the surviving spouse the authority to dispose in this way of the intended property;

c) that after our mutual death, the entire estate then existing, regardless of what it is, including what the survivor has acquired or saved for this purpose, be divided into two equal parts, one of which is to be given to the next legal heir of the man on the day of death of the last deceased and the other to the wife, both of them are to fall under the rules of intestate succession, according to the laws of the place where the last survivor last resided, which are prescribed for persons of the exercised jurisdiction. However, the surviving spouse shall be free to dispose otherwise by last will of the half of the joint property belonging to him or her.

§ 3.

The provisions of § 2 sub litt. b and c above shall cease to apply as soon as the last survivor enters into a second marriage. In this case, namely the intervention in another marriage, the last survivor is obliged, before the intervention in the second marriage, to draw up a complete inventory, to be confirmed by an oath, and to return the half part of the total property, to the closest relative of the deceased on the day of death of the deceased, or to their heirs within three months from the day of the judicially transferred inventory, but without paying interest thereon. However, the survivor is free to decide whether and which capital he wishes to retain for his part and whether and which assets he wishes to take over in whole or in part after a valuation to be made by court or to arrange for their public sale.

§ 4.

Both spouses expressly reserve the right to determine any legacies from the joint property during their lifetime and during the marriage, as they please, and to determine in this way both money and objects of monetary value and individual items of the joint property and to make special dispositions in this way both money and objects of monetary value and individual items of the joint property, but not more than half of the total property of both spouses, in the event of their death and to make special dispositions with regard to these assets etc. etc. the survivor hereby expressly renounces the right of inheritance as well as the usufruct and disposition to which he or she is otherwise entitled. In this respect and in as far as this is the case, all dispositions shall have force which are found signed by the disposing party himself with his first name and surname and which are found somewhere, whether in a court or out of court.

§ 5.

We request the court in which we have made our last will and testament to open it after the death of the first deceased, to observe its execution everywhere and to uphold it in all its parts as a will, codicilly, or other testamentary disposition valid according to the law. Thus it is done.

Stettin on June 28, 1828.

(L. S.) Read and signed by hand Johann August 'Sack

(L. S.) Marianne Gertrude Johanne Sack née Reiman.

b. Publication of the Reciprocal Testament Following the Death of Crown President Sack.

Royal Privy Councillor Dr. Johann August Sack and his wife Mrs Marianne Gertrude Johanne, née von Reiman, were present at the publication on June 28 of their mutual testament:

1. For Her Excellency the widowed Mrs Crown President Sack, Mr Privy Councillor Bourwieg, reserving power of attorney,

2. The Government Councillor Focke for his wife Gemalin Agnes née Sack, a brother's daughter of the deceased Mr Crown President Sack,

3. The Ref. Pitzschky, as the assistant assigned *ad actum publicationis ex officio* to the unknown heirs.

On June 29, 1828 the married couple August and Marianne Sack had handed over their mutual will to the court in Oberwieck near Stettin and the envelope was written:

Herein is our last will and testament and in it all impounding and inventorization is excluded in the event of death.

Stettin, June 28, 1828.

Johann August Sack

Marianne Gertrude Johanne

Sack née von Reiman

and is sealed three times with the combined arms of both testators.

The will was twice sealed with the court seal and the following acceptance note: Accepted for legal deposit and sealed twice with the Marian Council Court Seal, noting that the testators have forbidden the impounding and inventorization of the estate when the will is handed over.

Oberwieck near Stettin, on June 29, 1828.

The testament was presented to the gentlemen present and the seals were recognized by them as unbroken. The will was then excised and published by reading it out loud.

Comparenten trugen kein Bedenken die ihnen wohlbekannten Unterschriften der Testatoren zu recognosciren.

The Privy Councillor Bourwieg contributed to the drawing up of the will of his client
Read by: Focke
Approved: C. W. Bourwieg
Signed: Pitzschky. Holleben.

When questioned, Crown Government Councillor Focke stated that Mr Crown President Sack had died without children and that his next of kin had become heirs:

> 1. His brother the Privy Provincial Tax Director Ernst Heinrich Eberhard Siegemund Sack in Magdeburg,

2. His brother the President of the Higher Regional Court Justus Johann Leopold Maximilian Sack in Halberstadt,

3. His brother the Higher Regional Court Officer Ferdinand Johann Arnold Sack in Cleve.

Apart from these, the Chief President had four other brothers and sisters who had died before him, namely

a) The Government Councillor Carl Heinrich Theodor Sack in Magdeburg,

b) The Government Councilor Christian Cornelius Sack in Liegnitz,

c) The wife of the Consistorial Councilor Gillet, Friedericke Sophie Christiane née Sack in Berlin,

d) The wife of President Sethe in Berlin, Henriette Philippine née Sack,

all of whom have children who are still alive but whose names, age and whereabouts cannot be fully indicated at this time, so that if it should be necessary to do so, the details will be provided by the Lady Crown President.

v.   g.   sb.

Focke   Holleben.

VIII. Words Spoken at the Grave of the Immortalized Crown President of Pomerania Excellence Dr. Sack on July 1, 1831

In the Name of God, the Father, the Son and the Holy Spirit. Amen.

I would like to point out to all of us from this solemn place the words of the Scriptures, those words which were once spoken at a tomb and which were spoken by our Lord himself at Lazarus' tomb to the distressed sisters:

"Did I not tell you that if you believed you should see the glory of God." Joh. 11. 40.

Of course, unlike here, the glory of God revealed itself there, where the Lord called the sleepy Lazarus back into earthly life, just as everywhere where the Son of God walked in visible form, where he spoke his almighty words of life and performed his great deeds, the glory of God had to reveal itself in a different way than among us, who can no longer see him with physical eyes, but can lift up our hearts in faith to the exalted mediator. And yet, if only differently, if the true living faith in the Redeemer dwells in our hearts, then we will also see the glory of God at this tomb.

Admittedly, we no longer perceive anything of earthly glory when we look at this tomb but only the vanity and transitoriness of the world and of all earthly glory. It confirms to us so emphatically the earnest word of the Scriptures: "All flesh is like grass, and all the glory of men like

the flower of grass, the grass withers and the flower falls
away." This coffin encloses the earthly shell of a man who
was distinguished before many, who occupied an exalted
position among men. He was clothed with high dignity
and honour, equipped with exquisite gifts, enjoyed a prestige, a far-reaching efficacy crowned with fame and applause, which very few people can claim. He was rightly
counted among the noblest and best of our people. All this
outward glory is now gone, all that has earthly splendor,
majesty and prestige, beauty and excellence, has fallen
away, just as the flower of the grass falls away when the
wind blows over it. However, you say that what he has
done, worked and directed has not fallen away. The deeds
he has performed, the works he has accomplished and the
manifold good he has created and promoted will remain
and live on and will be remembered by his name for generations to come. And it is certainly right and praisewor-
thy that we receive the thoughts of the one who has fallen
asleep with a grateful heart.

Nevertheless, let us take care that we do not look at his life
and work with mere earthly eyes, with a carnal disposition, that we do not preferably dwell with our eyes on that
which was external in his life and work, that we do not
close our eyes to the higher light of the Gospel and make
much talk and praise of our own merits before the
Almighty, before whom a mortal is righteous only. No one
can earn merit otherwise we would profane rather than
honor the memory of our departed one. For if we look
upon a human life without enlightenment from above
from the lowly standpoint of our own righteousness
through the cloudy glass of an earthly and selfish mind,

we are in danger of living by the right to live and taking on the office of judge in a sinful and presumptuous way. Oh, we know the human heart, how inclined it is in its natural, unenlightened and unholy state, where so many things shine, where a life worthy of human merit is spread, to spy out defects and mistakes so as not to be too deeply humiliated by external greatness.

If we look at the man who has fallen asleep in the light of the Gospel, if we linger in his memory with a heart imbued with the power of a living faith, then we also realize that all that he shared in human weakness and fragility was forgiven by God for the sake of Jesus Christ. But where God has forgiven, how could man still be bold enough to judge what has been erased by the grace and merit of Christ, that is erased from the heart and memory of every believing Christian, and in a more beautiful, purer splendor of divine grace, the costly image of the one who has fallen asleep appears before our soul.

Now our believing eye sees the glory of God in his life and work. Yes, it was God's grace that was glorified in him, when he was active in the most diverse branches of various activities with such admirable power and fortunate success. It was God's grace that filled his heart with unshakable loyalty to his King and his fatherland, that equipped him under the most difficult and perilous circumstances with a firm courage, with prudence and wisdom, only to always recognize and do what was right, except for the good of the whole. It was God's grace that always preserved him in the various circles of his eventful life, in a comfort, a general goodwill towards the masses, which was made happy by the intimate warmth and friendly participation of the heart, not only among his near relatives but also winning the hearts of those who outwardly were less close to him. It was God's grace that always kept the pious spirit alive in him so that he did not forget the heavenly above the earthly. That which he was not by his own merit but by the grace of God, that which the Spirit of God worked in him and through him, that will last and remain and continue to work, even if all the works which he placed before the physical eye have long since disintegrated into dust and the memory of his name has faded from the earth.

But what better and for us more joyful thing can be said of a man who has completed his daily work on earth than that he does not resist the grace of God but that the glory of the Lord has been revealed in his life and work.

Yet no less was the glory of God revealed in him as the day of his life drew to a close and night approached when no one can work. If we look at the end of a human life, especially a life of much motion and action with a fleshly attitude, we see nothing but the sad, depressing picture of human weakness and powerlessness. There we see how the noblest forces tire, how under vehement upheaval the bond that unites soul and body is loosened more and more, how everything that gives us joy in the living sinks into death and destruction.

The picture becomes even more depressing when the departing person resists the grace of God, which wants to remove his soul from the earthly, when he does not want to let go of distant earthly thoughts, plans and aspirations and tries to hold on to the fleeing, earthly life with its goods with powerless hands. A completely different, beautiful and refreshing picture is presented to us. We see the glory of God when, enlightened by the light of the Gospel, we turn our gaze in faithfulness to the end of the one who has fallen asleep. He would have liked to have lived and worked even longer, if he had been granted this by the will of the Most High, just as he remained unceasingly active as long as his strength allowed. But when his earthly power ceased, higher, heavenly powers became active in him. The more his outer man disappeared the more beautiful his inner man appeared. When he clearly recognized several days before his end that he had completed his course, there was a wonderful silence in his soul. With calm surrender, submitting himself to the will of the Most High, he once again bid farewell to his loved ones with touching and friendly mildness. His reckoning with the earth was finished and his soul became more and more free from the earthly and physical. The same one ascended ever more powerfully to the Eternal and Immortal. With Christian self-denial, renouncing his dearest plans, endeavors and occupations, he placed his works into the hand of the Lord and, completely renouncing his own righteousness, he directed his hope to the grace and mercy of the heavenly Father and of Jesus Christ his Lord. He pointed to him as the way, the truth and the life, and with joyful trust he pointed out to his own. And after he had gently completed his mission, the tranquillity of the soul and the hope of eternal life, which was reflected in his lifeless features, still testified that he had died in the Lord and that his works had been done in God and followed him.

That, my listeners, is the transfiguration of faith and the revelation of glory in the death of the Christian.

Thus the glory of the Lord reveals itself even more beautifully and brightly to our believing hearts when we look beyond the darkness of this tomb to the bright heights of heaven, where God's angels have led the sleeping ones away. Yes, we assume that our Christian faith guarantees it, only what is earthly do we give back to the earth that which he himself is made of. His blessed spirit has returned to God, who gave it to him, and God will be gracious and merciful to him for the sake of Jesus Christ. From no one will be demanded more than that he is found faithful. And you, the one who has fallen asleep, have certainly been found true. You have kept house with the pound entrusted to you, you have not resisted the grace of God, which glorified itself so richly in you, you have fought a good fight, have kept faith and completed your course in God. The crown of eternal life is prepared for you, which the Lord, the righteous Judge, has promised to all those who love his glorious presence. There the Lord will place his servant, who has been so faithful to those entrusted to him here, above all else. There he will now see with a brighter gaze what he has believed here and will rejoice with inexpressible and blissful joy at the sight of the imperishable and eternal glory of his God and Saviour. This is the most beautiful consolation for the lonely wife and his bereaved loved ones and for all of us who were connected with the one who has fallen asleep, with the most diverse bonds of love, gratitude and veneration.

This, however, is also a powerful impulse for all of us to receive the grace of God in us in faith, and to allow it to work on us, so that it may be glorified in us in life and in death, and so that the glory of the Lord may be revealed to us in the highest and most blessed fullness. Thus may God, through Jesus Christ our Saviour, help us all to this end. Amen.

This imprint is based on the manuscript of Mr Richter, who wrote it by hand. By his hand is added:

"After the sinking of the coffin, the prescribed prayer from the agenda, followed by a free prayer at the end from the heart, which I am not not able to repeat".

R.

N.B. Any printing errors in both sections of this commemorative publication will be corrected on the next adhesive supplement to the "Silver Book of the Sack Family". Also a picture from the old Stettin "seen from the garden of the Sack family", which was made available to me after completion of my writing, will be printed on it, in order to be able to be pasted in at this place.

From The Taube No. 90 October 1931, p. 996:

The Memorial Publication for Dr. Joh. Aug. Sack.

Since I have so far, to my great regret, lacked the necessary leisure to thank for the numerous appreciative letters from the circle of *Taube* subscribers who have received the above memorial dedicated to the family of the Foundation, I take the opportunity of the Oktober *Taube* to fulfill this duty with pleasure. I need hardly say that it has given me great satisfaction to follow the traces of this important and noble ancestor in all still accessible sources and to show once again as a shining example in the present time such a warm and courageous patriot in his successful cooperation with Germany's liberators. Significant additions and at the same time documentary evidence of my work can be found in the two publications of letters initiated by the Historical Commission, the Province of Pomerania, also in this memorial year, as they were published in the 2nd volume of the book of letters written by Mr Dr. Erich Botzenhart, Berlin-Charlottenburg, which I have already mentioned in my essay on Cappenberg, and in the book by Dr. Wilh. Steffens, *Sacks Briefwechsel mit Stein von 1807-1817 und mit Gneisenau von 1811 bis 1819* (Sacks' Correspondence with Stein from 1807 to 1817 and with Gneisenau from 1811 to 1819), which was published on Gneisenau's birthday on August 24. (See advertisement in present issue).

That I, as I already announced in the April issue of this year, saw myself forced to charge a contribution from the *Taube* subscribers when my work was delivered in June and now again in October was unfortunately unavoidable, since the printing costs for such a small edition, as it represents the narrower circle of the foundation's family interested parties, even after payment of the enclosed payment cards, are still — as the publisher Mr Schwab can testify — two thirds of the total sum raised by myself.

I only take the liberty of mentioning this, since, contrary to the above-mentioned appreciative letters of thanks, there was no lack of suspicion, as if I had wanted to enrich myself in the dedication work for the foundation family, at their expense.

May it serve as proof that I have taken the noble words of the great ancestor as an example, that this complete misjudgment of my efforts has not misled me in this but that I will now, in accordance with my promise, have the second section delivered punctually on the birthday of my hero on October 7. I have taken the noble words of the great ancestor as an example: *Tu ne cede malis sed contra audentior ito*: Always going forward for the better! With my renewed thanks and kindred greeting!

Gertha von Dieckmann, née Sack (3014)

Arolsen, in October 1931.

Additional

Information

The French Republican calendar

Autumn:

Vendémiaire (from French *vendange*, derived from Latin vindemia, "vintage"), starting 22, 23, or 24 September

Brumaire (from French *brume*, "mist"), starting 22, 23, or 24 October

Frimaire (From French *frimas*, "frost"), starting 21, 22, or 23 November

Winter:

Nivôse (from Latin *nivosus*, "snowy"), starting 21, 22, or 23 December

Pluviôse (from French *pluvieux*, derived from Latin pluvius, "rainy"), starting 20, 21, or 22 January

Ventôse (from French *venteux*, derived from Latin ventosus, "windy"), starting 19, 20, or 21 February

Spring:

Germinal (from French *germination*), starting 20 or 21 March

Floréal (from French *fleur*, derived from Latin flos, "flower"), starting 20 or 21 April

Prairial (from French *prairie*, "meadow"), starting 20 or 21 May

Summer:

Messidor (from Latin messis, "harvest"), starting 19 or 20 June

Thermidor (or Fervidor*) (from Greek thermon, "summer heat"), starting 19 or 20 July

Fructidor (from Latin fructus, "fruit"), starting 18 or 19 August.

(from wikipedia.org)

Expansion of PRUSSIA 1807-1871

1. Alsace-Lorraine
2. Baden
3. Bavaria
4. Hanover
5. Hesse
6. Hesse-Nassau
7. Hohenzollern
8. Holstein
9. Mecklenburg
10. Oldenburg
11. Posen
12. Rhine Province
13. Saxony
14. Schleswig
15. Swedish Pomerania
16. Westphalia
17. Wurttemburg

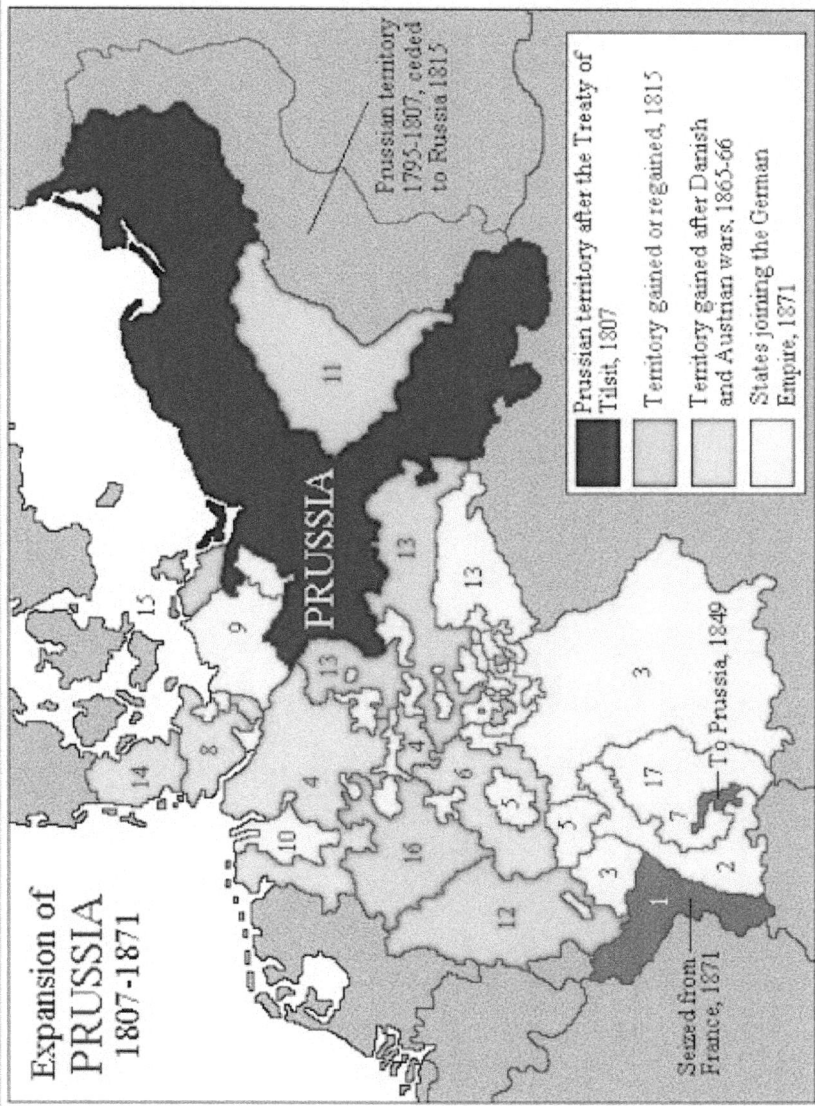

PRUSSIA

Prussian territory 1795-1807, ceded to Russia 1815

Prussian territory after the Treaty of Tilsit, 1807

Territory gained or regained, 1815

Territory gained after Danish and Austrian wars, 1865-66

States joining the German Empire, 1871

To Prussia, 1849

Seized from France, 1871

Illustrations

www.ingramcontent.com/pod-product-compliance
Lightning Source LLC
Chambersburg PA
CBHW031935090426
42811CB00002B/190